FOUR FACES OF BRITISH MUSIC

Norman Hyde

FOUR FACES
OF
BRITISH MUSIC

by

Norman Hyde

formerly Director of Music at
George Watson's College, Edinburgh

CHURCHMAN PUBLISHING
WORTHING
1985

FOUR FACES OF BRITISH MUSIC
was first published in 1985
by
CHURCHMAN PUBLISHING LIMITED
117 Broomfield Avenue
Worthing
West Sussex

© Copyright Norman Hyde 1985

Distributed to the book trade
by
Bailey Bros. & Swinfen Limited
Warner House
Folkestone
Kent

ISBN 1 85093 016 3

Typeset by CPJ Fotoset of Worthing, Sussex
Printed by Paradigm Print of Gateshead, Tyne and Wear

To
E. M. H.

ACKNOWLEDGEMENTS

When this book was in preparation I approached a number of former pupils for assistance in various ways. The response was quite wonderful and I wish to express my deep appreciation to them especially,

Dr. Eric Anderson, Headmaster of Eton College

John Cullen, Director of Music, Tonbridge School.

Donald Millar, Organist, St. Pancras Old Church, London.

Keith Millar, London Philharmonic Orchestra.

Brian Moyes, Philharmonia Orchestra.

Dr. Donald Nisbet, Oxford musical interests.

John Souter, The scene in Scotland.

Charles Stewart. On Music Staff of City of London Freemen's School, Ashstead.

My grateful thanks are due to Miss Hamilton and her excellent staff in the Music Room of the Edinburgh City Library. They gave me every facility during the period of research.

My thanks must also be accorded to the publishers, Churchman of Worthing and in particular to their Editorial Director, Mr. Peter Smith for his kindness and enthusiasm.

Norman Hyde

Goring-by-Sea
Sussex
Spring 1985

FOREWORD

by

JOHN CULLEN

MA FRCO ARCM

Director of Music at Tonbridge School

What is British about British music? How have the roots and branches developed over the centuries? What are the qualities for which music in Britain is renowned the world over?

These are questions often asked by a musical public and which Norman Hyde has set out to answer in this scholarly, yet immensely readable book. He has identified and brought together the principal contributors to our musical heritage, and traced the development of each from its origins to the present day. The book sets music against the backdrop of the time and the place in which it was created and evolved. We read lively accounts of the contributions to our musical heritage by every monarch from the Middle Ages to the present day, including the music of the Royal Wedding in 1981. The significance of the Court's contribution to our musical inheritance was great, and yet, the way in which music clubs and societies developed, from informal gatherings in the Inn to the countless number or well-organised societies which today offer music of a very high order, is of equal importance. Of the many thousands who patronise our concert-halls today, I wonder how many are aware of the origins of concert-going? Page after page of this book reveals such chronicles of the past, punctuated by quotations from contemporary observers.

The author has made many pertinent observations drawn from a lifetime's experience as a Director of Music. The section of the book concerning music in education is not only full of historical interest, but also makes compelling reading for anyone whose profession or interest involves music in our schools, colleges and universities. Although lamenting the decline of some of the traditions of previous generations, Mr. Hyde sees hope in the power of music to develop the corporate life of our institutions, through striving for high ideals and levels of attainment. Among the achievements he cites is a recent performance of Walton's *Belshazzar's Feast* by pupils almost entirely drawn from one school.

Norman Hyde is a born teacher, as I, and many thousands of pupils who have benefited from his vast knowledge of the arts which he communicates with charm and understanding can testify. This is a book for the reader who is concerned with music, be he amateur or professional, listener, performer or teacher. Its publication at the beginning of European Music Year is singularly appropriate.

CONTENTS

Chapter 1   Page
MUSIC IN THE COURT   1
    Henry V   4
    Henry VI   5
    Edward IV   5
    Henry VII   6
    Henry VIII   7
    Edward VI   13
    Mary Tudor   14
    Elizabeth I   15
    James I   21
    Charles I   25
    Cromwell   30
    Charles II   32
    James II   37
    The Scottish Court   39
        James I   39
        James II   39
        James III   40
        James IV   40
        James V   42
        Mary, Queen of Scots   43
        James VI   45
        James VII   46
    William and Mary   47
    Anne   48
    George I   48
    George II   49
    George III   52
    George IV   53
    William IV   54
    Victoria   55
    Edward VII   57
    George V   58
    George VI   60
    Elizabeth II   61
    The Royal Wedding 1981   62

Chapter 2   Page

MUSIC IN THE INN 64
     Seventeenth Century Catch Clubs 70
     Drinking Songs 74
     Mughouses 80
     Eighteenth Century Catch Clubs 80
     Free and Easies or Harmonic Clubs 84
     Concert Clubs 87
     The Early Music Hall 89
     Twentieth Century Taverns 91
     Hotels and Restaurants 92
     Music Clubs in Edinburgh 93
     Nineteenth Century Musical Societies 99
     The Village Inn 100
     Working Men's Clubs 111

Chapter 3

MUSIC IN THE SCHOOL 118
     Monastic Song Schools 118
     The Sang Scules 120
     The Reformation in England 123
     The Music of Friends 128
     The Lost Century 129
     Signs of Improvement 131
     The Twentieth Century 136
     The Schools Today 139
     Singing 142
     School Songs 145
     The Orchestra 145
     Listening 147
     Boarding Schools 149
     Local Authority Schools 153
     Grant Aided and Private Day Schools 157
     A Personal Note 161
     Competitons 162
     Specialist Schools 163
     A Sad Note 165
     Summer Schools 166
     The Church Tries Again 167
     Teacher Training Colleges 169
     Universities 169

Chapter 4
MUSIC IN THE CONCERT HALL 174
London 174
Edinburgh 188
Aberdeen 194
Oxford 200
Festivals 208
The Three Choirs Festival 210
Post War Festivals 212
The Edinburgh International Festival 212
Aldeburgh 214
Music in Wales 216
The National Eisteddfod 217
Llangollen 218
The Orchestral Scene: The Proms 221
Orchestras Today – London 225
The London Symphony Orchestra 227
The BBC Symphony Orchestra 228
The London Philharmonic Orchestra 229
The Royal Philharmonic Orchestra 230
The Philharmonia Orchestra 232
Chamber Music Ensembles 233
The Orchestral Scene – Outside London 234
The Hallé Orchestra 234
Bournemouth Symphony Orchestra 237
The Scottish National Orchestra 239
The Royal Liverpool Philharmonic Orchestra 241
The City of Birmingham Orchestra 243
The Northern Sinfonia Orchestra 244

CHAPTER 1

MUSIC in the COURT

And those musicians that shall play to you
Hang in the air a thousand leagues from hence.
King Henry IV, *Shakespeare*

IN former centuries music owed much to royal patronage. Kings vied one with another regarding the quality of their musical entertainment. This was particularly the case on the continent of Europe, where the majority of princely rulers made provision for musical performance at their courts. Much of this music-making was on a grand scale, with an orchestra, a choir and in a few places even a well-organised opera. In other courts the scope would be more modest, but whatever the size, each became a centre of the art in its own immediate neighbourhood. According to Tinctoris the Flemish theoretician, the great advance in musical knowledge in fifteenth century Europe was largely due to the ever-increasing number of royal chapels which used as their pattern the Papal choir at Rome.

Britain could not compete numerically with the large number of establishments on the continent, but the standard of court music reached great heights in spite of troublous times and the varying degree of interest shown by royal patrons. In early times the music tended to flow along two well-defined paths, the one represented by instrumental performers and the other by the singers of the chapel, a tradition which lasted many centuries.

The instrumentalists traced their origin to the strolling minstrels, who from time immemorial had been welcome visitors at court. A place was still found for them long after kings employed their own personal musicians. These early players were practical men, often able to perform on more than one instrument and able with equal facility to compose for those instruments.

1

Usually the most outstanding players were the best composers, enjoying in some respects lives less complicated than those of musicians today. They wrote for a small intimate circle consisting of their royal patrons and their professional colleagues, and not for a vast body of amateur listeners.

In Wales, music was an essential in the homes of the princes and noblemen such as Gruffydd ap Cynan of Anglesey. This was the music of the bards (harpists), a branch of the art not unlike that of the troubadors in France and the minstrels in England. The bards had of necessity to be of high birth and in the court of a prince the Bard of the Household, as with the King's Musician elsewhere, was considered a most important member of the retinue. He had certain obligations and duties to perform, not dissimilar to those in the courts throughout Europe. His art would be employed in singing genealogoies, of battles and heroes, whilst the Domestic Bard, attached to the princess would deal with gentler subjects, such as love and nature. Those bards who aspired to positions in the courts and great halls had to discipline themselves to a long and exacting period of preparation; consequently standards of performance were high. In addition to the bards who occupied what might be termed static posts in the great houses, there were those who travelled from place to place performing at banquets, marriage feasts and other important functions. Their journeyings and engagements were controlled by the chaired-bard, who by this means ensured that quality was maintained.

Probably the most fruitful musical periods in British court history were those of the Tudor and Stuart dynasties when many of the kings and queens were proficient in performance and generous in encouragement. They undoubtedly influenced the future course of music in the land, but many of the musicians who served them are now almost forgotten. Yet these were of considerable importance in their day, holding postions of privilege and responsibility befitting those living close to the sovereign.

From early times the greatest single influence on the music of the court in London was that of the Chapel Royal, first mentioned in household regulations of 1135. Owing to its special function it was always regarded as an integral part of the court rather than of the church. This is shown in the year 1200 when the chapel accompanied King John on his visit to York, and thus set a precedent for future royal progresses. During the last years of the reign of Edward I (1239-1307) the musical establishment of the

2

Chapel Royal was brought into line with the cathedrals by the introduction of boy choristers.

The history of the term chapel is of considerable interest. According to Grove it is derived from the *cappella*, or cloak of St. Martin which was treasured by the Frankish kings and carried before them into battle. Those responsible for the cloak were known as *cappellani* or chaplains, and the sanctuary in which it was retained became the *cappella*. Later the term was used for any private sanctuary or holy place.

Although the Chapel Royal produced the bulk of great music throughout the centuries, the Chapel of St. George at Windsor Castle played its part in a long history of outstanding achievement. It was founded in 1327 by Edward III with only six choristers and was known originally as the College of Windsor. Almost at once it became the centre for an active school of fourteenth century musicians, among whom William Excestre was a foremost composer and records of others, such as Cook, Burell, Aleyn and Chirbury appeared in the Wardrobe Books of 1413.

The Chapel Royal was not merely a building; it was an institution comprising chaplains, singing-men (Gentlemen of the Chapel) and singing-boys (Children of the Chapel), as well as a number of distinguished organist-composers. A description of the court in 1478 (*Liber Niger Domus Regis, A Collection of Ordinances and Regulations*) contains an excellent account of the constitution of the chapel, which in many respects has not materially altered to the present day.

The Master of the Children, chosen from among the Gentlemen of the Chapel Royal was a person of some position and dignity. His several tasks included training the boys in their singing and looking after their general well-being. This latter seems to have been quite an onerous duty. Although the choir normally contained not more than twelve boys, several adults were needed to care for them. In addition to the master, the staff consisted of an usher and another manservant to assist him. Also a woman servant was employed to keep the boys clean – it is indeed strange how little human natute has changed since those far-off days.

The master was also charged with obtaining suitable boys for the Chapel, a very real problem in the early fifteenth century. Good singing-boys were so difficult to come by that in 1420 a royal warrant was issued empowering the master, John Melynek to seize likely candidates by force from any church or cathedral in England, with the exception of St. George's Chapel, Windsor, Westminster

Abbey and St. Paul's Cathedral. This impressing of boys seems to have been repeated on numerous occasions in succeeding reigns until well into the sixteenth century.

Oddly enough, although there was establishment for the master of the children, the organist as a specialist was not mentioned until as late as the early seventeenth century. Each of the gentlemen of the choir was expected to play the organ and the *Liber Niger* records that their qualifications should include "sufficient in organs playing".

HENRY V

Benet, Markham, Cooke and Fonteyns were fifteenth century composers of whom little is known except that they were connected with the court of Henry V. They probably formed part of that "complete chapel full of singers" which accompanied the king on his campaigns in France. He certainly maintained a fully effective choir and it is considered likely that His Majesty was the composer of the Gloria and Sanctus for three voices entitled "Roy Henry" in the Old Hall Manuscript. This manuscript is in the safe keeping of the British Library, London.

After Agincourt, the members of the Chapel celebrated victory by singing a "Te Deum" and "In Exitu Israel". They also welcomed the king's entry into Rouen Cathedral at the capitulation of that city in 1419. On his return to London, Henry was afforded a great reception by the citizens. He was escorted by the Mayor, council and other notabilities to the city by way of London Bridge, where "the two towers of the bridge were dressed with banners bearing the royal arms, and at their foot was a band of trumpets. Alongside was a company of boys, dressed in white, with silver wings, who greeted the King with an anthem". (*The Streets of London*, Thomas Burke.)

Although John Dunstable was probably the most important musician of the fifteenth century, he does not come strictly within our terms of reference. He was musician to the Duke of Bedford, who later became Regent of France, but he never occupied a place in the royal household. According to an epitaph in John Weever's *Ancient Funerall Monuments,* Dunstable is described as "an astrologian, a mathematician, a musition, and what not".

4

HENRY VI

With the death of Henry V in 1422, England entered upon a period of intense unrest and internal strife which could not have afforded much encouragement to the musical section of the court. But in spite of the difficult times Henry took a keen interest in the performance of the Chapel Royal and he himself composed some excellent church music. If his reputation in history is that of a poor king, it must in fairness be recorded that his ability in music was considerable. Also to his credit Henry VI founded King's College, Cambridge with its famous chapel. This most beautiful building has been a treasure-house of the finest church music all through its history, and its present choir ably carries on the tradition.

How true is Wordsworth's sonnet written in praise of the chapel interior with its magnificent ceiling:

These lofty pillars, spread that branching roof
Self-poised, and scooped into ten thousand cells
Where light and shade repose, where music dwells
Lingering – and wandering on as loth to die.

EDWARD IV

Contrary to general expectation, Edward IV, who seized the throne in 1461, also paid attention to the music of the court, and it was in fact during his reign that the detailed organisation of the Chapel Royal took place. It consisted of twenty-six chaplains and clerks, thirteen minstrels, eight choirboys and their master, and a "Wayte" or musical watchman. The king was rewarded at his death in 1483 by the choir singing the whole of the Psalter over his body.

With the cessation of the Wars of the Roses and the crowning of Henry VII, some stability returned to the country. Almost at once there occurred a revival in the arts. Music again came into its own and many able composers found satisfaction and security in their service with the Chapel Royal. These included Henry Abyngdom, Robert Fayrfax, who, "in great renowne and accounted the prime Musition of the Nation" (Anthony Hood) and William

5

Cornyshe, not only a musician, but also an actor and producer of pageants. There were others of course, such as Richard Sampson, dean of the Chapel Royal, William Newarke and Gilbert Banestre, all of whom gained fame in the royal service.

HENRY VII

Henry VII encouraged music at his court, not merely for reasons of state, but from a genuine love of the art.

He was descended from the Welsh Tudors on his father's side and the Beaufort line through his mother. The Tudors, an ancient family from Gwynedd in North Wales made their first appearance in national history with Owen Tudor, who served with Henry V and was executed by the Yorkists in 1461. One of his sons, Edmund, married Margaret Beaufort and their son became Henry VII.

According to the records, his marriage to Elizabeth of York in 1486 was celebrated with much pomp and splendour, in which music played a conspicuous part. For this occasion Banestre, then Master of the Children, composed the five-part motet "O Maria et Elizabeth" which is preserved in the Eton Manuscript. As an example of his desire to secure the first talent for the court, it should be mentioned that the king sent to Italy for John Hothby, the distinguished musical scholar and composer. Hothby, an English Carmelite, who had travelled widely in Spain, Germany and France and was then living at Lucca, returned and entered the King's Musick.

As might be expected with so many brilliant composers in residence, religious music flourished. But secular music also played its part, as during the festivities of Twelfth Night 1487. An eyewitness on that occasion wrote: ". . . at the Table in the Medell of the Hall sat the Deane and thoos of the King's Chapell, which incontynently after the King's furst Course sang a Carall."

Minstrels had been welcome guests at the court for centuries – Berdic, mentioned in Domesday Book was probably one of them. Certainly Rahere, who founded the Priory and hospital of St. Bartholomew in London, was at one time minstrel to Henry I. It is well known that Richard Coeur de Lion introduced the art of the troubador into northern France, and the story of his imprisonment in Dürnstein Castle on the Danube and eventual discovery by Blondel de Nesle gives ample evidence of minstrelsy at that time.

Early records were not very detailed and often merely referred to "minstrels" in the king's service, but the harper would appear to have been an established post in the reign of Henry III. A Pipe Roll entry of 1252 makes mention of a payment to Master Richard *"Citharistae regis"*. At that time "Cithariste" was understood to mean "harper", although later the word became connected with the lute. The king's harper was on occasions given the title of "master" and Master Richard was sometimes known as King himself, a mark of distinction borne by certain other royal musicians during the period in question. Another of Henry's musicians was the royal trumpeter, Randolph.

During the reign of Edward III the royal music included five trumpets, two clarions, five pipes, three waits and a drum. Under Edward IV there were thirteen instrumentalists "some be trumpets, some with shawms and small pipes", whilst in addition a wait was employed to pipe at certain hours of the night.

In 1495 Henry VII had four "Shakbusshes" attached to the court. These were sackbuts, which in general principles resembled present-day trombones. It was at this time, during the fifteenth century, that the King's Musick as distinct from the Chapel began to develop. Even then, many wandering minstrels were at hand to supplement the resident musicians of the court.

HENRY VIII

By the end of the reign, in 1509, there was a permanent group of twenty instrumental players at court, but although the king had shown much sympathy with music and musicians, it was Henry VIII who placed the King's Musick on a really firm foundation. He was himself a keen musician, both as executant and composer, and being prepared to spend money, he attracted many of the most able performers of the day. These came from England, Wales and from the continent, and by 1547 there were fifty-eight musicians employed, including players of viols, sackbuts, flutes, lutes, harps, a rebec, a virginal and a bagpipe as well as singers, two instrument-makers and a copyist. Also, as something of a novelty the King introduced violinists from Italy in order to add variety to the instrumentation.

In fact during this time the King's Musick contained all the instruments important in the music of western Europe during the sixteenth and seventeenth centuries. Dr. Charles Burney, the eminent historian, had this to say of the king: "Our vindictive and voluptuous monarch, Henry the Eighth had studied Music very seriously in his youth, according to Lord Herbert of Cherbury: who tells us in his life, that 'his education was accurate, being destined to the Archbishoprick of Canterbury, during the time of his elder brother, Prince Arthur' — By these means, not only the more necessary parts of learning were infused into him, but even those of ornament, so that besides being an able Latinist, Philosopher, and Divine, he was (which one might wonder at in a king) a curious Musician; as two entire Masses composed by him, and often sung in his Chapel, did abundantly witness."

Hollingshead also gives us a picture of Henry during his progress from one place to another. "He exercised himself daylie in shooting, singing, dancing, wrestling, casting at the barre, plaieing at the recorders, flute, virginals, in setting of Songes, and making of Ballades."

In the early days of his reign the king spent much time at Hampton Court. Here he built the Great Hall — in some respects reminiscent of Westminster Hall — in order that he might keep a check on his powerful nobles. Henry insisted that everyone in attendance at court should dine together and those "noblemen, gentlemen and others who do much delight and use to dyne in corners and secret places" were brought to book in the Ordinances of Eltham, drawn up by Cardinal Wolsey. The Great Hall resounded to music during meal times and the arrival of each course from the kitchens was heralded by pipes and trumpets in the Minstrels' Gallery. When their work was done the court players and musicians repaired to the "Drynkynge House" adjoining the Wine Cellar, where they drew their daily allowance of ale and wine.

It seems that household regulations on every conceivable subject were constantly issued. An interesting one during this reign stipulated that Officers of the Bed Chamber "will not caress the maids on the stairs, as many household utensils are apt to be broken as a result. Such pages as seduce the maids of the King's Household, so that they become mothers, shall pay a fine of two marks, for the benefit of His Majesty, and shall go without beer for a month . . ."

Under the Tudors, the masque, always a popular royal entertainment, became even more elaborate and colourful than before. It was not a play so much as an amateur pageant, usually based on some legend and interspersed with music and processions. On occasions hundreds of people took part, including the ladies of the court and other prominent members of the household.

That worldly churchman Cardinal Wolsey, frequently provided Henry with the most lavish amusement of this nature, and Cavendish's *Life of Wolsey* contains a description of such an occasion at Hampton Court Palace. "The banquets were set forth, with masks and mummeries, in so gorgeous a sort, and costly manner that it was a heaven to behold. There wanted no dames or damsels meet or apt to dance with the maskers or to garnish the place for the time, with other goodly disports. Then was there all kinds of music and harmony set forth, with excellent voices both of men and children. I have seen the King suddenly come in thither in a mask, with a dozen of other maskers, all in garments like shepherds, made of fine cloth of gold and fine crimson satin paned, and caps of same, with visors of good proportion of visnomy; their hairs and beards either of fine gold wire, or else of silver, and some being of black silk; having sixteen torch-bearers, besides their drums, and other persons attending upon them, with visors, and clothed all in satin of the same colours."

The Cardinal decided to confiscate a number of the smaller monastries in order to endow a college at Oxford, the excuse for his action being the lax manner in which these houses were conducted. The original object of these religious houses was to provide a place withdrawn from the hurly burly of the world, where the monks might find sufficient seclusion to follow a life of prayer and meditation. During the course of time this ideal became somewhat tarnished; the spiritual and ascetic virtues coupled with the rigid code of physical austerity gradually diminished. As the abbeys became wealthy and powerful, so they changed into comfortable mansions and treasure houses for all that was finest in contemporary craftsmanship. Naturally many envious eyes were turned in the direction of these religious establishments, but to be quite fair many of them were ill-managed and had outlived their usefulness. Thus in 1524 several of the houses were suppressed and Wolsey founded his Cardinal's College at Oxford, later to be named Christ Church. With characteristic acumen he engaged John Taverner, one of the most influential composers of the day, as master of the choristers, and such was his ability that the choir of the college soon compared favourably with the Chapel Royal in the quality of its music – a fact not lost upon the King. Wolsey's own establishment was maintained on a princely scale and among his army of retainers were four minstrels, sixteen men singers, sixteen boy choristers and sixteen chaplains to conduct the daily mass. Meanwhile Taverner did not live an altogether monotonous life. He was imprisoned in 1528 for heresy and in 1530 he left the college, whether voluntary or not is unknown. He then gave up music, became an admirer of Thomas Cromwell and devoted himself whole-heartedly to the destruction of church property.

A section of the Chapel Royal accompanied the king on all his travels, as may be noted from the rules issued to the royal household in 1526, which state that "when the King is on journies or progresses, only six singing boys and six Gentlemen of the Choir, shall make a part of the royal retinue; who daylie in absence of the residue of the Chapel, shall have a Masse of the daie, besides our Lady-Masse, and an Anthempne in the afternoon: for which purpose, not great carriage of either vestments of bookes shall require."

In addition to travelling with the king to the various royal palaces, the Chapel Royal also attended him at the Field of the Cloth of Gold in 1520. Fairfax was in charge of the singing on this occasion and the music was of a particularly high standard. This may in part be attributed to the keen rivalry between the Chapel Royal and the private group of singers representing Wolsey. One ecclesiastical critic, in a letter to the Cardinal some two years earlier had written, "The King hath plainly shown unto Cornish that your Grace's Chapel is better than his, and proved the same by this reason that if any manner of new song should be brought into both the said Chapels to be sung ex improviso then the said song should be better and more surely handled by your Chapel than by his."

However, at the Field of the Cloth of Gold, the Chapel Royal combined with the Chapelle de Musique du Roi, and the two choirs sang together before Henry and François I. How pleasant it would be in this nuclear age, if international differences could be settled in so civilised and amicable a manner.

Although singing-boys in the royal chapel received no payment for their services, they were instead given a good education in music and general subjects. Academies and colleges of music did not then exist, but a valuable training was obtained at the Chapel, and many musical boys served their apprenticeship in this unique forcing ground and later achieved fame. When their voices changed the boys were able to choose between a further course of study at a university or becoming singers in other choirs. The *Liber Niger* states that "when they be grown to the age of eighteen years, and then their voices be changed, nor cannot be preferred in this chapel, nor within this court, the number being full; then if they will assent, the King assigneth every such child to a college of Oxford or Cambridge, of the King's foundation, there to be in finding and study sufficiently, till the King otherwise list to advance him." Henry VIII was generous in this respect and met the university expenses of the ex-choristers. Later, Elizabeth discontinued the practice.

The music of the royal chapel was undoubtedly of the highest level as might be expected with famous musicians such as Cornyshe, Fayrfax, Burton, Newarke and Farthing in command of affairs, but elsewhere severe criticism was often made regarding the manner in which church services were conducted. In the "Seventy-eight Faults and Abuses of Religion" presented to the King in 1536 there is mention of "the singing and saying of Mass, Matins or Evensong, as but a roarying, howling, whistleying, mummying, conjuring and jozeling and the playing of the organys a foolish vanite."

During the same year a further blow was to fall on the monasteries – the Dissolution by Act of Parliament of all the smaller houses remaining after Wolsey's confiscation. The King was now determined to suppress and destroy monasticism wherever it was to be encountered, and between 1538 and 1540 all the great abbeys were forced to surrender to him.

The church had not seen Henry's matrimonial escapades in quite the way he would have wished; in fact the authorities had been very unyielding. Consequently the king felt he had every right to stop such an uncooperative body in his own country. Also the monasteries were exceptionally rich and the nation's exchequer was in a low state.

The method of suppression, its callousness and bitterness is not part of our story, but its effect on religious music was immediate. Many of the great composers viewed with dismay the advent of Protestantism with its inevitable change-over from the long established liturgy in Latin to a new style of music more suited

11

to the vernacular. Furthermore, Henry directed that "the songs of the new short services should not be full of notes, but, as near as may be, for every syllable a note so that it may be sung distinctly and devoutly."

Much has been written regarding Henry VIII's ability as a composer, but there exists today strangely few worthwhile examples of his music. Certainly there is no complete edition of his work and as a result it is difficult to know precisely the position when attempting to asses his value in the field of composition. Odd pieces are to be found here and there, as for example a motet in the Baldwin Manuscript of 1581–1606, which forms part of the Royal Music Library presented to the British Museum by the present Queen Elizabeth in 1957.

The fine anthem "O Lord, the maker of all thing" for so long attributed to the King, is definitely of a later date. His songs "Pastyme with good companye", "In tyme of youth" and the three part motet "Quam pulcra es" are for the most part mediocre, although it is only fair to add that some authorities consider the last named to be a good example of English music of the period. On the other hand it is perhaps surprising that Henry's two songs "O my hart it is so sore sens I must nedys from my love depart" and "Alas, alas what shall I do for care is cast into my hart" suffer from neglect, as they seem well worthy of performance today.

It was Henry Peacham who wrote in the seventeenth century: "King Henry the eight could not onely sing his part sure, but of himselfe composed a Service of foure, five and sixe parts; as *Erasmus* in a certaine Epistle, testifieth of his owne knowledge." Also Anne Boleyn is said to have written the song "Oh Death, Rock Me to Sleep" shortly before her execution in the Tower of London. The manuscript was discovered recently in the Royal Library at Windsor amongst several hundreds by sixteenth century composers.

The writing and singing of simple three-part songs known as "freemen's songs" – a corruption of "three men's songs" – became popular during this period. William Cornyshe, already noted in connection with the Chapel Royal, was successful in this field, and as the king himself attempted several, we may assume that they found favour in court circles. An example of a typical three part song by the king is *Green groweth the holly, so doeth the Ivy*. This song and the instrumental piece are included in a beautifully produced edition of King Henry VIII's music presented in 1912 by Lord Beauchamp to the members of the Roxburghe Club.

In addition to composition he enjoyed playing the lute and in collecting keyboard instruments. This last named activity resulted in his owning between thirty and forty virginals and harpsichords at the end of his life.

There were seventy-five musicians in the court of Henry VIII, a number which rose to one hundred and fourteen during the reign of Edward VI. It is not surprising that such lavish patronage stimulated musical composition on a scale hitherto unknown. Some of the names of the more famous men have come down to us today. Richard Pygott, master of the children in Wolsey's private chapel, entered the Chapel Royal and served under Henry VII and Edward VI. Thomal Tallis first came into prominence as organist of Waltham Abbey before its dissolution in 1540. He was appointed a Gentleman of the Chapel Royal in 1537 and became a distinguished composer of church and secular music, both choral and instrumental. He was present at the Coronation of Edward VI and was listed an employee of the Royal household in the first year of Queen Elizabeth's reign.

John Merbecke, organist of St. George's Chapel, Windsor, had an exciting life even allowing for the exciting times. He was arrested as a Protestant heretic and only just escaped burning. Having been permitted a certain amount of freedom under Queen Mary, Merbecke produced several outspoken theological books in favour of Protestantism. He is now chiefly remembered for his "Booke of Common Praier Noted", and his Communion Service is still regularly used in the Anglican church today.

EDWARD VI

Edward VI shared with Henry VIII a love of music and from existing accounts he also appears to have been no mean performer. Cardan, in his character of the young king says that "he was not ignorant of logic, of the principles of Natural Philosophy nor of Music". In the King's own journal of July 20, 1550, which is found in the appendix to Burnet's *History of the Reformation* there appears the following: "M. le Maréschal St. André, the French Ambassador dined with me, heard me play on the lute, came to me to my study; supped with me, and so departed to Richmond."

MARY TUDOR

It may not be generally known that the tragic Queen Mary was an accomplished musician. At the age of ten she was sent to Ludlow as Princess of Wales and here arrangements were made for her "to use moderate exercise for taking open-air in gardens, sweet and wholesome places, and walks." The subjects to be studied were Music, Latin and French, but with the understanding "that the same be not too much, and without fatigation or weariness."

In 1557, Giovanni Michiel the Venetian Ambassador in France reported that Mary Tudor spoke fluently in English, Latin, French and Spanish and understood Italian. "Besides woman's work, such as embroidery of every sort with the needle, she also practises music, playing especially on the clavicorde and on the lute so excellently that, when intent on it (though she now plays rarely), she surprised the best performers, both by the rapidity of her hand and by her style of playing." (*Venetian Calendar*)

As well as being a good player of the virginal, Mary took part in many of the court masques and enjoyed those occasions when Thomas Heywood, the dramatist, brought the Children of the Chapel to perform before her. As already noted Edward VI's establishment consisted of one hundred and fourteen musicians and this number was maintained by Queen Mary.

Although the musicians attached to the Chapel Royal were normally of English stock, many of the members of the royal band were drawn from the continent. It is felt that the following list of names will not cause especial difficulty in deciding which countries supplied the majority of instrumental players.

Hans Hosenet, Fraunces de Venice, Mark Anthony Galyardo and Ambrose de Milano (viols). Mark Anthony Petalo and Anthony Mark Galiardello (sackbuts). Guillam de Trosse, Thomas Paginton and Piero Guye (flutes). Peter van Wilder and Philip van Welder (lutes), a rebec player John de Severnacke and five Bassanos – instruments not specified.

Some of these musicians lived in pleasant surroundings provided by the monarch. The Minories, near the Tower of London, formerly a convent of Minoresses of St. Clare was such a place. It had been intended as a store for ordnance and other effects for which there was no longer accommodation at the Tower. But gradually an assorted community of doctors, musicians, silk-weavers and others grew up in its precincts. Amongst the musicians we find Anthony Mary Galliardello, his son Caesar, John Lanier and Henry Truches, all attached to the courts of Elizabeth or James I.

ELIZABETH I

Many of what may be termed the rank and file musicians existed on less than £40 per annum. Between 1547 and 1577 a sackbut player, Robert May, received 6d. a day (£9:2:6 per year) with livery, and there were several instances of wages varying from 1/- to 1/4 a day. In fairness to the court however, it must be recorded that all such rates of pay had disappeared by the end of Elizabeth's reign. It must also be noted that musicians employed by royalty enjoyed certain advantages. According to a letter from the Lord Chamberlain to the Lord Mayor of London in 1573, they were not to be made churchwarden, constable, scavenger, watchman or charged with any taxes. Also most of them benefited from gifts at the appropriate seasons of the year. In 1600 fifteen musicians each received five ounces of gilt plate from Queen Elizabeth. The value of such presents was debatable on occasions, as the musicians often felt obliged to reciprocate. In this particular instance they presented the Queen with perfumed gloves.

In Elizabethan times the court musician had a busy and varied life. He was required for concerts, to play at dinner and to perform during the acts of the many plays given in the royal palace. Also dancing was popular and the Queen herself is reliably reported to have written music for this purpose. In connection with the plays it should be mentioned that several of the masters of the children also employed the boys as actors, a fact which gained some notoriety in the drama of Elizabeth's reign. The exploitation of these small boys caused grave discontent in many circles, not least in the families of the boys concerned. A warrant dated 1626 forbade the employment of the children on the stage, "for that it is not fit or desent that such as should sing the praises of God Almighty should be trained or imployed in such lascivious and prophane exercises."

Such a master was Philip Rosseter the English lutenist and composer who was associated with Jones, Kingham and Reeve in the training of children for the Queen's revels. Richard Farrant was another who wrote songs for plays performed by the choir boys. He was a Gentleman of the Chapel Royal until 1564, when he became organist and choirmaster of St. George's Chapel, Windsor. During his occupation of this post he composed a quantity of excellent church music, some of which is still performed.

A number of these musicians were also playwrights, as for example Richard Edwards. He was appointed Master of the Children of the Chapel Royal in 1561 and was responsible for the production of *Palamon and Arcite* performed for the pleasure of Her Majesty. He also wrote *Damon and Pithias* and contributed to a book of verse *The Paradise of Dainty Devices*.

Other outstanding musicians attached to the court at this time included Alfonso Ferrabosco an Italian composer who was granted a pension of £100 a year in 1569, John Johnson, lutenist, Robert Stone and the great Christopher Tye "the Father of the Anthem". His early years were spent as a choir boy at King's College Chapel, Cambridge; he then became music tutor to Edward VI and organist of the Chapel Royal. Tye, as a writer of church music exercised a profound influence on his successors, many of whom modelled their style on his compositions. This was a period of transition in which English was gradually taking the place of Latin as the language for church-singing. At the same time much adverse criticism was levelled against too complicated vocal music, particularly in those instances where the words proved difficult of hearing. As a result, Christopher Tye set the Acts of the Apostles to simple rhyming verses, not unlike the metrical psalms "with notes to eche Chapter to synge and also to play upon the lute". From this work come two well-known hymn-tune adaptations, "Dundee" and "Winchester Old". A manuscript by Anthony Wood in the Bodleian Library tells how "Dr Tye was a peevish and humoursome man, especially in his latter dayes, and sometimes playing on ye Organ in ye chap. of qu. Elizab. wh. contained much music, but little delight to the ear, she would send ye verger to tell him yt he play'd out of Tune: where upon he sent word yt her ears were out of Tune".

The "Royal Progress" was, and still is, an important function in the life of royalty. The monarch must constantly be seen by the people. Elizabeth understood this perfectly and spent much time in travelling about the country. Knowing her interest and delight in music, those who provided hospitality for the Queen did their utmost to obtain suitable entertainment. Perhaps the best-known example was the occasion of the Earl of Leicester's reception at his Warwickshire castle in 1575. Sir Walter Scott in *Kenilworth* describes how Her Majesty "found her way to the Great Hall of the castle, gorgeously hung for her reception with the richest silken tapestry, misty with perfumes, and sounding to strains of soft and delicious music!"

Then there was the occasion at Norwich where a musical surprise had been arranged for the Queen as she left the city. A large hole was dug at the riverside, covered with a green material and foliage. As the royal procession passed by, it was intended that water nymphs should appear and make suitable rhymed speeches to the accompaniment of underground music. But the weather of Elizabethan England seems to have been no more dependable than that of today and a very heavy rain-storm played havoc with the musicians in the pit. What should have been a delightful and original scheme fell somewhat flat.

As in earlier reigns the masque and pageant still enjoyed great popularity at the Court of Queen Elizabeth in spite of increasing adverse comment from Puritan sources. Many eminent people were averse to mummery and spoke against this form of entertainment in the strongest possible terms. Lady Bacon, mother of Sir Francis and Anthony, was moved to write on one occasion to the latter, hoping that "they will not mum or sinfully revel at Gray's Inn" where they both lived.

We have noted how the minstrels in England and the bards in Wales enjoyed the patronage of kings and the nobility, but co-existent with these fine musicians there was, on a lower artistic level, a mass of itinerant entertainers using the same titles. These normally performed for the benefit of the common people and not only played and sang but numbered among their members jugglers and story tellers. Many were the tales of happenings from far and near, with more than a hint of local gossip and not a little exaggeration to titillate their listeners. They were in fact the popular vocal newspapers of the times. By the sixteenth century their image had become somewhat tarnished and on receiving serious complaints from Wales regarding the bards, Elizabeth, herself a descendant of the Welsh Tudors, intervened and put an end to a discredited fraternity.

This was one of the greatest musical periods in the history of England, in which composers and performers of outstanding talent followed one another in court circles. Two of the most prominent were Thomas Tallis and William Byrd who described themselves as "generosis et organistic" on the title page of the *"Cantiones"* published in 1575. At one time master and pupil respectively, they later became joint organists of the Chapel Royal. Byrd continued to hold this position in spite of the fact that he was a Roman Catholic. He achieved much variety in his writing and was responsible for some of the finest church music of the century, as well as music for strings, keyboard instruments and madrigals, in which latter field he excelled. In fact, it might be said that his experiments laid the foundation for the music of the future. He was without doubt one of the most important English composers of his or any subsequent generation. This is perhaps the more remarkable when one considers his almost complete lack of composition from 1590 until 1603. During this period Byrd was occupied continuously in litigation with various members of his family over property.

William Blitheman was organist from 1585 until his death in 1591. He is chiefly remembered as the tutor of the brilliant John Bull and this fact is noted in Wood's *Fasti Oxon*: "This person, (Bull) who had a most prodigious hand on the Organ . . . was trained under an excellent master, Blitheman, organist to Queen Elizabeth." This same excellent master was buried at the church of St. Nicholas Olave's Queenhithe, and the following extracts are taken from an epitaph which formerly appeared above his burial-place.

Here Blitheman lies a worthy wight
Who feared God above
A friend to all, a foe to none
Whom rich and poor did love
Of princes chapell gentilman
Unto his dying day.
Whom all took great delight to heare
Him on the organs play,
Whose passing skill in musicke's art
A scholar left behind
John Bull by name his master's veine
Expressing in each kind.

Another of this brilliant group was Elway Bevin, a pupil of Tallis and teacher of William Child. He was made a Gentleman Extraordinary of the Chapel Royal in 1589. It was not until 1601 that the first appointment of organist was specifically mentioned in the Cheque Book, when Arthur Cock took the oath as "gentleman in ordinary and organist". He was followed by the famous composer Orlando Gibbons, who was described at the time as having "the best hand in England" at the virginal and organ.

The Chapel came under the direction of the Lord Chamberlain in Elizabeth's reign. He was "its chief governor under her sacred majesty" and maintained a general supervision of its affairs. The Secretary was known as the Clerk of the Check and this position enabled him to augment his income as a Gentleman of the Choir. This would seem most necessary as the daily wage was 7½d with 1/- for board, a total of £29:13:1½ a year, though later raised to £30.

In spite of the excellence, or perhaps because of the excellence of music in the Chapel Royal, an almost constant friction and bickering between musician and non-musician led to the publication of "The Injunctions of Queen Elizabeth". This was issued to Clergy and Laity in 1559, the first year of the new reign, and provided for the continuance and maintenance of church choirs and expressly forbade any infringements designed to weaken the musical life of the church. Later on, however, the Queen conveyed the lands intended for the support of the singers into the hands of deans and chapters and according to William Chappel (*Popular Music II*) "she did more injury to the cause she desired to advocate than all puritanism could effect".

During 1562, only three years after her Injunctions were issued, "six articles, tending to a farther reformation of the liturgy, were presented to the lower house of convocation, the last whereof was that the use of organs be removed from churches; which, after great debate, were so near being carried, that the rejection of them was owing to a single vote, and that, too, by the proxy of an absent member". *Hawkins History of Music.*

By using a technique which is not entirely unknown today, the gentlemen of the Chapel Royal banded together in 1596 to demand an increase in salary. An award of £10 per annum "to every man, so increasing their stipends from £30 to £40 was granted in 1604, after a long and chargeable suit". The Cheque Book made mention of this handsome gesture in the phraseology typical of the period. "Now it was thought meet that seeing the entertainment of the chapel was not augmented of may years by any one of his majesty's progenitors . . . that therefore his kingly bounty should be recorded, to be had even in remembrance, that thereby not only we (men and children now living), but all those which shall succeed us in the chapel should daily see cause (in our most devout prayers) to humbly to beseech the Divine Majesty to bless his highness, our gracious Queen Anne, Prince Henry and all and every of that royal progeny, with blessing both spiritual and temporal, and that from age to age, and everlastingly, and let us all pray Amen, Amen."

In the margin appeared the comment "Cursed be the party that taketh his leaf out of this book. Amen".

It will be noted that although this agitation started in Elizabeth's reign it was James I who acceded to the request. The Queen was inclined to be mean, or perhaps it would be more charitable to say that she was thrifty; consequently the musical establishment was smaller than in her father's reign. As far as can be ascertained she employed thirty-three musicians in 1570, about twenty-four in 1580 and this number had risen to some twenty-nine in 1590.

Certain of the Gentlemen of the Chapel, particularly those in especial favour, profited from being close to the monarch and to the noblemen of influence. The best known cases of royal patronage were the grants to Tallis and Byrd, and later to Morley, of monopolies for the printing of music. John Bull was made the first music professor at Gresham College in 1596 at the express wish of Queen Elizabeth despite his inability to give the lectures in Latin, as was then the custom. William Hunnis, a master of the children from 1556 to 1597 had in his charge the keepership of the orchards and gardens at Greenwich from 1562 and crown lands at Ilford in 1585. These may seem odd perquisites for musicians, but they had the desired effect of retaining valuable members in the royal service.

As might be expected during the Tudor period, several fine musicians of Welsh birth or descent were attracted to London to work for their royal kinsfolk. These included Robert Jones and Richard Edwards, both of whom have received mention in previous pages. There were also John Jenkins, a prolific composer and performer on several instruments and Thomas Tomkins, one of the outstanding madrigalists of the era.

As already remarked upon, this was a great time for music and we have seen how royal encouragement stimulated composers in their art. Towards the end of Elizabeth's reign, twenty-nine composers, under the editorship of Thomas Morley, produced twenty-nine madrigals in praise of the Queen. Entitled *The Triumphs of Oriana*, this represented one of the finest collections of music of the period. Unfortunately, by the time the book was published in 1603 Elizabeth had died.

JAMES I

At the Coronation of James I the Gentlemen of the Chapel Royal included "the sub-dean, then seven mynisters in order of seniority, and four officers of the vestry". Some of the gentlemen, owing to advanced age or infirmity were unable to appear regularly and were in fact members in name only. For example, Robert Stone was ninety-three years of age and probably past his best, William Byrd was eighty and Thomas Sampson had completed fifty-one years as a member of the choir at his demise.

Just about this time certain other malpractices came to light, as for instance the misappropriation of funds intended for the choirs of Cathedrals and Chapels other than the Royal Chapels. "The Occasions of the Decay of Music in Cathedral and College Churches", preserved in a British Museum manuscript, informed the King that despite all previous grants and Elizabeth's Injunctions, the money had been "swallowed up by the Deans and Canons, because they are the only body of that incorporation, and the singing men are but inferior members".

The whole sorry business was given an airing in a ballad *Sweet music mourns and hath done long* written by a music-lover shortly after the accession of the King. The difficulties and frustrations of the period received some outspoken comment. Although James was a somewhat dour and generally unpopular figure, he cannot be criticised for lack of interest in the royal music. In 1604 he restored the custom of Henry VIII regarding the further education of boys whose voices had changed, providing they had served at least three years in the chapel. These young men were given the opportunity of studying in any college of royal foundation at Oxford or Cambridge. The appointments of gospeller and episteller were given as preliminary offices to musicians waiting for gentlemen's places. During this probationary period they were expected to look after and support those boys who were on the point of leaving the choir. A record of the 1620s shows clearly a practice of appointing a man first episteller, then gospeller and finally gentleman, as vacancies occurred.

Many of the musicians who had served Elizabeth so ably were retained in the royal establishment of James. Robert Stone, Philip Rosseter, John Bull, Nathaniel Giles, Ferdinando Richardson and John Mundy together with Orlando Gibbons and Thomas Tomkins

21

formed a brilliant group capable of producing sacred and secular music of the highest quality. As an example *Parthenia,* a book of pieces for the virginal first appeared in 1611. It was compiled "by three famous Masters, William Byrd, Dr. John Bull and Orlando Gibbons, Gentilmen of his Majesties most Illustrious Chappell", The first part is devoted to the music of Byrd and consists of several pairs of dances, the pavana and galiardo. Thus is produced an excellent contrast between the slow dance in quadruple time and the more sprightly tune in triple time. John Bull is represented in the middle section and Gibbons occupies the third portion. This last part contains a "Fantazia of foure parts" which might almost have been composed by Bach himself. This music not only satisfied the exacting conditions of the times; much of it remains today and serves as a lasting contribution from the early years of the seventeenth century. In particular the fine madrigals of Orlando Gibbons and Thomas Tomkins are much enjoyed by those who delight in this superb form of vocal music.

John Bull was appointed a member of the Chapel Royal in 1585 and became the organist six years later on the death of William Blitheman. He was given the freedom of the Merchant Taylors' Company in 1606 and during the same year he was one of those to whom James I ordered "gold chains, plates or medals" to be given.

On the 16th July 1607 the King and Prince Henry were guests at the Merchant Taylors' Hall, on which occasion they were entertained with music. While they dined "John Bull, Doctor of Musique, one of the organists of His Majesties Chappell-royall and free of the Merchant-taylors, being in a citizens gowne, cappe, and hood, played most excellent melodie upon a small payre of Organes, placed there for that purpose onely". (Stowe)

In spite of his important position in the court and city, Bull seems to have committed some wrong which necessitated his rapid departure from England. The Cheque Book of the Chapel Royal dated 1613 records that "John Bull, Doctor of Musicke, went beyond the seas without license and was admitted into the Archduke's service, and entered into paie there about Michaelmas".

This was the Archduke of Brussels, in whose private chapel Bull became one of the organists. Thus was created an incident which caused some considerable feeling on both sides of the channel. The British minister, in a letter to James I, saw fit to explain how he had notified the Archduke "that it was notorious to all the world the said Bull did not leave your Majesties service for any wrong done unto him, or for matter of religion under which fained pretext he now sought to wrong the reputation of your Majesties justice, but did in that dishonest manner steal out of England through the guilt of a corrupt conscience, to escape the punishment, which notoriously he had deserved, and was designed to have been inflicted on him by the hand of justice, for his incontinence, fornication, adultery, and other grievous crimes."

John Bull later became organist of Antwerp Cathedral. His great importance in the history of music was as a composer for virginals, and as such he laid the foundation of the modern pianoforte repertory.

As in the reigns of Henry VIII and Elizabeth the masque remained a favourite entertainment at court. Many leading members of the aristocracy took part, including James's queen, who danced in Jonson's *Masque of Blackness* at Whitehall in 1605. Generally speaking a more serious quality was gradually introduced into this form, as might be expected from such expert writers as Thomas Heywood, Ben Jonson and James Shirley. However, on one occasion at least, a midnight masque at court failed ignominiously. This was at Theobalds, Cheshunt, during a state visit of the King of Denmark. The royal hospitality, being particularly lavish, took heavy toll of almost everyone present, including the ladies. As a result the "entertainment" was not strictly according to the general principles of the masque.

In 1613 the wedding of Elizabeth, daughter of James, was also celebrated by a masque, but this time in the best of taste. It was presented, according to Howes, in his *Annals*, "at the Banqueting House in Whitehall, by lords and ladies, with many delicate devices and much melodious music. It was in three parts: a rustic masque, the usual anti-masque in which the speaking parts and dances were performed by professionals, and the main masque. The last was a masque of knights wearing doublets of carnation satin decked with stars of silver plate, with spangles of silver lace, Venetian hose and silk carnation stockings, with garters and roses according to their orders. The chief masquers arrived at the Banqueting House by water in the King's barge." This was written by Thomas Campion, a poet and composer, though a physician by profession. He was responsible for several important masques ordered for specific occasions, such as that performed at Whitehall on Twelfth Night 1607 to celebrate the wedding of Sir James Hay. Another was given at Caversham House four years later to honour Queen Anne, wife of James I, and a third was held at Whitehall on the occasion of the marriage between the Earl of Somerset and Lady Frances Howard. Other masques given during this reign included Jonson's *Lovers Triumph* and *Chloridia*. This latter was performed by the Queen and her ladies who also enjoyed their parts in Townshend's *Temple Restored*.

The duplication of musical posts existed as in former reigns. Orlando Gibbons held two posts at court as well as that of organist to the Chapel Royal. Thomas Warwick was another who gained from this system of plurality as he later succeeded Gibbons in his various appointments. Alfonso Ferrobosco must have been specially well thought of, as he enjoyed no less than four posts, viz. "a musicians place in general, a composer's place, a viol's place and an instructor's place to the prince in the art of music." This information was discovered in a letter found after his death in 1627.

In addition to the everyday duties, the Chapel Royal played an important part in state functions such as coronations and funerals, and on these occasions members of the King's Musick usually augmented the choir. James I normally employed forty musicians, the Queen fifteen, and the Prince of Wales also fifteen. Therefore, apart from the Chapel Royal, about seventy musicians were at court during this period. Instrumental resources remained much the same as in the previous reign. There were those who played the cornett, hautboy and recorder, and in 1603 Gormock McDermott was engaged as court harper, the first for almost forty years.

John Cooper was eminent as lutenist and violinist and taught music to the children of James I. He changed his name to the more fashionable sounding Giovanni Coperario and thus proved that those present-day musicians who overcome their frustrations in a like manner are not so very modern after all. He will probably be best remembered for his *Songs of Mourning*, composed on the death of Prince Henry. Some of these musicians performed at what might be termed minor state functions, as for example the baptism of Princess Mary in 1605. The chorus of one anthem "was filled with the help of musical instruments" and at the banquet which followed "the chapel and the musicians joined together, making excellent harmony with full anthems". At Queen Anne's churching later in the year anthems were sung "with organ, cornetts, sackbutt and ohter excellent instruments of music".

Although John Dowland (1563–1626) was one of the greatest

composers for lute and voice in history, he had little opportunity of practising his art at the Court in London. In 1580 he became lutenist to the English Ambassador in Paris, where he remained for some years and became converted to Roman Catholicism. During the 1590s he applied for a position at the court of Elizabeth but was not accepted, probably on religious grounds. He thereupon left for Germany, first in the service of the Duke of Brunswick and later as lutenist to the Landgrave of Hesse. He returned home and reverted to the Protestant faith, but in 1598 he accepted the post of court musician to King Christian IV of Denmark. Apparently he was much appreciated in that country, his salary being commensurate with that of the Admiral of the Realm. He finally settled in England in 1606 and from 1612 to 1618 was employed at the court of King James I.

Dowland's disappointment at being refused admission into the court of Queen Elizabeth did not deter him from composing a number of pieces in her honour. Of these, *Queen Elizabeth's Galliard* and *Melancholy Galliard* were particularly charming.

The *Cheque Book* describes how the gentlemen of the chapel fared at the funeral of King James. "His dead corps were brought from Theobalds to Denmark House . . . where all his officers attended and waited during the time that his corps lay there, except the chapel, who waited upon King Charles at Whitehall. Two days before the day of the funeral the corps were brought into the said chapel in great solemnity with an anthem . . . and the gentlemen of the chapel from that time waited there, and performed solemn service with the organ brought thither for that purpose; they also waited with the corps night and day; by night, first decani side, and next cantoris side, and twice in the night, viz. at nine of the clock and at midnight, they had prayers with a first and second chapters, and ended with an anthem . . . The black hangings, chairs, screens, cloths and other furnishing of both the chapel set up in Denmark House and at Whitehall were fees to the gentlemen of the chapel and divided amongst them".

CHARLES I

Three days after his accession in 1615, Charles I effected an agreement with France which resulted in his marriage to Henrietta Maria, sister of Louis XIII. The wedding, which took place later in the year at Canterbury, was notable for its fine music, much of it written by Orlando Gibbons. The composer was commanded to be present at the service, but on arrival he became a victim to smallpox and died there on Whit Sunday.

At the commencement of the reign there was an immediate increase in the number of musicians at court. This was in some degree due to the fact that those who had served the Prince of Wales were now brought into the King's Musick. In 1625 there appear to have been seventy-eight with an additional musical establishment for Queen Henrietta of some fifteen men and a few boys. Immediately after the royal marriage Richard Dering was appointed organist to the queen, and in that same year his name also appeared as "a musician for the lute and voice" to the King.

The occasion of the coronation on Candlemas Day 1626, was outstanding both for its splendour and the quality of its musical accompaniment. "Upon which day all the chapel met at the College Hall in Westminster, where thay had a breakfast at the charge of the college, from thence they went by a back way into the church, and so into the vestry, where together with the quire of Westminster Abbey they put on surplices and copes and went into Westminster Hall, and there waited until the King came thither . . . by water . . . into the great hall, where a large scaffold covered all with cloth, and upon it a throne and chair of estate. The chapel followed the Knights of the Bath, next the quire of West-minster, then the church: when all the chapel were within the church they began the first anthem. After singing 'I was glad when they said unto me, we will go into the house of the Lord' and after the archbishop had 'done at the corners of the scaffold, and the people's acclamation ended' the choirs sang another anthem, 'Strengthened be thy hand and exalted by thy right hand . . .' A third anthem followed the sermon and after a further section of the service the choirs joined together in singing 'Sadock the priest and Nathan the prophet anointed Solomon King and joyfully approaching they cried, God Save the King . . . Allelujah!' This was performed during the king's anointment by the archbishop. Further anthems were sung at other points in the ceremony, the eighth and last being 'O hearken then unto the voice of my calling'. At the end of the service the king returned back again into Westminster Hall in the same manner as he went, the chapel going in their former order, and singing all the way till they came to Westminster Hall door,

and there they stayed, making a lane for the king and all the lords to pass betwixt them, and continued singing till the king was within the hall . . . the gentlemen and children now could take off their copes and surplices and return to Whitehall for what they must have welcomed, 'some allowance or diet for their suppers'."
A History of the English Coronation. Selramm.

It was during this same year, 1626, that Lanier was mentioned as Master of the Music. This is believed to be the very first use of the title, although the exact duties appertaining to the post are somewhat obscure. Presumably he would exercise some general control over the musicians at court, but whether musical, disciplinary or both is difficult to establish.

Although the number of musicians had increased, the instrumentation remained much as before, but with a new importance in the music for lutes and voices. In 1635 the Kings Musick consisted of nineteen viols and violins, seven flutes, nine hautboys and sackbuts, five recorders, eight cornetts, eighteen or more lutes and voices, two virginals and a harp. The salaries paid varied enormously. Fourteen received £40 a year and livery money, a total of £52:2:6. In contrast, the salary of Stephen Nau, a violinist and composer was £200 per annum. From 1626 Nicholas Lanier, composer, painter and favourite of the king received the same basic salary as Nau, but certain additions brought his total income to £272:5:0, a handsome sum.

Some of the musicians taught and trained boys for the royal service and a warrant of 1626 issued at Westminster gives some idea of the importance attached to this formal apprenticeship. "We will and command you that at the feast day of St. John Baptist next coming you deliver or cause to be delivered to our well beloved servant Andrea Lanier, one of our musicians, these parcels hereafter following for the summer liveries of two boys which we appointed to his custodie and keeping, for the training up, and to be made fit for our service, in the knowledge of the flutes and cornetts, to each of them severally nine yards of broad cloth for a cloak jerkin and breeches at thirteen shillings fourpence the yard; to each of them, two yards and a half of bayes to line their said cloaks at four shillings the yard; ten dozen of silk lace at three shillings fourpence the dozen for each of them; to each a quarter of a yard of velvet for a cape at six shillings. Five yards of fustian for doublets for them at four shillings the yard; twelve dozen of silk buttons for them at sixpence the dozen; two pairs of worsted stockings at ten shillings the pair to each of them; one pair of silk garters to each of them price six shillings; one hat with a band price ten shillings to each; and for shirts, bands and cuffs for one half year, six pounds for them both. And for the making of the said cloak, jerkin, doublet and breeches, and all small furniture, forty shillings. And further our pleasure and command is that you deliver or cause to be delivered to the said Andrea Lanier for the said two boys at the Feast of St. Andrew the Apostle next coming, after the date hereof the like parcels for their winter liveries, and so forth every half yearly''.

Despite the low wages paid to many a court musician, the position was much sought after on account of the several privileges then in being. For instance, a certificate issued to every new member of the King's Musick in 1640 stated that ''he should not be arrested, chosen into any office, warned to attend any assizes, impanelled on juries, charged with any contributions, taxes or payments''.

Charles I gathered together a group of outstanding musicians which included Nathaniel Giles, a famous organist and master of the children, Robert Johnson, a lutenist and composer, John Adson, composer whose *Courtly Masquing Ayres* were highly thought of, George Jeffries, organist to the court at Oxford during the Civil War, and Thomas Ford, another lutenist and composer whose music is still performed today.

The king himself more than dabbled in composition, and a manuscript in the British Museum *Mark how he blushful morne* bears the heading ''By his Majesty''. This song is found in Playford's *Second Book of Select Ayres and Diologues* which is attributed to Nicholas Lanier. A fashion of the period was that of self-deprecation or a sense of mock modesty where anything of a creative nature was concerned. However, there seems to be little doubt that Charles was the composer, although he would hardly have allowed that fact to become public.

Charles I had considerable resources not only in music but also in poetry and art. Together with Inigo Jones he laid the foundation of a new interest in art by starting a Royal Collection of pictures. Many fine paintings were bought, and others already in the household were carefully repaired and cleaned. Both Van Dyck and Rubens spent much time at the palace, the former being engaged in painting the king's portraits and the latter undertaking the herculean task of painting the great panels on the ceiling of the Banqueting Hall. A comment on the artistic interests of the king appeared in *The Musical Gramarian*, written by the Honourable

Roger North, who became Attorney General during the reign of James II.

"Charles I had a very ingenious virtuoso, one Nicholas Laniere, whom he employed into Italy to buy capitall pictutes; Mr Laniere was no less a virtuoso at music than pictures, for which the king greatly esteemed him. Being so qualified he must needs be a nice observer of the Italian music, especially that most valuable amongst them, the vocal. After his return he composed a recitative, which was a poem being the tragedy of Hero and Leander. The king was exceedingly pleased with this song and caused Laniere often to sing it. This was the first of the Recitativo kind that ever graced the English language".

York was a favourite city of Charles and he paid several visits to the northern capital before he became an exile there. It was due to his particular interest in the Minster that a large sum of money was made available towards a new and splendid organ.

The name Tomkins figured prominently in royal circles during the sixteenth and seventeenth centuries and the family is reputed to have included twelve musicians. Of these Thomas Tomkins was organist of the Chapel Royal, Giles was Musician for the Virginals to Charles; John became a Gentleman Extraordinary of the Chapel Royal and Robert remained a musician of the royal household for many years. Of William Gregory, Charles Coleman, William Child, Benjamin Rogers and Henry Lawes, some served under Cromwell during the Commonwealth and all were re-appointed royal musicians at the Restoration.

The execution of Charles was a melancholy occasion for his supporters and for none more than the musicians at court. They naturally had grave misgivings as to the future. Certainly there was an immediate recession in music-making, particularly by royal standards, but music did not cease by any means.

This might be a convenient place to mention briefly those indefatigable diarists Anthony Wood (1632) the antiquarian and Samuel Pepys (1633) the civil servant. Both were keen amateur musicians who mixed freely with their professional brethren and as a result gleaned much information denied to others less favoured. Students of the seventeenth century have cause to be indebted to them, as each possessed that gift of noting and recording every day happenings around them, even the seemingly unimportant things. Pepys normally surveyed the London scene, whilst Wood concerned himself with affairs in Oxford. Consequently their testimony regarding those two cities is of considerable value.

CROMWELL

In a chapter devoted to music in the court, any reference to the Commonwealth regime might seem out of place. But for eleven years Oliver Cromwell took the place of the monarch as head of state, and it is interesting to note what changes took place during this period. Contrary to general opinion the Puritans had no active dislike of music and in fact secular music flourished as never before.

Official objection was directed towards elaborate church music, in which highly trained choirs and organs had hitherto played so important a part. Again, there was no objection to organs as such, but only those connected with the church. Organs were often to be found in private houses and in taverns, and in such surroundings were not interfered with by the authorities. Indeed Cromwell enjoyed organ music and was himself responsible for the removal of the organ from Magdalen College, Oxford, where it was no longer necessary, and had it installed at Hampton Court Palace. Here John Hingston, private organist to the Protector, often gave recitals before his patron. He also trained two boys to sing the Latin motets of Richard Dering, which proved to be Cromwell's favourite music for voices. This in its way was surprising, as Dering was a Roman Catholic, and as such, one might have expected the Puritans to avoid contact with his music.

Cromwell also maintained a domestic body of musicians under the leadership of the same Hingston. Although this group did not compare numerically with those of royalty during the previous two centuries, many of the performers were highly talented. An embassy to Sweden in 1653 included some of these musicians, who on that visit created an excellent impression on the cultured Queen Christina.

Benjamin Rogers was well thought of as a musician at this time. He had been organist at Eton and a singer in St. George's Chapel until the choir was disbanded in 1644. Cromwell was interested in his music and helped him professionally on occasions. As an example, in 1658 the Vice Chancellor and Senate of Cambridge University were ordered to alter their rules of admission for

Bachelor of Music especially to suit Rogers. Some six years later he became organist and choirmaster of Magdalen College, Oxford from which appointment he was dismissed in 1685 for irregularities. He composed a considerable amount of vocal and instrumental music, but is now chiefly remembered for his *Hymnus Eucharisticus* which is still sung from Magdalen Tower at 5 a.m. on the first day of May every year.

Musically, the period was not as barren or as gloomy as has often been suggested. More secular music was published than at any time preceding or immediately following the Commonwealth. This was in part due to the suppression of stage plays and to the almost complete ban on church music.

The masque, so popular with a long line of kings and queens, maintained its position and in 1653 Shirley's *Cupid and Death* was first produced. This work, with music by Matthew Locke and Christopher Gibbons was performed by order of Cromwell in honour of the Portuguese ambassador.

Opera commenced in Britain with a performance of the quaintly named *The First Dayes Entertainment at Rutland House by Declamation and Musick; after the manner of the Ancients*. First tried out in 1656, it was in the nature of an experiment to see whether the authorities would allow its continuation. The work was written by Sir William Davenant, the Poet Laureate, who surprised but gratified by lack of official condemnation, immediately carried out further projects of a like nature. Within a few months *The Siege of Rhodes* was produced, generally considered to be the first real opera performed in the country. The music, which accompanied the dialogue throughout, was the work of no fewer than five composers, Charles Coleman, Henry Cooke, George Hudson, Henry Lawes and Matthew Locke. The title page of the programme bore the description *Made a Representation by the Art of Prospective in Scenes, And the Story Sung in Recitative Musick, At the back part of Rutland House in the upper end of Aldersgate-Street, London*.

Two other operas produced during the Commonwealth period were *The Cruelty of the Spaniards in Peru* and *The History of Sir Francis Drake*. If further proof were needed of the amount of music-making during Cromwellian times, mention might be made of an incident recorded by Roger l'Estrange in *Truth and Loyalty Vindicated* (1662) "Being in St. James his Parke, I heard an Organ touched in a little low room of one Mr. Hinckson's. I went in, and found a Private Company of some five or six Persons. They desired me to take up a

Viole, and bear a Part. I did so . . . By and by (without the least colour of a Design or Expectation) in comes Cromwell; he found us Playing and (as I remember) so he left us".

Hinckson (or Hingston) mentioned previously as leader of Cromwell's domestic musicians, was only one of many who carried on music clubs during this time. Organists, no longer allowed to play in cathedrals, churches or college chapels, installed small organs in their houses and invited musical friends to share an evening of pleasure. Several accounts exist of music-clubs flourishing throughout the country.

Also, surprisingly enough, dancing was not unknown during the Commonwealth, as will be obvious from the publication of the first three editions of Playford's *The English Dancing Master*. Cromwell is reported to have danced at the wedding of one of his daughters in 1657 on which occasion "they had forty-eight violins and much mirth with frolics, besides mixt dancing". The frolics and mixt dancing continued until five o'clock in the morning according to a contemporary newsletter.

One item on the agenda of the Council during the 1656–7 session referred to "the Advancement of Music" and resulted in the setting up of a small committee to enquire into the state of music and musicians. It is not known whether in fact this governmental attempt to improve conditions had much effect, but it does contradict the impression that the Puritans were rigidly opposed to the art. Even Anthony Wood, who loathed the regime, was forced to admit – unwillingly – that "they encouraged instrumental musick and some there were that had musick meetings every week in their chambers".

CHARLES II

After Cromwell's death and the dissolution of the Rump Parliament came the Restoration. Charles II arrived from France in 1660 and was given an hysterical welcome comparable to that afforded Henry V on his return from the same country in the fifteenth century. The streets of London were packed with those eager to see the new king. The procession consisted of 20,000 horse and foot, lords and noblemen, mayors and aldermen, and by members of all the City companies, with special music for the occasion composed by Matthew Locke.

According to Thomas Burke "All the bells of London were ringing; the roadway was strewn with flowers, and the windows of the houses hung with coloured tapestries. The conduits, as usual, supplied wine in place of water, and every section of the procession had its own accompaniment of trumpets, fifes and drums".

Such then was the auspicious start to the new reign. Theatres were re-opened and music and dancing reverted to the scale of pre-Commonwealth days. We are told that the Royal Palace was re-decorated, beautified and equipped with a lavishness in advance of any other in Europe. The court became the most colourful in Britain's history with a predominantly light-hearted approach to life. This change of scene to pomp and pageantry on the grand scale was much to the liking of the public. It was a tradition at that time for the citizenry to wander through the Palace at will, a Palace given over to music, laughter, revels and dancing; also intrigue.

A charming story is told concerning Charles II and Mark Carse, the 'Laird o' Cockpen' who fought for the royalist cause at the battle of Worcester in 1651. Being on the losing side, Carse felt it expedient to seek refuge in Holland for a time and there he was able to use his musical gifts to advantage, both as organist and teacher. At the Restoration he returned to Scotland only to find his estates occupied by Commonwealth supporters.

This was a not unusual state of affairs at the beginning of the new reign and was one of the serious problems which occupied the attention of King and Parliament. The House of Commons debated at length a situation causing disquiet throughout the country. Eventually legislation was brought in to restore all property previously owned by the Crown, the Church and a certain number of highly-placed individuals. But the vast majority of royalists were unable to claim their lands due to the complicated transactions involved. Carse decided on his own personal course of action and at once set off for London where he enlisted the help of the organist of the Chapel Royal. It was agreed that the laird should be allowed to play the organ on the next occasion the king attended service. He chose as his closing voluntary the old Scots melody 'Brose and Butter' in which Charles had shown great delight during that part of his exile at The Hague. The king was amazed, feeling certain that only one person was capable of playing the boisterous tune in such a manner. He made enquiries and the subsequent meeting was a joyous one, with Carse petitioning and succeeding in having his lands restored.

The musical establishment at court immediately increased and the Chapel Royal, which had ceased to function with the execution of Charles I, was now restored. A remarkable transformation took place in the service of the church, and nowhere was this more in evidence than in the Chapel Royal. The old rites were quickly brought back and within a fortnight the organ was playing again after a long silence. On December 20, 1661 the Book of Common Prayer was adopted by both Houses of Parliament and was given the Royal Assent on May 19th of the following year. It contained what to church musicians was a most important phrase, "In quires and places where they sing, here followeth the anthem". As a result of these changes the people of London travelled out of town every Sunday to hear the choir and see the King at Chapel, a sound and a sight which delighted them after the sombre days of the Commonwealth.

Captain Henry Cooke, that able musician and teacher, who had himself started as a chorister in the Chapel Royal, and who had served in the Royalist forces during the Civil War, now returned as Master of the Children. He was highly thought of as a composer for chruch and stage, and his works included coronation music and hymns specially written for the installation of the Knights of the Garter. With characteristic energy he applied an almost military discipline on the boy choristers and as a result the famous choir soon attained its previous very high standard. He also built up a fine choir at St. George's Chapel in less than four years.

Cooke was fortunate in having two exceptionally talented choir boys on hand at once, Pelham Humphrey and John Blow. Not only had they good voices, but at a very early age they showed unusual ability at composition. The new King, during his exile in France, had become a devotee of the type of music then popular at the court of Louis XIV. Determined to introduce a similar liveliness into his own surroundings and having no taste for Tallis, Byrd and Orlando Gibbons, he substituted the theatrical French style for the traditional music of England. Several of the more conservative composers from the previous reign complained bitterly of being ordered to "add Symphonies, etc., with instruments" to their anthems and strongly objected to the new music introduced by Charles. He thereupon sent some of the most brilliant younger musicians abroad to learn the new techniques. Included amongst these were Pelham Humphrey, then seventeen years of age and

34

John Banister, who on their return were appointed to responsible posts in the King's Musick.

Banister, who for a short time was leader of the King's band, committed some slight indiscretion and was removed from office. His place was taken by the Frenchman Louis Grabu. Pepys was present at a concert directed by this new favourite and made mention of it in his diary of October 1st, 1667: "To White Hall: and there in the Boarded Gallery did hear the musick with which the King is presented this night by Monsieur Grebus, the master of the music; both instrumental, I think twenty-four violins, and vocall: an English song about peace. But, God forgive me! I never was so little pleased with a consort of music in my life. The manner of setting the words and repeating them out of order and that with a number of voices, makes me sick, the whole design of vocall musick being lost by it. Here was a great press of people, but I did not see many pleased with it, only the instrumental musick he had brought by practice to be very just".

About this time some fine music for wind instruments was written. One particularly worthy of mention was composed "for his Majesty's Sagbutts and Cornetts" by Matthew Locke, and was performed at a progress of Charles II in London during 1661. It consisted of an Air and Courante in five parts, a Pavan-Almond in six parts and a Sarabande in four parts. This was typical of the seventeenth century suite. This same Matthew Locke is described most charmingly in Roger North's *Memoirs of Music* (1728). "Mr. Matthew Locke was the most considerable master of musick after Jenkins fell off. He was organist at Somerset House chappell as long as he lived . . . In musick he had a robust vein, and many of his compositions went about; he set most of the psalmes to musick in parts, for the use of some vertuoso ladyes in the city; and he composed a magnifick consort of 4 parts after the old style, which was the last made".

The number and importance of musical positions at the Court of Charles II make somewhat perplexing reading today. In addition to Henry Cooke, then Master of the Children, several other senior appointments were established at the Restoration. Nicholas Lanier, already mentioned as Master of the King's Musick to Charles I, was reappointed in a similar capacity to the new king. But he was then an elderly man and some two years later was succeeded by Edward Coleman.

Christopher Gibbons, son of the famous Orlando, became

private organist to the king as well as organist at the Chapel Royal. Other responsible posts were those of Composer in Ordinary, occupied by Matthew Locke, and that of Master of the King's Band, an appointment which should not be confused with that of Master of the King's Musick. Henry Lawes was another of the reinstated musicians of the previous reign and he set the words of *Zadok the Priest* to music for the Coronation of Charles II. George Hudson, previously mentioned for his part in the opera *The Siege of Rhodes* also became a member of the King's Band and Composer to the Monarch.

Other musicians who attended at the court were Thomas Tudway, Robert Smith, Michael Wise, John Lenton, Henry Eccles and John Blow. The last named bore out his early promise and achieved great fame as a composer. Among his successful works was the setting of Herrick's *Go perjur'd man* written in the style of Carrissimi at the king's request. He wrote three anthems for the Coronation of James II and was made a member of the Royal Band as well as Composer in Ordinary. In 1687 he succeeded Wise as almoner and choirmaster at St. Paul's Cathedral – not yet completed – and was then responsible for an anthem at the opening service in 1697. Other of his compositions included works in praise of William and Mary and odes on the death of the Queen. Blow's anthem *The Lord God is a sun* had been sung in 1689 at the Coronation of William and Mary and his *He will rejoice* was performed at a Thanksgiving Day on the discovery of a plot against the king in April 1696.

William Tucker, William Child and Nicholas Staggins also contributed much to the musical life of Charles II's reign. Staggins was especially famous, being in turn Master of the King's Band, then Professor of Music in the University of Cambridge and finally Master of the King's Music, a post he held until 1698.

But of this galaxy of talent the brightest star was undoubtedly Henry Purcell, one of the very greatest English composers of all time. He entered the Chapel Royal as a chorister and studied in turn under Cooke, Humphrey and Blow. Although organist of Westminster Abbey at the age of 16 Purcell was also composer for the violins and one of the organists of the Chapel Royal. He wrote a vast amount of music in his short life and not by any means wholly for the church. He in fact excelled at every type of music then practised. His output included a great deal of music for the stage, forty-nine different works in all. In some cases this consisted of incidental music for plays and in others the complete score for an opera, as for instance the magnificent *Dido and Aeneas* and *King Arthur*. He composed twenty-four odes, fiften of which were written in honour of Charles II, James II and Queen Mary. Those for the last mentioned took the form of birthday odes from the beginning of her joint reign with William III until the year of her death.

These odes include *Now does the glorious day appear* (1690), *Welcome, welcome glorious morn* (1691), *Love's goddess sure was blind* (1692), *Celebrate this festival* (1693), *Come ye sons of art away* (1694). They were written for solo voices and chorus with a normal accompaniment of flutes, oboes, trumpets and strings. On one or two occasions certain instruments were omitted as in 1692 when no oboes or trumpets were used. Other important items in his royal offerings were *My heart is inditing* for the Coronation of James II, *Blessed are they that fear* for the thanksgiving in 1688 "for the Queen's being with child", and *Thou knowest O Lord, the secrets of our hearts* sung at the funeral of Queen Mary in 1695. For this same occasion Purcell wrote a fine funeral march for "flat mournful trumpets" (slide trumpets). This was an adaptation from music originally written for *The Libertine* in 1676. He also wrote a mass of secular songs for solo voice, together with duets and trios, instrumental music for strings and keyboard; anthems, services, organ pieces and even catches.

JAMES II

In 1686, a year after James II came to the throne, a tune appeared in print in a book of lessons for the recorder or flute. This little melody which later received the spurious Irish name *Lillibulero* played an important part in current history. As a result of General Talbot being appointed Lord Lieutenant of Ireland, a number of highly satirical verses were published, set to the tune mentioned. This was a bitter party song ridiculing Talbot and the Irish Roman Catholics and has remained in the repertory of the Orange Party ever since. It is considered more likely that Purcell was the composer of the tune which is now known to many children for its association with the nursery rhyme "There was an old woman tossed up in a blanket, seventy times as high as the moon".

On Purcell's death in 1695 there appeared in *The Flying Post* the following announcement: "Mr. Henry Pursel, one of the most celebrated Masters of the Science of Musick in the Kingdom and scarce inferior to any in Europe, dying on Thursday last; the Dean of Westminster knowing the great worth of the deceased, forthwith summoned a Chapter, and unanimously resolved that he shall be interred in the Abbey, with all the Funeral Solemnity they are capable to perform for him, granting his widow the choice of ground to reposit his Corps free from any charge, who has appointed it at the foot of the Organs, and this evening he will be interred, the whole Chapter assisting with their vestments; together with all the Lovers of that Noble Science, with the united Choyres of that and the Chappel Royal, when the Dirge composed by the Deceased for her late Majesty of Ever Blessed Memory, will be Played by Trumpets and other Musick; And his place of Organist is disposed of to that great Master, Dr. Blow''.

Throughout the seventeenth century wind bands rose to eminence, none more so than those of the royal court. Shawms and trombones were still used, and althogh they formed a unit in themselves, cornetts were also introduced. The Stuart love of military display favoured the fife and drum band, whilst court pageantry gave full rein to royal trumpeters who numbered, during the century, from sixteen to twenty players as well as a royal kettledrummer.

At this stage we might pause for a moment or two and consider the very high standard of music in court circles during the Tudor and Stuart reigns. To some extent the pre-eminence of the Chapel Royal and the King's Musick was due to their considerable size, to the great ability of many of their members, to the instrumental and financial resources and perhaps most important of all, to the keen interest taken in the musicians by a surprising number of Kings and Queens. Tallis, Farrant, Tye, Dowland, Byrd, Bull, Gibbons, Morley, Lawes, Tomkins, Cooke, Locke, Humfrey, Blow and Purcell represent but a proportion of the outstanding composers who made reputations at the Chapel Royal.

As mentioned earlier when writing of the sixteenth century, far more foreign names appeared in the King's Band than in the Chapel Royal and in fact about two thirds of the instrumentalists came from continental countries or were the direct descendants of foreigners living in England. In a list of such musicians we should find the names Bassano, Galliardello, Truches, Ferrobosco, Nau and Lanier, some of which occur several times in succeeding generations.

THE SCOTTISH COURT

During the splendid days of royal music in England we find evidence of a similar vigorous policy in the Scottish court, despite the destruction of so many pre-Reformation records. The term "Chapel Royal" meant the same as in England, a body of clerics of various positions of importance, together with a group of singers, both men and boys. This unit, which was organised for ease of mobility, accompanied the king on his many royal progresses.

The first building which may claim to be the Chapel Royal in Scotland was that at Stirling Castle founded by Alexander I in 1120 and dedicated to his mother. Originally known as Queen Margaret's Chapel, it also bore the titles of the King's Chapel and St. Michael's Chapel at various times. Although little is known of musical establishment until the reign of James III, some information is available regarding the instrumental resources of the court before this time.

JAMES I

James I, whose reign lasted from 1406 until 1437 was himself a good musician, and as an executant he in many respects anticipated Henry VIII. He played the tabor, flute, trumpet, shepherd's pipe, psaltery, lute, organ and was particularly skilled as a harpist. He also sang well and had a reputation as a composer of ability. The evening before his assassination he spent "yn synging and pyping and harpyng and yn other honest solaces of grete pleasance and disport". The king was an expert piper and his personal interest in the instrument had a considerable bearing on the popularity of the bagpipe in the fifteenth century.

JAMES II

What might be termed domestic music suffered a setback and was relegated to the background during the reign of James II owing to the more pressing matters on hand. Apart from two of the "King's mimes and minstrels" Marco Trumpet and Ada Reeve, other mention of music is confined almost entirely to trumpets. This is not surprising having regard to the troublous mid-fifteenth century and the fact that the trumpet signified royalty and often royalty at war.

JAMES III

James III was a keen musician who gave much attention to the Chapel Royal, where the services were based on those of his contemporary, Henry IV. He was lavish in his endowment and maintained the highest possible standard. His enthusiasm was boundless and led him to coerce or detain William Rogers, a musical member of an embassy sent to Scotland by the English King. Rogers, by his teaching helped to foster a great interest in music throughout Scotland as well as at the court, and was later knighted by a grateful sovereign. All who delighted in music were drawn to the court, but owing to the destruction of the High Treasurer's Accounts little information is available regarding the names of those who entertained, apart from a solitary lute player, John Brown. In spite of his exceptional work, or perhaps because of it Rogers was seized by a section of the dissident nobility and hanged in 1482.

JAMES IV

It is possible that the idea of a collegiate church, on the lines of other great courts was suggested during the reign of James III, although this did not materialise until James IV came to the throne. Almost immediately after his coronation an increase in the number of priests and musicians took place, until the establishment of the Chapel Royal contained a dean, sub-dean, sacristan, precentor, sixteen canons, sixteen singing-men and six well-trained choirboys. This enabled one half of the chapel to travel with the king – when an organ was often carried – whilst the remainder maintained the services at Stirling.

James IV was obviously a talented musician and according to the Somerset Herald the king entertained Margaret Tudor on their wedding day by playing on the clavychordes and lute. This was at Holyroodhouse in 1503 and on that occasion the City Minstrels of Aberdeen were invited to attend and provide music at the Palace. Eight years later when the king visited the granite city, they greeted him with "the sound on minstrallis blaring into the sky" while "four and twenty madins young played on timberallis and syngand richt sweitlie". Apparently the queen brought some English minstrels with her to the Scottish court. In the first year of their marriage the records show that eight English minstrels were paid a total of £56. Harpers were particularly encouraged at the court, James Mylsoun, Sowles, Alexander, Henry Philip and Bragman being some of the more famous. The king also favoured the Highland clarsach and as a result Martin Clareshaw, Pate Harpur and "Odenelis" (Ireland man) all experts on that instrument were attached to the court.

Performers on the lute were accorded considerable royal recognition during this reign. The average players such as Adam Dickson, Robert Hay, John Ledebetar, Lindores Rankine, Robert Rudman and Gray Steil received 14/- a quarter. A certain Jacob, of whom there were several entries until 1503, when he pawned his lute, was paid 28/- a quarter, and specially gifted players, as for instance Knennar the queen's lutar, received £3:6:8 for the half year (1505).

Apart from the accounts dealing with the harpers there were also references to fiddlers. Three performers Adam Boyd, Bennet and James Widderspune were members of the court in 1503, but the instruments had been in use from about 1490. It is doubtful whether they were in fact violins as we know them today; they may well have been the somewhat harsh-toned three-stringed rebecs.

Itinerant musicians paid many visits to the castle and seem to have been well received. We read of "the Inglis pyparis that com to the castel yet and playit to the King" in 1489, and during the following year there was Blind Harry, the famous minstrel with only one hand. The court welcomed English minstrels and in "Ordinaire Feis and yeirlie Pensonis" are found several entries referring to such entertainers.

1503 "To Inglis menstrales". "To the trumpeters of Ingland". "to the Erle of Oxford's twa menstrales" and "to the Inglis harparis"

1504 "To twa Inglise wemen that sang in the Kingis pail-
zeouse."

Another item mentions an allowance of two liveries a year to five
"Etalians", quarterly sums to four violinists, fees for two labourers
and four performers on "the trumpettis of weir" (war trumpets),
and an amount for a new lute and two dozen strings. In addition
four drummers or tabronars, Ansle, Guilliam, Portuous and
Quhynbore were also on the establishment. Italians were popular
performers at court but many French and Irish musicians also
found favour with the king.

It was unusual for singers to be mentioned individually in the
records as they would normally be members of the Chapel Royal.
However, Nicholas Abernethy was "King's sangster" in 1512 at
£20 per annum and prior to this the "crukit vicar of Dumfreise"
was present at the court as a vocalist. The poems of David Lyndsay
were set to music and sung to the king, thus establishing something
of the quality found at the court.

At this time some interesting higher officials were in residence
at the Chapel Royal. The Dean was James Beaton, who later
achieved notoriety as Archbishop of St. Andrews. John Major, a
famous historian, was canon and treasurer, and the sacristan
Alexander Paterson was part author of an important work *For
Singing the Mass*. An inventory of the chapel taken in 1505 tells of
"Three pairs of organs, one of wooden, and two of tin or lead pipes".
In the music library were "Four large music books written on
parchment having divers capital letters gilt . . . Two volumes on
parchment, with notes in counterpoint . . . Three graduals written
on parchment, and the large gradual, written on parchment, given
to the king by deceased Abbot of St. Columba".

JAMES V

James V continued this tradition of music-making and his
daughter Mary Queen of Scots sang to her own lute accompaniment
and was an accomplished performer on the virginals. About this
time there was a proposal in royal circles to move the court from
Stirling to Edinburgh. The Abbey of the Holy Rood, built by David I
in 1128, was the attraction. James IV lived there for a time and began
the domestic building which was later to figure so prominently

MARY, QUEEN OF SCOTS

The Palace of Holyroodhouse, attached to the well-endowed abbey became the principal residence of Queen Mary and her son James VI until his accession to the English throne. But the Chapel Royal was not installed there immediately and was in fact in attendance at the baptism of James VI at Stirling in 1561, on which occasion "the choristers sang appropriate airs accompanied by the organs". The Reformation of 1560, which in Scotland was so uncompromising, resulted in enormous damage to the cathedrals and abbeys. Practically all the organs were destroyed and all but the simplest Church music was abolished, although the Chapel Royal was spared for a while.

Although ecclesiastical music was at a low-ebb, domestic music flourished at the court. This was largely due to the Queen's love of the art and to the fact that she was a performer of considerable skill. In addition to possessing an excellent singing voice, Mary played the cittern, harp and harpsichord and was also an accomplished dancer. In this last respect and to the everlasting scandalisation of a large number of her subjects, she organised a masked ball at which several ladies of the household appeared in complete male attire.

Many musicians were attracted to the court, mostly foreign and of this group one was destined to play an important and tragic part in its history. This was David Rizzio, a native of Piedmont and a member of the staff of Morvette the Ambassador from Savoy. His ability in the sister arts of music and poetry had gained for him high regard, particularly in France, where he was considered responsible for many of the popular airs of uncertain parentage. "A merry fallow and a gud musition", he ingratiated himself with the royal musicians, the majority of whom were French. After performing with them on several occasions he succeeded in pleasing the Queen and obtained a permanent situation in the music of the court. A man of ambition, Rizzio did not long remain satisfied with his relatively humble position. He arranged a number of masques at the court and his influence steadily increased until he was appointed her private secretary in 1564. Two years later he was stabbed to death.

One of the criticisms levelled in the Dumfries Declaration by the Protestant Lords, to justify their opposition to Mary, was her "leaving the wholsom advice and counsell" of her nobles and barons, and following instead that "of suche men, strangers, as have nather judgement nor experience of the ancient lawes and governance of this realm, not naturall love towards her Majestie nor subjects thereof, being men of base degrie, and seeking nothing but their own commodities". Of these base foreigners, the most hated was Rizzio.

A warrant dated 9th December 1566 tells of the payment for maintenance of lutes at the Palace: "Maister Robert Rychardson Thesaurer that ye incontinent efter the sycht heir of ansueir to our servant Jhon Hume ten poundis, usual mony of Scotland, for luit stryngis that he has bocht, and for to by otheris alsua, and for to pay for the caryage of the luitis and raparyng of thaym; and it salbe weill all ouit to yow, ye schawand this our precept at your comptis for your warrand.

Subscrivit wyth our hand, at our Paly of Holyroudhous, the IX day of December, the yeir of God a.m. Vclxvi yeris.

Marie R."

The following year the Queen returned to Stirling for a short stay and on Sunday, September 14th, her chaplains intended to sing high mass in the Chapel Royal, but "the Earl of Argile and the Lord James so disturbed the quire, that some, both priest and clerks, left their places with broken hands and bloody ears. It was a sport alone for some that were there to behold it. Others there were that shed a tear or two, and made no more of the matter". *Keith's History*.

In 1571 Parliament decreed "that the said Chapel should be purged of all monuments of idolatory or other things whatsomever dedicated to superstition", and to the Earl of Mar was given the responsibility of carrying out the order. Although much was destroyed the chapel still functioned. Thomas Hudsoun was appointed Master of his Majesty's Chapel Royal in 1586 and was commanded that the service there should conform with "the religion presently professed within the realm". The chapel was futher guaranteed its status as a musical institution by three acts of Parliament passed in 1592, 1594 and 1606 respectively.

JAMES VI

James VI, who came to the throne in 1567 was undoubtedly a great music-lover and there remain many examples of his outstanding assistance to musicians and musical bodies. He was petitioned on various counts and rarely turned away empty-handed those musicians who required his help. He also took a lively interest in re-establishing several of the old sang-scuils which once had flourished throughout the country.

The wedding of James and Anne of Denmark was solemnized in 1590 at the Abbey of Holyrood, but the baptism of their first son Henry took place in the chapel at Stirling. This was in 1594 and the occasion caught briefly some of the brilliance of former days. With the subsequent removal of the entire court to Edinburgh however, the chapel and its music ceased to operate. For a time the king kept up a high standard of music at Holyrood, but on his departure in 1603 to become King of England as well as Scotland a period of stagnation set in, during which time only a small staff was maintained at the Palace. In 1612 James suddenly became interested in Holyrood Chapel again and as a result William Birnie was appointed as Dean and Master. He was instructed to engage prebendaries "skillfull in music" and by 1617 it was obvious that James VI of Scotland was determined to enjoy the type of music provided for him as James I of England.

This entailed the introduction of the Anglican Service and the building of a new organ in the Chapel Royal. These innovations did not please the people, who in their straight-forward Scottish manner made no attempt to conceal their feelings. The king's enthusiasm waned somewhat and on his return to London the chapel music again lapsed into its former dismal state. It was recorded in 1623 that of sixteen canons, nine prebends and six choirboys, only seven put in an appearance and their contribution was merely "the Common Tune of a psalm".

The varied fortunes in the music of the Scottish court took yet another turn with the accession of Charles I in 1625. His first act was to appoint Edward Kellie as Director of Music with sufficient financial backing to enable him to obtain first rate musicians. "The Chapel Royal almost immediately came to life again. An organist, sixteen men and six boy choristers, several instrumentalists and a quantity of suitable music were collected together in London and transported to Holyrood. The orchestral resources included performers on the flute, viol, pandore, cornett and sackbutt. With this considerable array of talent the Chapel Royal was in business again with a service similar to that in London, but instead of being held daily it was on Sundays only. This state of affairs contined for twelve years, until in fact the king attempted to introduce Laud's liturgy. The Scots refused to accept this new move and according to the Spalding *Memorials,* "all the chaplains, choristers and musicians were discharged and the organ broken".

During the Commonwealth period the chapel naturally remained silent, but with the Restoration, Charles II learning nothing from history tried to reproduce something of its previous glory. We have seen how his liking for the theatrical French style of music had alienated many people in London, so it is difficult to understand how the introduction of a similar type was to succeed in Edinburgh. The king expressed the opinion "that the chapel within the palace of Holyroodhouse did not please him", and the Privy Council announced that the Abbey Church was to be "the Chapel Royal in all times coming", a somewhat rash assertion as events proved.

James, Duke of York, who acted as Commissioner to the Scottish Parliament for his brother the king, took up residence at Holyroodhouse in 1679, together with his Duchess, Mary d'Este and the Princess Anne. The court was distinctly lively, and among the various festivities, the masquerade caused the gravest misgivings to the Calvinists. This form of amusement was many-sided and often included a masked ball accompanied by a degree of revelry. The royal family frequently took part with members of the household in such pieces as Dryden's *Indian Emperor* and *The Spanish Friar.*

JAMES VII

The very last attempt to revive the music of the chapel was made by James VII of Scotland and II of England, who also re-introduced the Order of the Thistle. He originally decided to turn the largest apartment – the Picture Gallery – into a chapel and the Privy Council granted a sum of money for "persons appointed for the service of music employed for our Chapel in Holyroodhouse". In 1687 the king changed his mind and restored the Abbey instead.

During the early months of the next year a large organ was completed and the Roman Catholic ritual established. This so incensed the people that in the following December "a rabble of all sorts" broke into the Abbey and pillaged and destroyed with the utmost fury. This was the death blow to the Chapel Royal in Scotland, an institution which, with an unusually troubled history had lasted for five hundred and sixty-eight years. In 1768 during a storm the roof fell in, leaving the building a ruin, in which state it still remains today.

WILLIAM AND MARY

The great days of the Stuarts were over and although music continued in the court of William and Mary, it lacked the drive and vigour of previous reigns. Purcell had gone and no one of comparable ability had come to the fore. Blow was still alive and still attached to the Chapel Royal, but he may not have received the same encouragement from the new sovereigns, who were probably engaged in duties requiring more immediate attention.

William Croft was the outstanding musician of the period. Having studied under Blow he succeeded him in his positions at Westminster Abbey and as Master of the Children and composer to the Chapel Royal. He was organist at the chapel during the reigns of William III, Queen Anne and George I, dying in 1727, the same year as the last named king. He was especially famous as a composer for the church and much of his music is still in use. A number of his works appeared in a collection named *Musica Sacra* published in 1724. Interest attaches to this publication as it was the first example of ecclesiastical music engraved in score on plates. Its full title read *Musica Sacra, or Select Anthems in Score, consisting of 2, 3, 4, 5, 6, 7 and 8 Parts. To which is added The Burial Service, as it is now occasionally perform'd in Westminster Abbey.* The publishers were Walsh and Hare of London, a famous firm which produced many of the best works during the eighteenth century.

The family of Shore was active in musical circles at this time. Matthew Shore occupied the position of Sergeant Trumpeter at the courts of James II and William III and his two sons William and John followed in his footsteps. The last-named invented the tuning-fork in 1711.

Several other able, rather than brilliant musicians flit across the scene, such men as Weldon, Clarke, Eccles and Aldrich, but they pale into insignificance with the arrival of the mighty George Handel. There was undoubtedly a dearth of British composers and apart from Croft only Turner was of any stature at this time. This was the great opportunity for foreign musicians, who now began to settle in London in increasing numbers, a movement which in a few short years was to become a veritable invasion.

ANNE

As Kapellmeister to the Elector of Hanover, Handel obtained leave of absence to visit London in 1710, an event which was to prove so important a landmark in his life. His opera *Rinaldo* was produced and achieved a success quite remarkable in England. Two years later he returned and again created a sensation with the opera *Teseo*. Handel found London life far more stimulating than that of the small princely state of Hanover and on this occasion he failed to return to his duties, much to the annoyance of the Elector. He wrote a birthday Ode for Queen Anne for 6th February 1713 which gained gracious approval and he marked the Peace of Utrecht with a *Te Deum* produced on July 7th of the same year. As a result of these musical offerings the queen settled on him a life pension of £200 a year. This might seem rather surprising as Anne was completely unmusical and never even bothered to listen to the Royal Band.

This was a great time for Thanksgiving Days. The victory at Blenheim in 1704 and the Navy's success in 1708 were both commemorated by Croft. The Union with Scotland in 1707 was celebrated by Tudway in an anthem "Behold how good and joyful".

GEORGE I

At first, life was kind to Handel. He had many friends in high places and was the object of a considerable degree of adulation by the masses. But the accession in 1714 of the Elector of Hanover as King George I created some problems for the composer and it was Croft who wrote the coronation anthem. The king showed a certain coolness towards Handel and there was a withdrawal of the royal pension. Croft again came forward with another suitable anthem in 1715 "for the Thanksgiving upon suppressing of the Rebellion at Preston".

Handel was eventually forgiven and with forgiveness his pension was not only restored but doubled. Also he was appointed music master to the little princesses at a further £200 making his total emoluments from royal sources £600 per annum. Furthermore George I contributed to the scheme for Italian opera, in which Handel was particularly interested.

However, at this stage we witness a marked change from the Tudor and Stuart conception of royal music and musicians. It had become increasingly obvious during the seventeenth century that much of the political power was being wrested from the kings by successive parliaments. This in turn led to a new situation regarding the arts. Patronage no longer remained the sole privilege of the monarchy; instead, members of the aristocracy came to the fore in increasing numbers as patrons of art and music. As an example Handel for some time lived at Canons near Edgware as composer and organist to the Duke of Chandos. Although some of the patronage seemed a little misplaced at times, in general this widening of interest was probably a good thing. Court music still functioned, but not on the same scale as hitherto. Public concert-giving was now beginning to have its effect and the members of the royal household found pleasure in attending and being seen at the theatre and concert hall. Musicians attached to the court undertook more and more commissions outside and apart from the Chapel Royal there was a definite lessening of the ties which had in the past bound monarchs and musicians together in so close a friendship.

GEORGE II

The domestic strife between each succeeding king and Prince of Wales became almost an accepted mode of royal behaviour during the Hanoverian dynasty. The relationship of George I and his son was nothing but a public scandal. They quarrelled on every possible topic; even the choice of god parents for the prince's first child became a political issue. It is not surprising therefore that members of the royal family took opposing sides in the musical intrigues of the day and helped to build up artificial dislikes and even hatreds between composers and their followers. On the accession of George II in 1727 the newspapers informed the public that the famous Mr. Handel was appointed to compose the anthems for the coronation. These were respectively *Zadok the Priest, The King shall Rejoice, My Heart is Inditing* and *Let Thy Hand be Strengthened.* Frederick, Prince of Wales who had been at daggers drawn with his father for some years, immediately supported a rival group led by Buononcini, Pepusch and Senesino. Squabbles continued throughout the reign and whatever effect they may have had on their royal perpetrators, they certainly adversely affected the health of Handel. He, although not particularly renowned for diplomacy, made an effort to overcome the enmity of the Prince of Wales by composing an anthem on the occasion of his wedding in 1737. This so incensed the king that he withdrew his patronage from the composer. As a result Covent Garden ceased to function and Handel wrote no more opera. So history is made. This might seem an over-simplification of a difficult problem, but more space than is available would be needed to treat the matter fully.

Another piece of history was made three years later, when Arne's masque *Alfred* was performed for the same Prince of Wales at Cliveden, the house he rented in Buckinghamshire. The masque contained the famous song *Rule Britannia* which became virtually a second British national anthem.

Handel was later restored to royal favour. The defeat of the Jacobite Rebellion in 1745 caused so much relief and considerable rejoicing in Hanoverian circles and Handel made the most of the opportunity by composing the "Occasional Oratorio". "Judas Maccabaeus" was written to commemorate Culloden and was ready for its first performance on April 1st, 1747. These works so pleased the king that he gave the composer *carte blanche* for the next public occasion, the celebration of the Peace of Aix-la-Chapelle. Here Handel excelled himself with the famous Music for the Royal Fireworks. This accompanied a massive fireworks display given in St. James's Park on 27th April 1749 and watched by George II from his library. A manuscript description prepared for the king mentioned: "After a Grand Overture of Warlike Instruments composed by Mr. Handel a Signal is given for the Commencement of the Fireworks, which opens by a Royal Salute of 101 Brass Ordnance".

Although Handel played so important a part in the musical life of the early Georges he never held an official position at court. Desiring freedom of action, he was not anxious to tie himself to any one patron and in any case he earned a considerable income from his royal countrymen.

One of the most influential English musicians during the reign of George II was Maurice Greene who occupied several important positions. After serving as a chorister at St. Paul's Cathedral, he was made organist there at the age of twenty-three years. Early in life he was friendly with Handel but became involved in the bitter dispute between that composer and Buononcini and took the latter's side. Greene succeeded Croft as organist of the Chapel Royal, became Master of the King's Music and Professor of Music at Cambridge. He composed a quantity of music, which included the usual odes for festal occasions and settings for the theatre. His reputation as a composer was based chiefly on the volume of *Forty Select Anthems,* some of which still receive an airing today. Although Greene was an excellent musician and an outstanding teacher, he was a man of uncertain temper whose actions were sometimes perplexing. He retired in middle life and in 1750 having inherited an estate in Essex, he devoted his time to the collection of anthems and services which was to prove of great value to the church. With commendable modesty he refused permission for any of his own compositions to be included, and being unable to finish his self-imposed task, he left everything in order for William Boyce, his most famous pupil to bring to completion.

Greene and his pupils must be given credit for the uphill task of maintaining some semblance of native music amidst the mass of German and Italian compositions and their imitations which were now proving so popular in the country. His influence was predominant in the church, where his example was so ably followed by John Travers and James Nares, both of whom spent part of their lives as organists at the Chapel Royal. The latter was a worthy successor to his teacher and in addition to his more serious works, amongst which must be mentioned the Dramatic Ode *The Royal Pastoral,* he wrote a number of catches and glees.

Other instrumentalists who made reputations during the reign of George II were William Corbett, Michael Festing, both members of the King's Band and Valentine Snow who followed John Shore as Sergeant Trumpeter to the king. The trumpet obligato parts in Handel's oratories were written specially with this famous player in mind.

William Boyce commenced his career in a similar manner to his illustrious master by becoming a chorister in St. Paul's Cathedral, which at this period seems to have overtaken the Chapel Royal as the training ground of young musicians. For some time he held the post of Composer to the Chapel Royal, jointly with Greene and in 1755 he was appointed Master of the King's Music. As well as being a fine organist, he composed a large amount of vocal and instrumental music. Later in life he was a victim to deafness and as already mentioned he gave of his great ability to the continuance of Greene's work in collecting together the finest compositions of the Anglican church. This work was known as *Cathedral Music, being a Collection in Score of the Most Valuable and Useful Compositions for that Service, by the several English Masters of the last Two Hundred Years.*

Handel's great innings came to an end in 1759 just one year before the death of George II. He had dominated the musical scene since his arrival in London and had risen like a colossus above his contemporaries in eighteenth century Britain. Whether this was a good thing from the standpoint of British vocal music is debatable. Most of the composers of his time and indeed later, instead of copying Purcell's meticulous care in the setting of words, took as their model Handel, who never really mastered the English language.

GEORGE III

We have seen that public and semi-public concert-going was now becoming popular and George III, who was a great lover of music, helped materially to accelerate this course of events. He did little to encourage the Chapel Royal, spending more time at Windsor than in London and with St. George's Chapel being readily available the choir at St. James's Palace suffered as a result. It is possible that the music performed in the chapel did not appeal.

However, if royal interest was lacking in this particular respect enthusiasm for the monthly meetings of the Concerts of Ancient Music knew no bounds. This society which had its beginning in 1776, met at the King's Concert Rooms in Chapel Street. Its object was to perform music of not less than twenty years old, which meant that the works of Handel could be included as often as required. The king, as a staunch Handelian (and as a director of the society) saw to it that his favourite music appeared with regularity. An unusual feature of these concerts was that applause and requests for encores could only come from the royal box. The conductor always received strict instructions to take his cue from the king, who invariably stood up beating time.

From 1784 to 1791 a series of monster Handel Commemorations were held in Westminster Abbey. This was the music which appealed to the king and he was always present. The famous historian Dr. Burney, wrote a book on the first great Handel Festival and included certain items of criticism on some of the performers. George III, hearing of this publication, asked to see it in proof form and included a few of his own views, particularly on the playing of Fischer, the great oboist.

Two outstanding musicians of this period were John Stanley and Samuel Arnold, but although they held positions in the King's Music, much of their most important work was produced in the wider field of public life. Stanley, completely blind from the age of two, became organist at the Temple Church in London where he remained for over fifty years. His remarkable memory enabled him to play a new oratorio after hearing it played only once. He was Master of the Band during the reign of George III but he is remembered today for his music for the organ. Arnold was a man of many interests and in addition to being organist of the Chapel Royal and Westminster Abbey he composed much music for the theatre as well as for the church. He edited the works of Handel in thirty-six volumes and also published a continuation of Boyce's work *Cathedral Music* mentioned earlier in these pages.

William Shield was another excellent musician and an expert viola player. He was Master of the King's Music and achieved great success as a theatrical composer. James Nares, at one time organist of York Minster, became one of the organists at George III's Chapel Royal. He is chiefly remembered for his compositions of Anglican church music, some of which are still performed.

GEORGE IV

So far the reign of the Georges had not been especially noteworthy for the furtherance of British music and with the accession of George IV in 1820 there was faint hope of any improvement.

He, like his father was a confirmed Handelian but he was also an accomplished 'cellist. The new king also possessed a useful singing voice which he used to good effect at the famous Noblemen and Gentlemen's Catch Club. During his reign military bands improved enormously and special mention should be made of the Royal Artillery Band under Mackenzie and the Court Military Band conducted by Kramer. These were both magnificent and no doubt reflected the German regard for wind bands. Many historians find nothing but ill to report of this short and chaotic reign, but as with most people, there was a redeeming feature in George IV. This was his great and genuine love of music and his generosity to many musicians – he sent Beethoven £200 when that composer was in financial straits. It has been said that this devotion to the art was one of his most attractive attributes – some may think his only attribute.

Two musicians who served him in the royal music were William Hawes and Sir George Smart. The former shared the duties of master of the choristers at St. Paul's and the Chapel Royal. As with so many others of this period he had many interests which included the publishing of music, direction of the opera at the Lyceum Theatre in London, the composition of a great deal of music for the stage and a number of popular glees which were so fashionable at that time.

Smart started his musical career as a chorister at the Chapel Royal and later became an expert conductor of the music of Handel. He was appointed one of the organists at the Chapel Royal. He numbered amongst his friends and acquaintances Beethoven, Weber and Mendelssohn and he played an important part in bringing into operation the Mendelssohn Scholarship.

WILLIAM IV

Both of these musicians overlapped into the following reign, that of William IV who in 1830 took over an unenviable task. The image of royalty was distinctly tarnished by now. Yet this quiet, friendly man who disliked all forms of fuss, did much to regain respect and indeed popularity for the throne, but there is little evidence of any great music-making at the court during his seven years as king.

VICTORIA

Queen Victoria was crowned in 1837 at the age of 18. The young queen was fond of music and paid her initial state visit to Covent Garden in the first year of her reign. So many people wished to see her that the event became something of a problem in crowd control: "An enormous mob packed the cheaper seats, causing such tumult, fainting and screaming that a great number of women had to be lifted over the boxes in an exhausted condition". Later she attended Covent Garden again, this time for a performance of the Magic Flute. This must have been a splendid occasion. The Grand Foyer became the Queen's retiring room: "at each extremity of this saloon, crystal curtains intermingled with ruby drops, most brilliantly lighted up with gas, were suspended, and large mirrors were placed in every panel".

The people were delighted with the new queen; she was young, attractive and unspoiled and as a result she had quickly gained their affection. When in 1840 she married Prince Albert the future of music seemed assured. His musical education was sound; he played the organ, sang and composed. The court orchestra was revived and Mendelssohn, a personal friend and distinguished pianist, was a welcome guest to Buckingham Palace where he often played for the royal couple. About this time dancing was a popular pastime in court circles, for which the band of M. Henri Laurent, considered the very best for its purpose, was regularly engaged.

The Prince Consort, who was largely responsible for the Great Exhibition in Hyde Park was said to have suggested the design for the Royal Albert Hall (1867–71) which became and still is London's largest concert hall. The tragedy of Albert's death in 1861 threw a blight over the court and the queen went into almost complete retirement for several years. However the Chapel Royal and St. George's Chapel, Windsor continued their activities. Elvey, organist at St. George's Chapel was in office for nearly fifty years, first to William IV and then to Victoria. He was followed by Parratt whose period of service was almost as long. Both were knighted by the queen.

Although some clever musical boys still received their education at the Chapel Royal – Sullivan and S. S. Wesley were two outstanding examples – a change was on the way. Music in Britain had been at a low ebb during the early years of the nineteenth century, but there were encouraging signs of improvement in the latter half. Schools, colleges and universities were beginning, in some cases, to treat the teaching of music much more seriously than hitherto. The Royal Academy of Music, founded in 1822 as a boarding establishment, with Crotch as its first principal, and the National Training School of Music in 1873, nine years later to be reorganised as the Royal College of Music, played an important part in this movement. Standards of instrumental and vocal performance improved and more attention was paid to the art of composition. Both of these institutions held a charter from the crown and under a succession of able men they prospered. Among the musicians who directed these colleges were Grove, Sullivan, Parry and MacKenzie, all of whom were knighted by the queen. Also Professors of Music at Oxford and Cambridge were singled out for the highest honours and the following list makes impressive reading. Crotch, Bishop, Ouseley, and Stainer at Oxford and Walmisley, Sterndale Bennet, Macfarren and Stanford at Cambridge. The queen also knighted Oakely, Professor of Music at Edinburgh and Composer to her Majesty in Scotland.

Another interesting innovation was the commencement of the Royal Military School of Music at Kneller Hall in 1857. Its object was to train bandmasters and bandsmen for the army. In the course of time these players became highly professional and were in great demand for state occasions. Queen Victoria had long appreciated the sterling work of the bandmasters and in 1887 she conferred an honorary commission on Dan Godfrey then in charge of the Grenadier Guards Band. In 1898 four staff band-masters were promoted to full commissioned rank.

Possibly a little known event in court life was the queen's invitation to William Jackson, born in Masham, who entertained Her Majesty at Buckingham Palace with a choir of two hundred Yorkshire singers.

All in all, the Victorian age was one of musical expansion with three outstanding men, Parry, Stanford and MacKenzie largely responsible for a renaissance in British music. As a result of their pioneering work and tilling of the musical soil, a new composer, Edward Elgar came to the fore towards the end of the queen's reign, one destined to play an important part in royal music for some time to come. His first commission was for the Diamond Jubilee in 1897 when he composed the cantata *The Banner of St.*

George and the *Imperial March.* The latter was performed again later in the year at a state concert by special request of the queen. Two years later Elgar was invited to Windsor to conduct at a concert to celebrate the eightieth birthday of Queen Victoria. For this he wrote a madrigal *To her beneath whose steadfast star,* also a song *Like to the Damask Rose.* Later in the year a concert was given in the private chapel at Windsor, in which no fewer than ten Elgar works were performed and on 20th October his *Sea Pictures* were given by command of the queen at Balmoral.

In the outside world, on the evening of 10th August 1895 the first of the Promenade Concerts at Queen's Hall was given under the baton of Henry J. Wood.

EDWARD VII

Queen Victoria died in 1901 amidst great and genuine mourning and Edward VII took over the responsibilities of what was to prove a short reign. Apart from putting an end to the tradition of holding state concerts, resulting in the disbandment of the court orchestra, the king did nothing to discourage the new wave of enthusiasm for British music. The nation was in great heart; patriotism was not then a dirty word and the prevailing love of pageantry demanded the stimulation of suitable music. This was provided in full measure by Stanford, Parry and Mackenzie and in particular by Elgar, who rapidly took on the mantle of what might be termed *musician laureate.*

For the king's coronation in 1902 Elgar was commissioned to write a *Coronation Ode,* but on the day previous to the coronation the king was taken ill with appendicitis and with an immediate operation necessary, the event had to be postponed. On 26th October, a National Thanksgiving Concert was arranged by Henry Wood at Queen's Hall to celebrate the recovery of His Majesty. The programme contained items specially written for the coronation in Westminster Abbey: *Coronation Marches* by MacKenzie and Cowen were featured together with the *Coronation Ode* by Elgar. This last named work caught the imagination of the audience and met with an enthusiastic reception.

The king was now to be seen at public concerts and according to Wilfrid Blunt "every night of his life he was to be seen at theatres and operas and music-halls". However, not only did he attend the Union Jack concerts at the Royal Albert Hall, but also those where new music was being performed for the first time. He seemed able to assimilate new works far more successfully than many of us can do today. The Elgar Festival at Covent Garden in 1904 was attended by the royal family who also appeared at His Majesty's Theatre for Ethel Smyth's new opera *The Wreckers,* conducted by a young genius, Thomas Beecham. The first London performance of Richard Strauss' *Elektra* was given at Covent Garden, also conducted by Beecham. We are told that at the close of the performance "Covent Garden had known few if any ovations like it within living memory. In the royal box, King Edward, who usually left the theatre at the first curtain, sat and applauded until the sixth, Queen Alexandra, with Prince Henry of Prussia and his Princess, were still there at the twelfth curtain".

The movement noticed during the reigns of the early Georges, when there was a distinct lessening of the ties between kings and the musicians in their courts, was now complete. No royal band as such existed any more; for state banquets and the like the incidental music was provided usually by a military band or its string section. The monarchy and the people now shared in common their musical experiences, either on the great occasions such as coronations or when royalty patronised concerts, operas and festivals and Royal Command performances were to become increasingly popular.

GEORGE V

King Edward VII died in 1910 and in June of 1911 the coronation of King George V and Queen Mary took place at Westminster Abbey. Elgar was again employed. He wrote a *Coronation March* for the royal procession at the conclusion of the service. This was interesting as one section was in ¾ time, an unusual deviation from normal.

George V did not evince the same interest in avant garde music as did his late father; possibly he could, in more recent parlance, be described as a "square". We have already seen what popularity the opera *Elektra* gained at its London premier. As a result Bandmaster Williams of the Grenadier Guards made an arrangement of the music and conducted it on one occasion in the forecourt of Buckingham Palace after the Changing of the Guard. He was perhaps a little surprised to receive a note from the king immediately the piece had ended. It read "His Majesty does not know what the Band has just played, but it is *never* to be played again".

The king, not unnaturally, showed more than a passing interest in the playing of *God Save the King*. He often complained of tempi and interpretation. In 1930 an Army Order was introduced laying down detailed instructions regarding its orchestration and performance. Elgar was still the outstanding composer, not only of music for kings, but also of music for the people. However much the so-called intelligentsia turned up their elegant noses – and some still do – the music from a vast quantity of his compositions, the Enigma Variations, Falstaff, the Violin Concerto, the Cello Concerto, the two Symphonies and a little-known short work, Sospiri as well as The Dream of Gerontius and other Oratorios *is* very beautiful and is listened to with keen appreciation by modern audiences. This is great music which appeals to the heart. I remember talking to a hardened orchestral player on one occasion who confessed to having a lump in the throat whenever he performed the Nimrod Variation. The Pomp and Circumstance Marches are splendid of their type and what is wrong with a fine rousing march?

In 1911 came the first performance of Elgar's Second Symphony. He had wished this to be a musical offering to Edward VII, but the king died before its completion and the work bore the following inscription: Symphony No. 2 in E flat, for Full Orchestra, Edward Elgar (Op 63). Dedicated to the memory of His late Majesty, King Edward VII.

At the beginning of 1912 he commenced work on the masque *The Crown of India* written for the visit of King George V to India. On the death of Sir Walter Parratt in 1924 Elgar succeeded to the position of Master of the King's Music, some think rather belatedly. He had previously been knighted by Edward VII and had also been awarded the Order of Merit. Although by now he was not writing very much, he treated his new duty seriously and his first action was to attempt to trace the instruments which had lain dormant since the court orchestra's disbandment. He then attended to the library of music and brought some order out of chaos. Another of his duties was to be in attendance on royalty when they appeared at concerts or the opera.

Elgar was responsible for only two other works connected with his courtly office. One was the carol *Good-morrow* written as a thanksgiving for the king's recovery from serious illness in 1929. The composer went to Windsor and conducted the choir at St. George's Chapel on this occasion. Two years later he completed the score of the *Nursery Suite* and the title page reads: "Dedicated by permission to Her Royal Highness the Duchess of York and the Princesses Elizabeth and Margaret Rose". The Duchess of York, later Queen Elizabeth and now the Queen Mother has always shown a keen understanding of music and musicians and is patron of many worthwhile enterprises.

GEORGE VI

Other British composers were now emerging, one in particular, Ralph Vaughan Williams, was destined to take over much of the role of his great contemporary. Elgar died in 1934 and his place as Master of the King's Music was taken by Walford Davies. King George V died two years later and the Duke of York was crowned as George VI at Westminster in 1937. Several eminent organists were involved on this occasion, including W. G. Alcock, Ernest Bullock and Walford Davies. Vaughan Williams was commissioned to write two works, *A Flourish for a Coronation* and a festival setting of the *Te Deum*. In the Birthday Honours of 3rd June 1935 Vaughan Williams was awarded the Order of Merit, a personal honour from the sovereign. He never accepted a knighthood and although he did not become Master of the King's Music, he certainly took over from Elgar the position of principal composer of his time.

The Chapel Royal still maintains an important place in the service of the sovereign, though it is now much depleted numerically. There are chapels both at Buckingham Palace and at Marlborough House, but one normally associates the Chapel Royal with St. James's Palace. This building dates from 1532 but has not been in use continuously through the centuries for its original purpose. The later Stuarts held their court at Whitehall Palace, but when the chapel was burned down in 1691 the building at St. James's returned to royal favour and to the glory of its former past. This small chapel is a gem with its decorated ceiling by Holbein and its wonderful atmosphere, enhanced by the candlelit choir stalls.

Never shall I forget the thrill, just prior to the second world war, of being invited to sit at the organ by Dr. Stanley Roper, then organist of the chapel. On glancing around, one could not help musing on the fact that this was in the direct pattern of centuries of splendid tradition and dedication. The boys, ten in all, in their scarlet uniforms; the six men, more correctly described as Gentlemen of the Chapel; the fine singing of music from a vast repertoire, some of it heard by monarchs from the sixteenth and subsequent centuries brought vividly to mind a great sense of continuity. On more recent visits to the chapel this impression has only been heightened and one has come away hoping and trusting that nothing will be allowed to destroy this superb act of worship.

ELIZABETH II

The coronation of Queen Elizabeth in 1953 was seen and heard by millions all over the world through the medium of television and radio. The pageantry was magnificent and the music equally so, to which Vaughan Williams contributed an anthem *O taste and see*. To celebrate the coronation Benjamin Britten was commissioned to write an opera. This work, *Gloriana* was first performed on 8th June 1953 at Covent Garden before the royal family and a distinguished gathering. It caused something of a stir and in fact received a certain amount of adverse criticism at the time. But the grand old man of British music, Vaughan Williams came to the fore with a spirited observation. "I do not propose, after a single hearing, to appraise either the words or the music of *Gloriana*. The important thing to my mind, at the moment, is that, so far as I know, for the first time in history, the Sovereign has commanded an opera from these islands for a great occasion. Those who cavil at the public expense involved should realise what such a gesture means to the prestige of our music".

The demands made on the time and energy of modern royalty might seem excessive by any standards. The frequent journeys abroad, the constant progresses in Britain, the increasingly complex affairs of state and attention to the many and differing aspects of life today, must be extremely burdensome. In spite of these duties Queen Elizabeth and Queen Elizabeth the Queen Mother contrive to attend concerts and to act as patrons of many worth-while musical enterprises. But generally speaking the commissioning of new works and the upkeep of orchestras have passed from kings and queens and private patrons. These important functions are now in the hands of the B.B.C., the Arts Council, certain enlightened municipalities and a few sponsored concert-giving bodies. In this democratic and sometimes rather grey age, may we retain the pageantry and ceremonial associated with royalty. The staff band, both horse and foot; the state trumpeters; the great occasions full of colour and music that have been a part of the British heritage for centuries.

THE ROYAL WEDDING 1981

Prince Charles has long been interested in music and during his school days he was a valued member of his school orchestra. More recently he has become patron to several great musical bodies which he supports on every possible occasion.

The wedding of H.R.H. the Prince of Wales and the Lady Diana Spencer on 29th July 1981 caught the imagination of the British people and those of most overseas countries as well. A glorious day, a vast crowd in wich affection for the young couple was so obvious, coupled with magnificent pageantry, created a wonderful atmosphere tinged with emotion. And this was marked by the service itself. The choice of St. Paul's Cathedral was perfect. The great Wren church, following its recent highly successful re-decoration, proved an ideal setting for the colourful congregation.

Prince Charles paid special attention to the choice of music and attended several meetings with Sir David Willcocks, who was in overall control. The various musical items were conducted by Sir Colin Davis, Mr Richard Popplewell, Mr Barry Rose and Sir David Willcocks. It was a joy to hear an entire programme of British music at this service, if one may stretch a point to include Handel. He certainly lived much of his creative life in England and is often claimed as British.

The choirs of St. Paul's Cathedral, the Chapel Royal, the Bach Choir, together with the Royal Opera House Orchestra, Covent Garden, the English Chamber Orchestra and the Philharmonia Orchestra.

The State Trumpeters of the Household Cavalry were directed by Major Anthony Richards of the Life Guards. The Fanfare Trumpeters of the Royal Military School of Music, Kneller Hall, were directed by Lt. Col. George Evans.

Before the service Mr. Christopher Dearnley, organist of St. Paul's Cathedral and Mr. John Scott, assistant, played works by Arthur Bliss, Benjamin Britten, Geoffrey Bush, Edward Elgar, Herbert Howells, Michael Tippett, Ralph Vaughan Williams and Malcolm Williamson.

The Trumpet Voluntary by Jeremiah Clarke was played during the bride's procession. The first anthem "Let the people praise Thee" taken from Psalm 67 – was specially composed by William Mathias.

After the Archbishop of Canterbury's address the anthem "I was glad when they said unto me", Psalm 122, v. 1–3, 6, 7, Charles Hubert Parry.

After the Blessing. The National Anthem arranged by Sir David Willcocks.

During the procession to the Dean's Aisle for signing the register, the March from the Overture to Handel's Occasional Oratoria was played. This was followed by the Aria and chorus "Let the bright Seraphim" from the same composer's *Samson*. The solo parts were taken by Kiri Te Kanawa (soprano) and John Wallace (Trumpet) with the Bach Choir and orchestral accompaniment.

On the conclusion of the signing of the register, the orchestra played the Pomp and Circumstance March No. 4 in G – Elgar and Crown Imperial – Walton.

Thus ended a great occasion, fairy-like in retrospect and one which created joy for millions of people. The behaviour of the great crowds in the streets was admirable and there seemed to be no disturbing incident of any kind to spoil the day.

CHAPTER 2

MUSIC in the INN

If all be true that I do think,
There are five reasons we should drink,
Good wine – a friend – or being dry –
Or lest we should be by and by –
Or any other reason why.

Henry Aldrich
Dean of Christ Church, Oxford 1647–1710.

Although the court, church and castle at various times in their different ways have contributed towards the progress of music in Britain, so the inn, in its more earthy way has also played an important role in what might be termed the "music of the people". This association between music and the inn, although perhaps not as strong now as formerly, had far-reaching results of historical significance.

It would not be strictly correct to claim that the type of music heard in the public-house of today compares with that performed in the average concert-hall of any large city. But public concerts as we know them are of comparatively recent date, certainly not earlier than the second half of the seventeenth century. Before that time, apart from the music to be heard in private houses and churches, the inn often provided the chief opportunity for the itinerant musician and for communal singing by the local inhabitants.

In many of our villages and small towns the two most important buildings are frequently the church and the inn, often at no great distance one from another and indeed on occasions occupying adjacent positions. Here again there was a close association in spirit as well as physical proximity, the inn oftentimes having been provided for the benefit of pilgrims and visiting clergy. Also, adult members of church choirs and teams of bellringers have from time immemorial found their self-imposed but pleasant duty to be thirst provoking. With the task of performing the musical portion of the service safely behind, what could be more natural than to find the same worthies joining together in something of a more secular nature, aided and abetted by the cup that cheers.

Many bellringers rehearsed their hand-ringing exercises in the local hostelry and made it their headquarters. Some of these teams became highly proficient and so well-known in their districts that at various seasons of the year they made a habit of visiting other public houses to demonstrate their art. For at least two centuries parties of handbell ringers from nearby parishes assembled at Bassett Down in Wiltshire in smocks and gaiters and played throughout December nights. No doubt this work demanded a modicum of cheer at the local.

It is interesting to note the number of what might be termed "church inns" whose names include a reference to bells. In travelling around the country one frequently notices *The Bell, The Ring o' Bells, The Eight Bells* and many others. According to one authority on the subject, there are no fewer than four hundred and eighty-three houses in England alone bearing the name *Bell*. In those instances where *Bell* found a place additional to the original title, such as the *Bull and Bell, Raven and Bell* and *Dolphin and Bell*, it was to honour the local bell-ringers who regularly used the house for their refreshment.

The lovely church at Norton-sub-Hamdon in Somerset bears strange witness to its centuries of bellringers and their age old habit of drinking the local beverage. At the foot of the tower the Ham stone has been worn away by successive generations of bell-ringers attending to their natural functions. "The acid in the cider was responsible" laconically remarked a late vicar who acted as my guide on one occasion.

While on the subject of inn names and their association with music, mention should be made of the *Hautboy and Fiddle* at Peterborough. It is assumed that this house was so called either because the landlord was a performer on the instruments concerned, or amongst his regular customers were musicians who would accept engagements as waits.

There are one or two examples of the *Jew's Harp* in London. Ben Jonson stated that it was at one time the custom to keep a clown or fool in certain taverns to amuse the clientele. The fool would sit on a stool and play the Jew's Harp. The licensee displayed a sign outside his house to signify to would-be customers that he catered for their entertainment in addition to their nourishment. Thus the instrument became a recognised sign for a licensed house.

One very unusual name was the *Three Organ Pipes* in Walbrook. During the reign of Queen Elizabeth in the year 1574, this house was owned by a certain John Howe, a grocer and churchwarden "of S. Stevens in Walbroke within the Cyttie of London". The parish register of 1548-9, records that Mr. Howe was paid "his fee for mending the organ iij.s." Obviously he was a man of parts.

In the past there was a definite line of demarcation between the inn and the tavern which does not obtain today. The former was a house given over entirely to the entertainment of travellers by day or night and had to be open at all hours. At the same time the inn was not allowed to be used as a place for casual drinking by the local inhabitants. The tavern, on the other hand, supplied food and drink, but was forbidden to accept guests. Also the tavern had certain hours of closing which were strictly enforced. The special function of the inn was to supply food and sleeping accommodation to the visitor. The essential business of the tavern was to provide refreshment and recreation for its townspeople. Here, in an atmosphere of informality, the ordinary citizen met his friends, exchanged views on current topics, enjoyed his drink and sang songs.

Many are the accounts in literature of musical evenings spent in such surroundings. Chaucer, in *The Miller's Tale* makes reference to conditions of his day when writing of a parish clerk well-known for his dancing, singing and performances on musical instruments:

In al the toun nas brewhouse ne taverne
That he visited with his solas.

During the sixteenth century, as distinct from the seventeenth and eighteenth centuries, it would appear that 10 p.m. was the normal hour for ending musical and club meetings. One of the *Tatler* papers refers to a group of men, self-styled critics, who met regularly every night to discuss music, poetry and politics. Their meeting-place was the *Smyrna Coffee House* in Pall Mall, where they talked for the benefit of any who cared to listen, between the hours of eight and ten.

Many of these old houses had a fascinating history. For instance, the original *Ship Tavern* in Little Turnstile was famous in the sixteenth century as a shelter for Catholic priests who had used the premises for their religious services. Bishop Challoner is recorded as having sat at a table with his congregation scattered about the room smoking and enjoying their mugs of beer. Should any enemy agent find his way into the saloon he would see only a group of ordinary folk spending a quiet evening at their local hostelry.

The inn often provided musical entertainment as well as refreshment and accommodation. Usually the local waits would be at hand to play during the evening meal, and a wandering fiddler or ballad-singer could always be found to brighten up the period between supper and bed.

In London, three great coaching inns of this nature were *The Swan with Two Necks* in Lad Lane, *The Golden Cross* in the Strand and *The White Hart* in the Borough. They were associated almost entirely with travellers and took little part in the daily life of the neighbourhood.

Shakespeare made mention of this type of music when Falstaff, entertaining some ladies at a tavern, ordered a servant to "find out Sneak's noise because Mistress Tearsheet would fain hear some music." Another account, this time by Deloney, a contemporary of Shakespeare reads, "To the Tavern they went . . . The old man called for wine plenty, and the best cheere in the house . . . They had sitten long, but in comes a noise of Musitions in tawny coats, who (putting off their caps) asked if they would have any musicke". *(Jack of Newbury)*.

In his *History of Music* Sir John Hawkins adds to our general information on this subject: "Fidlers and others, hired by the master of the house; such as in the night season were wont to parade the city and suburbs under the title Waits . . . Half a dozen of fidlers would scrape *Sellenger's Round,* or *Iohn, Come Kiss Me,* or *Old Simon the King* with divisions, till themselves and their audience were tired, after which as many players on the hautboy would in the most harsh and discordant tones grate forth *Greensleeves, Yellow Stockings, Gillian of Croydon,* or some such common dance tune, and the people thought it fine music".

It seems obvious that the local musicians had an understanding with the inn servants who no doubt received a suitable commission for giving the latest information regarding the arrival of guests.

The musicians were not always welcome however; indeed they were often a source of annoyance to travellers, who frequently were pestered with their attentions. Thus Bishop Earle in *A Poore Fidler* (Microcosmographie 1628) writes: "He is in League with Tapsters for the worshipfull of the Inne, who he torments next morning with his art, and has their names more perfit than their men". It was the custom for the musicians to stand outside the bedroom doors before breakfast, call out the names of the guests and play them a tune. Pepys, when staying at Reading on one occasion was disappointed with his morning serenade: "Musicke, the worst we had had, coming to our chamber door, but calling us by our wrong names, we lay".

From time to time laws were made to safeguard the public from this nuisance and musicians were forbidden to perform unless invited by the guests to do so. At least one example exists of an apprentice in music, who on wishing to leave his master, gave as a reason that he had been sent "up and down to proffer music in taverns and alehouses, being not sent for, contrary to law".

However, in every age people have enjoyed music with their meals and the custom is of great antiquity. According to Isaac Walton in *The Compleat Angler* "The Romans at the height of their glory . . . had music to usher in their sturgeons, lampreys and mullets". In a report on one of Sir Francis Drake's voyages his chaplain mentions that "neither had he omitted to make provision also for ornament and delight, carrying with him for this purpose expert musicians".

Sixteenth and seventeenth century British literature abounds in references to music as an accompaniment of meals. Deloney mentions this fact in several of his books and of Tom Dare he remarks: "It was as sure as an Act of Parliament that he could not digest his meat without music". As might be expected, in any discussion dealing with food and music Samuel Pepys cannot be left out. On a visit to the town of Marlborough in 1688 he notes: "Then to supper and had musique, whose innocence pleased me, and I did give them 3 shillings. So to bed". On another occasion, this time in London, "I expected musique, the missing of which spoiled my dinner". About this time the Cambridge Waits had a reputation for excellent music and attention to business. One meets with many allusions to their playing at local inns, particularly for anyone able to pay well for their performance.

MUSIQUE HOUSES

Cromwell's regime was unwittingly responsible for a great increase in tavern music. During this period organs were removed from the churches and either destroyed or bought by private persons for use in their homes. A few astute inn-keepers decided to install some of these instruments in their establishments. The fashion, once started, spread rapidly and such inns became known as "Musick Houses", where often a small orchestra was provided in addition to the organ. Many were to be found in and around London, particularly in riverside districts and there is evidence that several provincial towns followed suit.

Stepney boasted a Musique House with an organ and a group of fiddlers and hautboys, and at Wapping *"The Mitre"* was famous for its musical evenings. This house was the subject of a detailed description by Ned Ward in *The London Spy.* "Remembering we had heard of a famous Amphibious House of Entertainment, compounded of one half *Tavern* and t'other *Musick House,* made us willing to Dedicate half an hour to what Diversion we might there meet with . . . As soon as we came to the *Sign of the Spiritual Helmet (The Mitre)* such as the High Priests us'd to wear when they bid Defiance to the Devil, we no sooner enter'd the House, but we heard *Fidlers* and *Hautboys*, together with a Humdrum *Organ* make such incomparable Musick, that had the Harmonious Grunting of a *Hog* been added as a *Bass* to a Ravishing Concert of Caterwauling Performers, in the Height of the Extasie, the unusualness of the sound could not have render'd it, to a Nice Ear, more engaging. Having heard of the Beauty and Contrivance of the Publick *Musick Room,* as well as other parts of the House, very highly Commended, we agreed, first to take a view of that which was likely to be most remarkable. In order to which we Ascended the grades, and were Usher'd into a most Stately Apartment, Dedicated purely to the Lovers of *Musick, Painting, Dancing* and t'other thing too. No *Gilding, Carving, Colouring* or good *Contrivance* was here wanting to illustrate the Beauty of this most noble Academy; where a good Genius may learn with safety to abominate Vice; and a bad Genius as (with as much danger) to Practice it. The Room by its compact Order and costly Improvements, looks so far above the use its now converted to, that the seats are more like Pews than Boxes, and the upper-end being divided by a Rail, looks more like a *Chancel* than a *Musick-Box;* that I could not imagine it was Built for a *Fanatick Meeting-House,* but that they have for ever destroy'd the Sanctity of the place by putting an Organ in it; round which hung a great many pretty *Whimsical Pictures . . .* "

A French visitor quoted by Evelyn in 1659 was not impressed with the Musique Houses and delivered himself of some uncomplimentary remarks regarding them. "Nothing may be wanting to the height of luxury and impiety of this abomination, they have translated the organs out of the Churches to set them up in taverns, chaunting their dithyrambics and bestial bacchanalias to the tune of those instruments which were wont to assist them in the celebration of God's praises".

SEVENTEENTH CENTURY CATCH CLUBS

During the second half of the seventeenth century, as a contrast to the general rowdines of the London night scene and the rather juvenile behaviour of some sections of the community, many of the more sedate citizens formed themselves into singing groups. These amateur musicians met either in private houses or at taverns and became proficient in the performance of madrigals, glees and catches. Pepys was a leading light in this movement and on occasions he attended the Music Meetings at the *Black Swan,* Bishopsgate, in addition to the normal domestic singing-parties with his friends and servants. If one may generalise in this matter, madrigals were sung at home and in polite society, whilst catches and glees found their spiritual home in the tavern where the society was almost entirely masculine.

A word or two of explanation regarding the musical style of the catch and glee might be of value. The catch followed closely the tradition of the round, though with the principal difference that it was usually of a humorous nature. The various voices entered at intervals and were so arranged to give an amusing twist to the words, in which the pun often played a part. As an example "Ah how Sophia" might well become "Our house afire". It is feared that the sentiments expressed in many of the early catches are far too indelicate to be performed today.

The glee was strictly for male voices with an upper part designed for male altos. It was an unaccompanied work, but unlike the catch, the parts moved in chords, being therefore harmonic in construction rather than polyphonic. In this way, the glee, an essentially English composition, afforded an excellent foil to the catch. The first mention of the word Glee occurred in Playford's third collection of *Ayres and Dialogues* published in 1659. It was a three-part work by Thomas Brewer entitled *Turn Amarillis to thy Swain*.

One of the earliest clubs devoted to the singing of catches and glees started about 1670 and met regularly in Old Jewry. This society published a book entitled *The Catch-that-Catch Can* or the *Musical Companion*. Thus commenced a fashion that was to remain in favour for a very long time.

Henry Playford, head of the publishing firm which first produced Purcell's music, was keenly interested in a movement for promoting catch and glee clubs throughout the country. His motives may not have been entirely unconnected with business, but according to existing records this scheme met with considerable success and such clubs were very popular during the seventeenth century.

Ned Ward made many observations on the tavern life of his day. He was at one time licensee of the *King's Head* in Gray's Inn, but this did not prevent him from visiting other hostelries of the neighbourhood. In describing a typical evening spent with friends he mentions that: "Songs and catches crowned the night, and each man in his turn elevated his voice to fill our harmony with the more variety. Amongst the rest, we had one song against music which, because of its being the first essay in this nature, I have thought it worth inserting."

Verse

Music's a crotchet the sober think vain;
    The fiddle's a wooden projection
Tunes are but flirts of a whimsical brain,
    Which the bottle brings best to perfection,
Musicians are half-witted, merry and mad;
    The same are all those that admire 'em;
They're fools if they play, unless they're well paid;
    And the others are blockheads to hire 'em.

The organ's but humming, Theorba but thrumming,
    The viol and the voice,
Is but jingle and noise. The bagpipe and fiddle,
    Go tweedle and diddle,
The hautboy and flute, Is but toot-atoot-toot,
Your scales and your clefs, keys, moods and dull rules,
Are fit to please none but madmen and fools.

There are many other examples of this rather strange cult of writing against music and there exist equally as many in defence of the art. The fashion continued for some time.

The Theorba, mentioned in the previous song, was the largest instrument of the lute family. Sometimes known as the Archlute it appeared in Engish literature over a lengthy period. Being portable, it became particularly associated with inns and taverns as a useful accompaniment to singing, as the following lines by Thomas Jordan suggest.

Let us drink and be merry, dance, joke and rejoice,
    With claret and sherry, theorba and voice.

An interesting work published in 1700 was *Amphion Angliens* by John Blow. This was a "Work of many Compositions, for One, Two or Three or Four Voices; with several Accompagnements of Instrumental Music; and a Thorow-Bass to each song: figur'd for an Organ, Harpsichord or Theorboe-lute".

The next paragraph or so might give some cynical satisfaction to those rather narrow-minded and self-righteous individuals who still look upon musicians as vagabonds, n'er-do-wells and sturdy beggars. Although many musicians are abstemious and some are tee-total, nothing is gained by attempting to disguise the fact that there would appear to be a close association between music and drinking, an association that has continued through many centuries. However, to be perfectly fair, if careful research were carried out, this might be found to be no greater than that existing amongst certain other professions, medicine, journalism and perhaps even the law.

But to return to our subject and another quotation from the *London Spy* (1700). "Music and wine are usually held to be such inseparable Companions, that the true Relish of the one can never be Enjoy'd without the Assistance of the other". Although this may be an exaggeration, it is true that many taverns had long connections with music, and records still exist from the past as in the case of the famous *Crosskeys*. Its name was changed to *The Queen's Head* on the accession of Queen Elizabeth and it was mentioned in a tract of 1691, *The Last Search after Claret in Southwark* or a *Visitation of the Vintners in the Mint.*

> To the Queen's-head we hastened, and found the House ring,
> By Broom-men a-singing old Simon the king;
> Besides at the bar we perceived a poor Trooper
> Was cursing his master and calling him Cooper.

Other well-known taverns of the period were *The Three Crowns in the Vintry* described in literature as "the most topping tavern in London", *The Mitre,* the *Mermaid,* the *Falcon,* the *Boar's Head* and the *Devil Tavern.* Several of these hostelries were mentioned in the plays of Ben Jonson, who had his own Apollo Club in the great room at the *Devil Tavern.* He drew up twenty-four rules of behaviour, written in Latin and placed on a board hung above the fireplace. This board still exists and is now to be found in a bank which occupies the original site of the tavern. The colourful inn-sign of this house depicted St. Dunstan pulling the Devil's nose with a pair of tongs.

The *Crown and Anchor* in the Strand achieved fame as being the first meeting place, in 1710, of the Academy of Ancient Music. This consisted of a group of eminent musicians formed for the study and performance of older music, particularly that of the sixteenth century. The fortnightly meetings often included motets and madrigals sung by the choirs of St. Paul's and the Chapel Royal. These famous choirs together with that of Westminster Abbey receive frequent mentions in records of the eighteenth century as performing at taverns in central London.

In 1731 Maurice Greene, the Master of the King's Music, withdrew from the Academy of Ancient Music and provided opposition at the *Devil Tavern.* Known as the Apollo Society Concerts, this action gave rise to the saying that "Dr. Greene has gone to the Devil". He took with him the boys of St. Paul's Cathedral and Michael Festing as leader of the orchestra, but by this time several organisations were engaged in concert-giving and the Apollo Society Concerts did not last for more than a few years.

The Castle Society began its series of Castle Concerts in 1724, so named because of its meeting place, the *Castle Tavern* in Paternoster Row. According to Dr. Thomas Busby in his *Concert-room and Orchestra Anecdotes* of 1825, "both auditors and performers subscribed to their support; several singers from the Italian Opera assisted; and the subscription was raised from two to five guineas, for the purpose of enabling the society to introduce the performance of oratorios". Sir John Hawkins observed perhaps a little unkindly that "many young persons of professions and trades that depended upon a numerous acquaintance were induced by motives of interest to become members". The Society moved to the Haberdasher's Hall in 1764 where it continued for fifteen years before making another change. This time the venue was the *King's Arms,* Cornhill, but the title of "Castle Concerts" was still used in spite of these changes. Soon after the move to the *King's Arms* the concerts were discontinued.

Another London tavern is still remembered in the words of a popular song.

> Up and down the City Road
> In and out the *"Eagle"*
> That's the way the money goes
> Pop goes the weasel.

The last line of this song had for a long time been a source of mystery. According to Christopher Pulling in his *They Were Singing,* the "weasel" was a slang term in the East End for a tailor's "goose" or heavy iron. As this was an article which could easily be pawned, there seems no need to look further for an explanation.

DRINKING SONGS

There is a fascinating history of drinking songs. Many catches and glees were written in praise of wine or ale, and some of these songs lasted, with minor alterations, for several centuries. The drinking songs of the fifteenth century were of cheerful character, as will be noted from the following example "Song of the Taverner" which I have taken from the delightful *Old Inns of England* by A. E. Richardson.

> I am a taverner, wytty and wyse,
> That wynys have to sell gret plente.
> Of all the taverners I bere the pryse
> That be dwelling with-inne the cete;
> Of wynys I havve grete plente,
> Both whyte wynne and red that ys so cleyr;
> Here ys wynne of mawt and Malmeseyn,

Clary wynne and claret, and other moo,
Wyn of Gyldyr and of Galles, that made at the grome,
Wyn of Wyan and Vernage, I seye also;
Ther be no better, as ferre as ye can goo.

Here, lady, is wyn, a repast
To man, and woman a good restoratyff;
Ye shall not thynk you mony spent in wast
From stodys and hevynes it woll you relyff.

Another song, taken from the same source, refers to a group of
women who met together in a tavern every week unknown to their
husbands.

Good gossip mine, where have ye be?
It is so long sith I you see.
Where is the best wine? Tell you me.
Can you ought tell, (then say) full well.

I know a draught of merry-go-down,
The best it is in all this town;
But yet would I not, for my gown,
My husband it wist, ye may me trist.

Call forth your gossips by and by,
Elinor, Joan and Margery,
Margaret, Alice and Cecily;
For they will come both all and some.

And each of them will somewhat bring,
Goose, pigeon, or capon's wing,
Pasties of pigeons, or some other thing;
For a gallon of wine they will not wring.

Go before by twain and twain
Wisely, that ye be not seen;
For I must home, and come again,
To wit ywis where my husband is.

A stripe or two God might send me,
If my husband might here see me.
She that is afeared, let her flee.
Quoth Alice then: I dread no man.

75

Now we be in tavern set,
A draught of the best let him go fet,
To bring our husbands out of debt;
For we will spend, till God more send.

Each of them brought forth their dish
Some brought flesh, and some (brought) fish.
Quoth Margaret meek, now with a wish,
I would Anne were here, she would make us good cheer.

How say you gossips, is this wine good?
That it is, quoth Elinor, by the rood;
It cherisheth the heart, and comforteth the blood;
Such junkets among shall make us live long . . .

(Wright's *Songs and Carols,* published by the Percy Society)

A better known example is taken from the Jacobean tragedy: *The Bloody Brother; or Rollo, Duke of Normandy!*
Then let us swill, boys, for our health,
Who drinks well loves the commonwealth
And he that will to bed go sober,
Falls with the leaf, still in October.

In his book *Victorian Songs,* Maurice Willson Disher points out that this verse is used a century later in a glee (a) and then a further century ahead forms part of the famous song *Come, landlord, fill the flowing bowl* (b).

(a) He who goes to bed and goes to bed sober
   Falls as the leaves do and dies in October
   But he who goes to bed and goes to bed mellow
   Lives as he ought to do and dies an honest fellow.
(b) The man who drinketh small beer,
   And goes to bed quite sober,
   Fades as the leaves do fade
   That drop off in October,
   But he who drinketh strong beer
   And goes to bed quite mellow
   Lives as he ought to live
   And dies a jolly good fellow.

76

Another, though perhaps not as well known is *The Wassail Song*.

Wassail, wassail all over the town,
Our bread it is white and our ale it is brown,
Our bowl it is made of the green maple tree;
In the Wassail bowl we'll drink unto thee.

Here's a health to the ox and to his right eye,
Pray God send our master a good Christmas pie,
A good Christmas pie as e'er I did see,
In the Wassail bowl we'll drink unto thee.

Here's a health to the ox and to his right horn,
Pray God send our master a good crop of corn
A good crop of corn as e'er I did see,
In the Wassail bowl we'll drink unto thee.

Here's a health to the ox and to his long tail,
Pray God send our master a good cask of ale,
A good cask of ale as e'er I did see,
In the Wassail bowl we'll drink unto thee.

Come butler come fill us a bowl of the best;
Then I pray that your soul in heaven may rest;
But if you do bring us a bowl of the small,
May the Devil take butler, bowl and all.

Then here's to the maid in the lily white smock,
Who tripp'd to the door and slipp'd back the lock;
Who tripp'd to the door and pull'd back the pin,
For to let these jolly Wassailers walk in;

Wassail, wassail all over the town.

Even the great Henry Purcell, famous for his compositions in connection with the church, royalty and opera, was not averse to writing catches, some of which were quite as bawdy as popular opinion then demanded. The following example however is one that could not give offence.

Drink on till night be spent and sun do shine,
Did not the gods anxious mortals wine
To wash all care and trouble from the heart?

Why then so soon should jovial fellows part?
Come, let this bumper for the next make way;
Who's sure to live and drink another day?

Then there was the famous "Here's to the maiden of bashful fifteen".

Here's to the charmer whose dimples we prize;
Now to the maid who has none, sir:
Here's to the girl with a pair of blue eyes,
And here's to the nymph with but one, sir
    Let the toast pass
    Drink to the lass
I'll warrant she'll prove an excuse for the glass.

And how many a riotous evening has concluded with "Beer, beer, glorious beer".

The following three verses form the opening of a work by Robert Burns who excelled at drinking songs.

SCOTCH DRINK

	Let other Poets raise a fràcas
	'Bout vines, an' wines, an' drucken Bacchus
torment	An' crabbit names an' stories wrack us,
vex; ear	An' grate our lug,
barley	I sing the juice Scotch bear can mak us,
	In glass or jug.
	O thou, my Muse! guid, auld Scotch drink!
winding; dodge	Whether thro' wimplin worms thou jink
cream	Or, richly brown, ream owre the brink.
foam	In glorious faem.
	Inspire me, till I lisp an' wink,
	To sing thy name!
valleys	Let husky wheat the haughs adorn,
oats; bearded	An' aits set up their awnie horn,
	An' peace and beans, at e'en or morn,
	Perfume the plain.
Blessings on	Leeze me on thee, John Barleycorn,
thee	Thou king o'grain.

But not all references to strong drink were of a favourable nature. Though perhaps not the most rabid prohibitionist, Macheath, the notorious highwayman in the *Beggar's Opera* remarks "I have the Rat's-bane ready, I run no risk; for I can blame her death upon the Gin; and so many die of that naturally, that I shall never be called in question!". And that was probably a reasonable assessment of the situation in the early eighteenth century.

Excessive drinking occupied the attention of reformers during the late nineteenth century, and one method adopted to counteract the evil was the publication of a number of temperance ballads. As noted in my *Music Hath Charms* this practice had roots in a much earlier period, where songs lauding virtue and setting forth warnings against a particular vice frequently appeared when deemed necessary.

One well-known Band of Hope song *Please Sell No More Drink to My Father* was published in *The Temperance Vocalist* of 1866 and dedicated to Sir Wilfred Lawson, who did so much for temperance.

> Please sell no more drink to my father –
> It makes him so strange and so wild.
> Heed the prayer of my heart-broken mother,
> And pity the poor drunkard's child.

Three years later another temperance song *Don't Go Out Tonight, Dear Father* was published. This ballad had great popularity and probably had a considerable influence on its public.

> Don't go out to-night, dear Father,
> Don't refuse this once, I pray;
> Tell your comrades Mother's dying,
> Soon her soul will pass away;
> Tell them, too, of darling Willie.
> Him we all so much do love,
> How his little form is drooping,
> Soon to bloom again above.
> Don't go out tonight, dear Father;
> Think, oh think, how sad 'twill be
> When the angels come to take her,
> Papa won't be there to see.

The Drunkard's Lone Child, and *Father, Dear Father, Come Home With Me Now*, were but two others written in a similar vein.

MUGHOUSES

It seems probable that the eighteenth century Mughouses were a continuation of the earlier Musique Houses. They were taverns, with certain characteristics of clubs, in which regular customers had their own mugs, and where singing was a special feature of the convivial evenings. The first of these met twice a week during the winter at a house in Long Acre. John Timbs, in his *Club Life of London* describes a typical meeting at this rendezvous: "They have a grave old gentleman, in his own gray hairs, now within a few months of ninety years old, who is their President, and sits in an arm'd chair some steps higher than the rest of the company to keep the whole room in order. A harp plays all the time at the lower end of the room; and every now and then one or other of the company rises and entertains the rest with a song, and some are good masters . . . The room is always so diverted with songs, and drinking from one table to another to one another's healths, that there is no room for politics or anything that can sour conversation".

The last sentence of this quotation is particularly interesting as the mughouses later took on a distinctly political flavour. They became notorious as the meeting-places of the Whigs and were the means of serious trouble, even riots on occasions.

EIGHTEENTH CENTURY CATCH CLUBS

Although in the vast majority of cases the eighteenth century singing clubs were organised by and for the wealthy and aristocratic, at least one example of a madrigal society formed for working men is on record. This was started by John Immyns, secretary to Dr. Pepusch, for a group of people who appreciated the older type of music and "not less distinguished by their love of vocal harmony than the harmless simplicity of their tempers, and their friendly disposition towards each other".

The Noblemen and Gentlemen's Catch Club was founded in London in 1761, and as its name implies, membership was drawn largely from the aristocracy. Among the earlier members were the Duke of Kingston, the Marquess of Lorne, Lord Bolingbroke, Lord Ashburnham and Lord George Sutton. Later the club included the Duke of Clarence (afterwards William IV) and the Dukes of Cambridge, Cumberland, Sussex and York. There were several quaint regulations in connection with this club. For instance each member was bound to sing a song at every meeting. One bottle of sherry was shared between every three members and one bottle of Madeira to every seven. No one was allowed to take to the table "coffee, tea or such heterogeneous beverages – on any account", and as in the case of the early mughouses, political argument was forbidden. Several members of the royal family attended the meetings and George IV took his turn with the rest in acting as chairman and singing a song. One most valuable provision of this club was to offer prizes for new and worth-while compositions.

The Catch Club at the exclusive *Thatched House Tavern* was instituted in 1762 by the Earl of Eglinton, the Earl of March and some of their friends. It met with immediate and prolonged success and was in part responsible for the considerable improvement in the performance of catches, canons and glees of every type. Many of the members wrote songs and sang them at their convivial evenings.

Tom Moore, the popular composer of Irish songs commenced with translations of Anacreon, and this resulted in his being known as "Anacreon Moore". He will be remembered for his *Let Erin Remember, The Last Rose of Summer, The Harp that once through Tara's Halls* and *The Minstrel Boy*.

A supper, given by the Duke of Sussex in honour of the Prince Regent, was perhaps typical of this period and this famous club. The eating started at 9 o'clock and continued until 1 a.m. after which came the singing. Apparently the Prince was in great form and sang his vocal item with gusto.

In his *London Journal* of 1763 Boswell makes reference to the pastime of singing catches. Under his entry for March 23rd which refers to Lord Eglinton, we read: "He begun and taught me to sing catches, of which he is very fond. He gave me much encouragement, and said there were not five people in the whole Catch Club who had a better ear than I have". Then again on May 10th: "My Lord Eglinton made me very welcome, and immediately he and I began singing catches, which is really a most enlivening thing. There some lively sentiment well accompanied with suitable music, and when sung in parts a fine harmony is produced.

I take a lesson from him whenever I can, and I make very good progress".

The Anacreontic Society had a short life compared with the Noblemen and Gentlemen's Catch Club. It commenced in 1766 at the *Crown and Anchor* in the Strand, as an aristocratic club of amateur musicians with a leavening of professional members. The club had a special claim to fame – its own club song. This was sung by all members with great vigour. The tune of Anacreon is perhaps better known today as the "Star-spangled Banner".

> To Anacreon in heaven, where he sat in full glee,
> A few sons of harmony sent a petition,
> That he their inspirer and patron would be;
> When this answer arrived from the jolly old Grecian;
> 'Voice, fiddle and flute, no longer be mute,
> I'll lend you my name and inspire you to boot;
> And besides, I'll instruct you like me to entwine
> The myrtle of Venus with Bacchus's vine.
> And besides, I'll instruct you like me to entwine
> The myrtle of Venus with Bacchus's vine.

This was followed by songs in every possible style and by catches and glees sung by the finest singers of the day. Membership of this club was considered a great privilege and a long waiting list testified to its popularity. The Society came to an end in 1794 during the Presidency of Sir Richard Hankey. Apparently the Duchess of Devonshire, at that time one of the foremost leaders of society, expressed a wish to be present at a meeting and although placed in a private box under the orchestra, her presence rather cramped the style of the illustrious members. Some favourite comic songs were omitted from the evening's programme as being unfit for the lady's ears. This caused resentment among the clientele and many gentlemen resigned at once in indignation.

Haydn once visited this club, an honour he also conferred on another – the Graduates Meetings – after receiving his Oxford degree of Doctor of Music. This club consisted of musicians, all of whom possessed a musical degree. It failed after a few years and was replaced by another, the Concentores Sodales. Here the members were composers and the normal gatherings consisted almost entirely of performances of their own music. This society did not last long either and an attempted revival proved short-lived.

On the emergence of a popular movement of any kind, there has never been a dearth of those able and willing to cater for it, and no doubt to profit from it also. The glee and catch phase was no exception to this rule. Several composers devoted themselves almost exclusively to the writing of this music and supplied countless members of music clubs with charming examples of the style.

Of these composers, Samuel Webbe was probably the most important. He held high office at the Catch Club and the Glee Club for many years, and was successful in gaining a large proportion of the prizes offered. John Smith, one of the musicians employed at the Chapel Royal was also responsible for a number of glees, as was also Richard Stevens, organist of the Temple Church and the Charterhouse. Stephen Paxton and his brother William made reputations for themselves in this field and the Earl of Mornington, father of the Duke of Wellington and Professor of Music at Dublin was a distinguished composer of catches and glees. John Callcott was another whose talent brought many prizes at the Catch Club. The son of a bricklayer, he received a rather irregular musical training at first, but was fortunate in knowing both Arnold and Cooke from whom he gained considerable knowledge. In 1785, as a young man of nineteen he gained three of the four prizes presented by the Catch Club. Two years later he caused something of a sensation by submitting nearly one hundred glees in one of the competitions. As a result of this youthful enthusiasm it was decided that three entries should suffice in future from any one competitor. In this same year, 1787, Calcott, together with Samuel Arnold founded the Glee Club. At a later date his son-in-law William Horsley also achieved a reputation as a writer of glees and catches.

During this century the reading of serious poetry developed as an evening entertainment in the taverns of London and other large cities. It had quite a vogue, which might seem a little surprising as the audience could not participate to the same extent as in the songs. But first class readers were engaged and according to contemporary records they held their audiences spell-bound. This confirms an opinion that not all public-house entertainment was necessarily lewd or questionable despite the fact that most taverns and clubs at this time catered entirely for males.

The citizens of places other than London enjoyed music in their favourite drinking-houses. In the early years of the eighteenth century, public musical entertainment in Edinburgh was centred in one or two inns, in particular that known as Steil's near the Parliament Close, of which more later.

In Cambridge, Christ's College had its music club dating from 1710, in which the members met once a week. This was one of the earliest clubs of its type in the country.

The Canterbury Catch Club began in a tavern in 1779 and later built its own premises, the "Apollonian Hall". All records of this club make special mention of the refreshments "gin punch and mutton pies", but perhaps almost as important was the fact that it did not confine its activities to catches and glees. Instrumental and organ music found a place in the weekly meetings. Similar clubs flourished elsewhere, three of particular note being at Bath, Belfast and Dublin.

FREE AND EASIES
OR HARMONIC CLUBS

"A Free and Easy kept here every Friday". Such notices became more common in public-houses as the century drew to a close. The "Free and Easy" or "Harmonic Club" as it was often known, had no printed programme; instead, each item was introduced by a chairman. This gentleman, imposing in manner and slightly over-dressed, did not lack personality. The position of chairman was not always an enviable one, and personality was essential in order to keep a grip on the somewhat high-spirited clientele of these establishments. He sat in a commanding postion at a high table facing the customers. From time to time he would invite some special guest to sit at his table and take refreshment. Henry Angelo, the fencing master, in his *Reminiscences* describes the scene at *Jacob's Wells*, in Barbican: "The long room, if I may depend on my memory, was on the ground floor, and all the benches were filled with motley groups, eating, drinking, and smoking . . . There was a president who, from a rostrum, knocking with an ivory mallet, hoarsely bawled 'Will any gentleman favour the company with a speech, a recitation, an imitation, or a song?' Half a dozen candidates for fame, in each department proposed, started up; when the moderator, from his lofty seat, decided who was first on his legs. The parties then retired, a bell was rung, the curtain was raised at the end of the room, and the spouter or singer, making his bow, commenced his part . . . The entertainment, as Lord Barrymore often said, was the most prolific of fun that his lordship, whose very being was to seek frolic, had ever witnessed in all his peregrinations. The night was waning fast, and we sat until exhilerated by copious draughts, and urged by his lordship, I yielded to my vanity, and undertook the part of Mother Cole, from Foote's celebrated farce of *The Minor* . . . Lord Barrymore, entering heartily into the mirth which surrounded us, obeyed the general call for a song, a speech, or a recitation, and gave them a convivial strain with great glee",

A similar kind of entertainment, though catering for a rather different type of patron was the Pic-Nic Society, which had its meetings at the Tottenham Rooms near Tottenham Court Road. This consisted of a group of the stage-struck aristocracy, who gave dramatic performances in which their own amateur orchestra took part. This orchestra seems to have caused especial merriment and as a result of its popularity the established theatres suffered much competition. Again, according to Angelo: "Here, some descendant from the great and mighty baron of old, instead of being cased in armour, drew forth the fiddle-case; and he whose redoubtable ancestor wielded the battle-axe at Cressy, here figured with the long-bow on a larger fiddle still; whilst one whose blood flowed through his thrice-noble veins, transmitted from the days of the Conqueror, conquered all hearts by his soft strains upon the flageolet. Here, too, quoting the audacious caricaturist, a giant lord warbled on the tiny flute, and a tiny lordling thundered on the double-base. The gorgeous Lady Albina's dimpled fingers pressed the ivory keys of the grand piano, and Lady S....... delighted the patrician auditory with a flourish on the French Horn".

Another masterly description of a Harmonic Meeting is that by Dickens in his *Sketches by Boz*. It is so charmingly portrayed that I feel it must be included. "In a lofty room of spacious dimensions are seated some eighty or a hundred guests knocking little pewter measures on the tables, and hammering away with the handles of their knives as if they were so many trunk-makers. They were applauding a glee, which has just been executed by the three "professional gentlemen" at the top of the centre table, one of whom is in the chair – the little pompous man with the bald head just emerging from the collar of his green coat . . . To hear him growling away, gradually lower and lower down' till he can't get back again,

85

is the most delightful thing in the world, and it is quite impossible to witness unmoved the impressive solemnity with which he pours forth his soul in "My 'art's in the 'ighlands", or "The brave old Hoak". The "professional gentlemen" are in the very height of their glory, and bestow condescending nods, or even a word or two of recognition, on the better-known frequentors of the room, in the most bland and patronising manner possible. "Gen'l'men" says the little pompous man, accompanying the word with a knock of the president's hammer on the table – "Gen'l'men, allow me to claim your attention – our friend Mr. Smuggins will oblige". – "Bravo!" shout the company; and Smuggins, after a considerable quantity of coughing by way of symphony, and a most facetious sniff or two, which afford general delight, sings a comic song, with a fal-de-ral-tol-de-rol chorus at the end of every verse, much longer than the verse itself. It is received with unbounded applause, and after some aspiring genius has volunteered a recitation, and failed dismally therein, the little pompous man gives another knock, and says "Gen'l'men, we will attempt a glee, if you please". This announcement calls forth tumultous applause, and the more energetic spirits express the unqualified approbation it affords them by knocking one or two stout glasses off their legs – a humorous device; but one which frequently occasions some slight altercation when the form of paying the damage is proposed to be gone through by the waiter".

Quite apart from the often rough and ready performances and the somewhat "popular" musical fare mentioned in this chapter, some serious music of a high order took place in London taverns during the nineteenth century. For instance, the City of London Classical Harmonists Society was an association of amateurs devoted to great choral works, many of which were of considerable technical difficulty. Included in their repertoire were Weber's "Oberon" and Spohr's "Mass in C minor". This society, which began in 1831, met at the *Horn Tavern* and should not be confused with the Classical Harmonists, an even older group which favoured the famous *Crown and Anchor* in the Strand.

Then came the Choral Harmonists Society which seceded from the City of London Classical Harmonists and first met at the *New London Hotel*, Blackfriars on 2nd January 1833. It subsequently performed at the *London Tavern* until 1851. Among the splendid programmes were included performances of Beethoven's "Mass in D", Haydn's "Seasons" and Mendelssohn's "Walpurgisnacht".

86

These works were accompanied by a complete orchestra.

CONCERT CLUBS

The *Cyder Cellar* in Covent Garden, sometimes known as the Midnight Concert Room, attracted a great deal of custom. As its name implied the accommodation was actually in a cellar and the principal drink was cider. The entertainment consisted of the usual free and easy, at which the landlord led off followed by the company. It was conveniently placed for journalists and attracted the Bohemian and intellectual element of the city. The *Queen's Head* in Newgate Street had a concert club composed of professionals and amateurs. This, unlike the normal sing-song was really a concert with admission for the public at a charge of two shillings. Supper was obtainable after the concert at which the artists and audience met and discussed musical matters at length.

At the *Coal Hole,* Fountain Court, kept by Rhodes, the Singing Collier, Edmund Kean formed his Wolves Club. It consisted almost entirely of men associated with the theatre and there they passed their time in eating, singing and conversation. Kean delighted in such places. There he met those of similar outlook who spoke the same language as himself. Also they enjoyed his brilliant wit and looked upon him as one of the outstanding personalities of the day. Another house frequented by the great actor was the *Harp Tavern* near Drury Lane Theatre, where dramatic performances were given by all sorts and conditions of men. Everyone present had to take some part, however humble, in the evening's entertainment. Mass television had not then cast its blight over the nation and good conversation was still an art indulged in by a large number of enthusiastic devotees.

Another well-known song-and-supper rendezvous was Offley's in Covent Garden. Here, the singing, always led off by the proprietor himself, was exceptionally hearty. So much so, that the supper rooms had to be fitted with double windows in order to overcome the nuisance to the neighbours. In near-by King Street was the famous house owned by Joy, and taken over in 1820 by Evans, who transformed it into a supper and singing room. But this was a singing-room with a difference. The type of music associated with Offley's was not encouraged; instead, professional musicians provided the basis of these programmes and occasionally a dining member would be invited to give a solo item during the evening.

Nineteenth century song and supper rooms on the pattern of the *Coal Hole* and the *Cyder Cellar* increased rapidly throughout the country, and it was from these earthy but quite natural forms of recreation that the popular entertainment of the future was to spring. Unfortunatley in 1851 both of these establishments were taken over by "Chief Baron" Renton Nicholson, of whom Thomas Burke wrote "Whatever he touched he soiled". True it was that the *Coal Hole* and *Cyder Cellar* deteriorated and very soon disappeared. But they had given a lead and taverns in every district had their harmonic meetings, in some places nightly and in others once a week. They became ever more crowded and as a result, rooms reserved solely for singing and music were added to countless public-houses. The following might be considered a typical tavern chorus of the period.

> We're jovial, happy, and gay, boys!
> We rise with the moon, which is surely full soon,
> Sing with the owl, our tutelar fowl,
> Laugh and joke at your go-to-bed folk,
> Never think but what we shall drink,
> Never care but on what we shall fare –
> Turning the night into day, boys!

In 1841, rather in the style of the early seventeenth century, a group of former choir boys of Westminster Abbey formed a club for the cultivation of glee singing. At first the meetings were held at the Herbert Hotel, Westminster on the second and fourth Saturdays in every month. An older club, the Adelphi Glee Club, founded in 1832, merged with the Abbey Club about 1845 and the newly constituted group met at the *Freemason's Tavern* and later at the Caxton Hall. This society, which limited its membership to one hundred and fifty, maintained a high standard of glee singing until well into the present century, and in fact only ceased to function in 1932.

Some of the tradition and much of the bonhomie of the clubs mentioned earlier have been carried over to the present day Savage Club which celebrated its centenary in 1957. First situated in Adelphi Terrace, long famous as the London address of several great literary figures, it later moved to its present home in

Carlton House Terrace. Speculation has been caused by the rather unusual name given to this club and from time to time suggestions have been put forward to account for it.

According to A. P. Herbert, himself a member "a number of bright sparks were choosing a name, *The Addison* said one; *The Johnson* said another. *Goldsmith* and even *Shakespeare* were suggested. But at last one said 'who are we to take such mighty names? Let it be something modest'. Someone said 'Why not Savage?' And it was so".

Members of the Savage Club have to be connected with Art, Drama, Literature, Music or Science, and on Saturday nights the greatest men in the world of music and entertainment give freely of their talent to amuse and edify their brother Savages.

Still in London and not a great distance from Carlton House Terrace we find the City Glee Club with its headquartes at St. Ermin's Hotel, Westminster. Here, during the winter, are held the monthly meetings for the singing of glees, madrigals and part-songs. Membership of the club is limited to two hundred and the singers are mostly choirmen from Westminster Abbey, St. Paul's Cathedral and the Chapel Royal. The club, which owns an extensive and valuable library of music, still maintains the happy and friendly spirit of the informal smoking-concert and remains one of the most important glee-singing institutions of today. Its history may be traced back to 1853 when it succeeded the much older Civil Club dating from the reign of Charles II.

THE EARLY MUSIC HALL

The earliest music halls of about the mid-nineteenth century were very different from those of today. The audience was accommodated on one floor and sat at tables upon which rested their liquid refreshment. Between the turns, waiters darted around taking orders – in some cases almost compelling them. From the owner's point of view this was most important as the sale of drink provided his profit. Much of the entertainment consisted of comic songs. These were earthy and vulgar but without the double-entendre which serves so often as humour today. Disraeli described this type of hall in *Sybil*, in which the picture is taken from a typical north country town. The room, known as the Temple of the Muses, was part of a public house and although the price of admission was only 3d. this was returnable on the customer ordering a drink.

"The room was very full; some three or four hundred persons were seated in different groups at different tables, eating, drinking, talking, laughing, and even smoking, for, notwithstanding the pictures and the gilding, it was found impossible to forbid, though there were efforts to discourage this practice in the Temple of the Muses. Nothing, however, could be more decorous than the general conduct of the company, though they consisted principally of factory people. The waiters flew about with as much agility as if they were serving nobles. In general the noise was great, though not disagreeable; sometimes a bell rang, and there was comparative silence, while a curtain drew up at the farther end or the room, opposite to the entrance, where there was a theatre, the stage raised at a due elevation, and adorned with side screens, from which issued a lady in fancy-dress, who sang a favourite ballad; or a gentleman elaborately habited in a farmer's costume of the old comedy, a bob-wig, silver buttons and buckles, and blue stockings, and who favoured the company with that melancholy effusion called a comic song. Some nights there was music on the stage; a young lady in a white robe with a golden harp, and attended by a gentleman in black moustachios".

The transition from tavern to music-hall came with the erection of a stage for the performers, and an upper-hall for the "quality" with prices suitably raised to discourage the masses. The ground floor, with its tables, kept the tavern-like atmosphere for some time, but as accommodation became more pressing the tables disappeared and ledges for refreshments were attached to the backs of the seats. The Chairman remained a powerful influence in the early days of the music-hall and acted as a compere or link between artists and audience.

The first real music-hall was the Canterbury Arms Tavern, Westminster Bridge Road taken over by Charles Morton in 1848. A first-class business man, he saw the possibilities of providing entertainment on the grand scale with professional artists, particularly singers and comedians. In 1851 Morton built a new hall adjoining the tavern, which was enlarged three years later and opened as the New Canterbury Music Hall. There was seating accommodation for 1500 and women were made welcome as patrons. The tradition of glee singing was wisely retained, and one particularly interesting feature was a performance of excerpts from Gounod' *Faust*, given several years before its first production at the Opera House in the Haymarket.

Charles Morton, although probably the most spectacular showman of his time, did not always play down to his public. At the Canterbury he installed a picture-gallery which included paintings by many reputable and indeed famous artists. Here then, we observe the subtle change-over from the tavern to the hall. The public which previously had met nightly in a small intimate circle and whose entertainment consisted almost entirely of the "do it yourself" brand, now began to favour the more impersonal atmosphere of a large building and to appreciate the professional entertainer. Morton moved on to become the brains behind several West End halls, the Oxford, the Alhambra, the Tivoli and the Palace.

the modern music-hall, where it still survives, has little in common with the old "free and easy" of the nineteenth century apart from a tendency on the part of the audience to join in the chorus of a well-known song. But even this feature is not always as easy to attain as one might expect. Entertainers often attempt, and sometimes work very hard to re-create hearty chorus singing, but it must be confessed, with varying degrees of success.

TWENTIETH CENTURY TAVERNS

Music still plays a part in the tavern life of this century, though it may not have the uninhibited approach of former days. Such places have now become more refined, and any undue boisterousness is looked upon with disfavour. There may be many good reasons why the full-blooded musical entertainment of earlier centuries has declined, but public-houses may yet be found which advertise sing-songs. They are mostly in districts famous for splendid voices, such as the north of England, and to some extent in Wales, another home of choral singing. In the latter instance Nonconformity has probably had an adverse effect on this form of entertainment, but the Union Hotel at Bangor is possibly only one of many which displays the sign "Licenced by Act of Parliament for Singing" above its front door. In Devonshire I rather unexpectedly came across somewhat similar notices in connection with inns at Budleigh Salterton and Ottery St. Mary.

The tavern music-room in the tradition of the seventeenth and eighteenth centuries has not then entirely disappeared. In addition

91

to those in areas mentioned, several exist in the environs of London, particularly in riverside resorts. As in former days the customers sit at tables, while on a dais at the far end of the room may be found a small group of versatile musicians. Waiters dart about serving the patrons, during which time the orchestra plays popular tunes of various periods. The company is encouraged to join in the singing of well-known choruses, and at intervals one of the musicians goes around taking a collection on behalf of his colleagues and himself.

The majority of houses do not provide so lavish a musical entertainment and it is perhaps more usual to find a somewhat battered piano, together with a pianist ready to oblige the customers. Some of these pianists are extraordinary beings. They are capable of performing from memory, or by ear, any popular melody that may be called for, and they will continue to play all the evening for a glass or two and a few coins thrown into a hat or other receptacle.

As a general rule now-a-days however, the nearest approach to live music found in the precincts of most taverns is the rather down-at-heel and pathetic character who serenades from without, on trumpet, trombone or thin-toned fiddle. Although in direct descent from the waits of the sixteenth century and earlier, one imagines that the present-day busker is now suffered rather than sought after.

HOTELS AND RESTAURANTS

The famous Pagani's Restaurant in London's Great Portland Street opened in 1871 as a small coffee shop kept by a Mario Pagani. It is worthy of mention here because it became a centre for musicians – in the early days primarily Italian. Edward Cecil, in his Jubilee Souvenir remarks: "They dropped into the habit of signing their names, sketching their friends, scribbling some bars of melody they had found in the music floating through this happy contentment, on the grey distempered walls, now preserved under glass panels". These inscriptions, which ran into hundreds, became a feature of the restaurant and included such famous names as Caruso, Tchaikovsky, Melba and Paderewski. During the second world war the building was destroyed by bombs, but the inscribed walls remained undamaged. A move was made to temporary quarters not far away, where business was carried on under difficult conditions of much restricted space. The management still contrived to supply excellent meals and as before, numbered musicians amongst its clientele. Unhappily Pagani's has now closed its doors.

In the late 1880s, by the example of the then Prince of Wales, public entertaining became more general. In London by that time the Ritz, Savoy and Carlton Hotels supplied music in their restaurants. The dining-rooms still remained aloof from this new intrusion, but orchestras appeared in the lounges where coffee was taken.

Since eating-out has become almost universal, many good-class restaurants and hotels now provide music. Orchestras of varying sizes, from the large "Corner House" type resplendent in fancy dress, to the discreet Palm Court trio, perform anything from popular to rather more serious items. The playing is often of an excellent quality and the musicians enter into the spirit of the occasion, by playing "A happy birthday to you" to a medley of national airs in honour of a group of people from another country. This form of background music is much to the taste of a large section of the community, but is disconcerting to others. Some seem not to listen at all and simply converse in a rising crescendo as the circumstances demand; when the music stops they tend to look a trifle surprised. To be strictly fair, it must be recorded that not a few restaurants gain patronage by advertising NO MUSIC.

The chromium-plated snack-bar often boasts a juke box which, upon being fed with a few coins, will oblige with the latest "pop" numbers. This canned music, though not to everyone's taste, has proved popular in a certain type of cafe catering mostly for young people.

MUSIC CLUBS IN EDINBURGH

The Edinburgh Society of Musicians, which still meets every Saturday evening, is very much in the tradition of the ancient Musique Clubs. The comfortable and dignified club room is gained by a long turret-like stair case. The panelled walls are covered by photographs and drawings, consisting largely of important figures in music. During the winter months a roaring fire at each end of the room adds to the atmosphere of cheeriness. The members, drawn from many walks of life, sit at tables upon which rest their refreshment. A sense of friendliness and informality pervades the club and warm appreciation is shown to the various artists who perform there. I have been particularly fortunate in obtaining much interesting information regarding the Edinburgh Harmonists Society. Mr. John Molphy, the President since 1932 has given every possible assistance and has allowed me to browse amongst the early manuscripts and records of this famous club. As a result its history is dealt with here in some detail. The Catch Club, as it was then known, started as an offshoot of the Musical Society which was established in 1728 at Steil's in Old Assembly Close. The Earl of Eglinton played an important part in the formation of this aristocratic club, in connection with which a meeting is known to have been held at his house in 1725.

Arnot, in his "History of Edinburgh" writes: "Before that time several gentlemen, performers on the harpsichord and violin had formed a weekly club at the *Cross Keys Tavern* (kept by one Steil, a great lover of musick and good singer of Scots songs), where the common entertainment consisted in playing the concertos and sonatas of Corelli, then just published, and the overtures of Handel. That meeting becoming numerous, they instituted, in March 1728, a society of seventy members, for the purpose of holding a weekly concert".

This would appear to be the oldest music club of its kind in the world. The Catch Club was a great success. It contained many members with excellent voices, capable of singing a difficult part at sight. The atmosphere was one of happiness and good spirits, as was usual in such assemblies during the eighteenth century.

The Governor of the Edinburgh Musical Society, Lord Drummore, and the gentlemen of the Catch Club entertained the Prince of Hesse in 1745. An able musician himself, the Prince was unfamiliar with Scots songs and English catches, but according to reports he thoroughly enjoyed this new experience.

An entry in the minutes for December 4th, 1771, mentions James Boswall, advocate, as being elected to membership. As noted earlier in the chapter, he had received useful tuition at the hands of Lord Eglinton.

Although the Catch Club officially closed down at the end of the eighteenth century, glees and catches were now held in private houses. In 1822, at such an occasion in Mr. Nicholas Swift's house, it was decided to start another club. Such was the interest aroused that the resolution was put immediately into operation and Mr. Gilbert Innes of Stow was elected the first President of the Harmonist's Society, a position he occupied until his death in 1832. The present Harmonists' Society is therefore a direct successor of the original Catch Club.

During the early nineteenth century many interesting personalities became members of the Society. According to the minutes for December 7th, 1829, "Mr. Richard Carte, a professor of the flute, late of London, was admitted as a professional member. He was one of the brothers who comprised the firm of Rudall Carte, London, Musical Instrument Makers and Music Publishers. He had a son Richard Carte, who adopted the name of his mother a member of an old Suffolk family named D'Oyly. As Richard D'Oly Carte he became the impressario of the Gilbert and Sullivan Operas".

Of other members special mention might be made of Charles Horn, the singer and composer of many glees, who was elected on June 7th, 1830. As a point of interest he was the first important English composer to visit the United States where he eventually settled.

The following account of the meetings of the Society shows a regular and unvarying ritual that was maintained over a considerable period. The members sat with the President round a table on which was provided a decanter of whisky with water carafe, silver spirit measure and glasses. Members toasted the President and their fellows and the Company indulged in some general conversation while the Librarian selected the music for the evening. Music stands were used for the formal meeting and a piece of music having been placed on each of the four stands, and on one provided for the Conductor, the Librarian approached the Chair and announced "Mr. President, the Glee (or part song) is up (meaning the piece and its composer).

The President then announced to the meeting "Gentlemen, the Glee is up, Mr. Conductor will you please call a caste". The Conductor then called upon one or more of each part, by name, or for a "full caste" and those so nominated proceeded to the stands and performed the works.

At the finish of the piece the performers were rewarded by applause from the others, resumed their seats – and where necessary, replenished their glasses. The general conversation was then resumed until the Librarian again broke in to announce the next piece in the manner before described.

The formal meetings closed at 10 p.m. and at that hour the Chair was vacated and the stands abandoned, the company then singing some of the simpler glees sitting round the table.

The Secretary saw to it that the decanter was kept filled from the jar – and as Treasurer received the dues at the close of proceedings".

Practically all the original music of the Edinburgh Catch Club is still used by the Harmonists Society thanks to Gilbert Innes of Stow, who bought it at an auction sale and presented it to the society.

There must be much interesting history to be told of musical clubs throughout the land. Some may not be famous or known widely outside their own circle of members. As a rule societies of this nature do not welcome the glare of publicity; nevertheless they have influenced the course of music far out of proportion to their numbers, as has been noted. Such a one was the quaintly named Geoghegan Sofeggio Club of Edinburgh. This grew out of the ashes of the Solfeggio Musical Society conducted by Joseph Geoghegan, a teacher of singing. When this society ended officially, several of the members met at regular intervals and eventually decided to form another club.

The first meeting was held on November 24th, 1883. The members asked Goeghegan to become its patron and requested that his name should be associated in its title. The membership card contained a picture of the patron, together with the first few notes of Wainwright's glee "Life's a Bumper". It was the tradition in the early days for all members to sing this glee at every meeting. Although it was essentially a social club, lectures were given at the monthly meetings, usually by the members. A John C. Grieve, who taught musical theory at the Heriot Watt College was one member who occasionally obliged. There exists a good story regarding this gentleman. One of his pupils at the College insisted that had Bach been a member of his class, Mr. Grieve would not have approved of his counterpoint. It appears that this pupil, on one occasion, had introduced a short passage from the B minor Mass into his home exercise, and Mr. Grieve had condemned it.

A Club Outing was held on the first Saturday in June for many years and took the form of an excursion into the country. The members drove in a four-in-hand, with several important stops for refreshment, and from all accounts a most lively day resulted. The following verses were sung at Edgelaw on June 1st 1901, and they give an excellent picture of this fraternity in festive mood.

A RETROSPECT

'Twas in the year one-nine-ought-ought
On a bright June Saturday
The Geoghegan Club, in smart array,
Set out for their annual ploy,
                              Brave boys
With a fal-la, etc.

Away they hied to fair Glencourse
In a splendid char-à-banc,
With sprigs so gay upon each horse,
And President T. on the box
                              Brave boys
With a fal-la, etc.

On board was Secretary A.,
And near him Johnnie B.,
J. K. L. and a jolly lot more
Not to mention yours trulee
                              Brave boys
With a fal-la, etc.

They drove along right merrily,
With song and jest well worn,
And tho' they'd left their girls behind,
Not a soul was there forlorn.
                              Brave boys,
With a fal-la, etc.

But a little rift within the lute,
Well nigh made the music mute,
For tho' not time for "Round the First"
Some began to feel a thirst
                              Brave boys
With a fal-la, etc.

And when good Straiton hove in sight
The thirsty cried "Let's have a drink"
But the Secretary said "We won't alight
We shall pass *straight-on*, I think
                                        Brave boys
With a fal-la, etc.

Then Johnnie B. sprang on the poop –
"Secretary", says he, "you're too cock-a-hoop;
You go to blazes mighty quick
For a drink we'll have right slick"
                                        Brave boys
With a fal-la, etc.

So down they leapt, and stormed the inn,
And sipped their whiskies quite the thing,
While the Secretarym in high dud-ge-on,
Said "I'll stop their grog at Bil-ste-on"
                                        Brave boys
With a fal-la, etc.

And when they got to that stronghold,
Some said "We'll go by Roslin old"
But Secretary had them there of course,
"No, no" says he, "we're for Glencorse".
                                        Brave boys
With a fal-la, etc.

Arrived at last at the old, old church,
They chopped a tear at M'Kean's last couch,
Were photographed, both short and tall,
With the Dominie's dog on the wall
                                        Brave boys
With a fal-la, etc.

But malt without meal's a trifle headee,
So sandwiches were called for quite brisklee,
And some got one, and others got two,
And some got none at all.
                                        Oo-ooh.
With a fal-la, etc.

These sought about like men in a dream,
And jumped from side to side of the stream,
Till they didn't know which side they were on,
Gave it up, and started for town

                              Brave boys
With a fal-la, etc.

All the way home they echoed the cry,
"Too much water in the reservoir!"
But J.K.L. said "I'll put that right,
With five goes of "Pherson's tripe"

                              Brave boys.
With a fal-la, etc.

This high resolve was met with acclaim,
And each guest also did the same;
And the effect was such upon them all,
Their girls didn't think they'd been away at all.

                              Brave boys.
With a fal-la, etc.

Not great poetry perhaps, but a splendid account of a club outing. Anyone who has ever suffered or enjoyed – according to taste – such an occasion, will recognise all the types. I seem to remember, many years ago as a young organist of a West of England church, the incredible annual choir outing. To this day I have a most vivid recollection of the "stores" taken aboard the coach, and wondering how on earth so much could possibly be consumed by so few. The return journey was inevitably enlivened by hearty singing, though the choice of music might sometimes have been other than the ecclesiastical modes, thus proving the broad taste of this particular choir. It was certainly an important occasion, one necessitating many serious meetings in advance, at which, according to reliable information, much useful preparation was undertaken.

NINETEENTH CENTURY MUSICAL SOCIETIES

It is interesting to note that at least one famous choral society started, and continued for some years on club lines. The Huddersfield

Choral Society was founded in 1836 and met once a month on a night near full moon, in order that members might walk home in safety. Male members were charged 2/6d. per half-year but the ladies had nothing to pay. Everyone was allowed "three gills of ale and bread and cheese" at every meeting. The object of the Society was enjoyable rehearsal rather than public performance, and members had in turn an opportunity of choosing the Oratorio next to be performed. Criticism was encouraged and any member was allowed to give his opinion after the performance of any piece of music on the condition that it was given "in a respectable, friendly and becoming manner". Here then were the beginnings of a choir destined for the highest honours in the realms of choral singing. It might be added, as an incentive to others, that the Huddersfield Choral Society has reached its present position by a quite outstanding devotion to duty.

The Cambridge University Musical Society had its beginnings in 1843 as a club, then known as the Peterhouse Musical Society. Its original object was the performance of instrumental music and the University Musical Club still holds weekly meetings at which its members provide chamber music of a high standard.

Oxford University also has its Music Club, founded in 1872 for the intimate playing of chamber music. In 1915 it amalgamated with another similar group, the Oxford Musical Union and the combined clubs occupy premises which are claimed to be the oldest devoted to music in Europe. A Musical Society used this building from 1748 until 1836 when it then became devoted to other purposes.

The two Universities of Oxford and Cambridge have a joint music club in London for their members. Regular weekly meetings, much in the seventeenth century style, are held at their Bedford Square club house.

THE VILLAGE INN

In the rural districts the village inn continued to be the centre of communal life and sing-songs were a regular feature. These did not aspire to the high standard of music performed at the *Crown and Anchor* mentioned earlier, nor was their singing comparable to that of the metropolitan catch and glee clubs. But heartiness compensated for lack of finesse. Harvest suppers, church ales and other occasions of revelry were held in the "big room" of the inn, while the bar parlour resounded nightly to the lusty, earthy songs of the country folk, often ballads containing references to local people and affairs.

Where wine and English liquors brew'd
Of malt were sold for human good
Which drew the rural slaves from plough,
From treading Hey and Barlew-Mow,
And swains and shepherds from their herds,
With sunburnt looks and bristled beards,
To wet their whistles with the liquors,
And make their heavy souls the quicker.
A crowd of these were got together,
With faces tanned like bullock's leather,
Roaring out country songs and catches
Over their belly jugs and gotches;
Sometimes *The Children in the Wood*
Was sung, till some both cry'd and spew'd
And then, *The Pie Sat in the Pear Tree*,
Was bawl'd so loud it would have fear'd ye,
And when that good old ditty's done,
The Fox, We'll Catch Him, Boys, Anon.
As they were thus in merry mood,
Consuming malt for the' public good,
The fiddler . . . . .
Was courting in a room hard by,
Dandling his mistress on his thigh
And to engage her fickle mind,
Was singing *Oh, My Dear, My Kind* . . . . .

Anyone who has lived in a small country place is only too aware of the simmerings just below the surface, and of the characters and wits who form so natural and interesting a part of the daily life. This is nothing new. Although less sophisticated, the pleasures have always been hearty and often coupled with an almost childlike delight in "dressing up". Long ago the traditional communal festivals such as May games, church ales and harvest suppers were attended by music and much boisterous behaviour.

Philip Stubbs, in his *Anatomie of Abuses* of 1583, describes the scene as he saw it. "First, all the wild heads of the parish, conventing together, choose them a grand-captain . . . and him they crown with great solemnity . . . This King anointed chooseth twenty, forty, threescore or a hundred lusty girls (who) bedeck themselves with scarfs, ribbons and laces . . . they tie about either leg twenty or forty bells . . . Thus all things set in order, then they have their hobby-horses, dragons and other antiques, together with their bawdy pipers and thundering drummers to strike up the devil's dance withal. Then, march these heathen company towards the church and church-yard, their pipers piping, their drummers thundering, their stumps dancing, their bells jingling, their hand-kerchiefs swinging about their heads like madmen, their hobby-horses and other monsters skirmishing amongst the route: and in this sort they go to the church (I say) and into the church (though the minster be at prayer or preaching), dancing and swinging their handkerchiefs, over their heads in the church, like devils incarnate, with such a confused noise, that no man can hear his own voice . . . Then, after this, about the church they go again and again, and so forth into the churchyard, where they have commonly their summerhalls, their bowers, arbors and banquetting houses set up, wherein they feast, banquet and dance all that day and (per-adventure) all the night too . . ."

From the sixteenth and seventeenth centuries there come many accounts of attempts to limit and indeed to suppress this form of letting off steam. At the Devonshire Quarter Sessions of July 1595 the magistrates declared that "All Church or Parish ales, revels, May-games, plays and such other unlawful assemblies of the people of sundry parishes unto one parish on the Sabbath Day and other times, is a special cause that many disorders, contempts of law, and other enormities, are there perpetrated and committed, to the great profanation of the Lord's "Saboth", the dishonour of Almighty God, increase of bastardy and dissolute life, and of very many other mischiefs and inconveniences, to the great hurt of the commonwealth".

When I read of a case brought at the Somerset Sessions in 1607, I blushed for the goings-on in my own home town at that time. Apparently two church wardens of Yeovil were proceeded against for taking part in disorders at their church ale. The prosecution alleged that minstrelsy and dancing normally occurred on Sundays and that the accused willingly allowed themselves to be carried to the church "upon a cavell stafe". In the following year, the Somerset justices ordered "all bull baitings, bear baitings, church ales, clerk ales, woodward-ales, briales and all kinds of such like ales whatsoever" to be discontinued throughout the county. As the order was repeated in 1624 we must assume that the first injunction was not entirely complied with. Similar pronouncements were made by local magistrates about this time in other parts of England, notably in Worcestershire and Staffordshire.

The Church Ale of early times was the responsibility of the churchwardens. They bought a large amount of drink as cheaply as possible and sold it to their parishioners at a profit in order to swell "Church expenses". Originally there were several Church Ales in the course of the year, but by the eighteenth century only one remained, that being the Whitsun ale. By this time it had become a business proposition on the part of innkeepers and its connection with the church had been severed.

In an age when "live and let live" was remarkable only for its absence, it is perhaps not surprising to find a great cleavage of opinion and diversity of behaviour, particularly concerning religion and morals. Feeling ran high in many parts of Scotland and Robert Burns caught the atmosphere perfectly in his poem, "The Holy Fair". This was a satire on the "tent-preaching" outside the kirk while Communion was taking place within. At Mauchline the preaching tent was situated in the churchyard, with a back entrance to Nance Tinnock's tavern. As the poem is of considerable length, twenty-seven verses in all, I have felt obliged to use seven only, in the hope that the reader may wish to become acquainted with the others.

THE HOLY FAIR

V	My name is Fun – your cronie dear,
	The nearest friend ye hae;
	An' this is Superstition here,
	An' that;s Hypocrisy.
going	I'm gaun to Mauchline Holy Fair
flirting	To spend an hour in daffin:
If; wrinkled	Gin ye'll go there, you runkl'd pair
	We will get famous laughin'
	At them this day.

IX	keep off	Here stand a shed to fend the show'rs
		An' screen our countra gentry,
two or three		There, Racer Jess, an' twa-three whores,
leering		Are blinking' at the entry.
whispering		Here sits a raw o' tittlin jads
jades		Wi' heaving breast an' bare neck;

103

weaver   An' there a batch of wabster lads,
Blackguarding frae Kilmarnock
For fun this day.

X
clothes
soiled

sample

busy

Here some are thinking on their sins
An' some upo' their claes;
Ane curses feet that fyl'd his shins
Anither sighs an' prays:
On this hand sits a chosen swatch,
Wi' screw'd-up, grace-proud faces;
On that, a set o' chaps, at watch,
Thrang winkin' on the lasses
To chairs that day.

XII

climbs

the Devil

hot

Now a' the congregation o'er
To silent expectation;
For Moodie speels the holy door,
Wi' tidings o' damnation.
Should Hornie, as in ancient days
'Mang sons o' God present him,
The vera sight o' Moodie's face,
To's ain het hame had sent him
Wi' fright that day.

XIV

But hark! the tent has chang'd its voice;
There's peace an' rest nae langer:
For a' the real judges rise,
They canna sit for anger.
Smith opens out his cauld harangues
On practice and on morals;
An' off the godly pour in thrangs,
To gie the jars an' barrels
A lift that day.

XIX   My
   blessings on
wakens;
crams
small beer

Leeze me on drink! it gies us mair
Than either school or college:
It kindles wit, it wankens lear,   learning
It pangs us fou o' knowledge.
Be't whisky-gill or penny wheep,
Or onie stronger potion,
It never fails, on drinkin deep,

tickle	To kittle up our notion,
	By night or day
XXVII Bell-	Now Clinkumbell, wi' rattlin tow,
ringer; rope	
ring and sound	Begins to jow an' croon;
can	Some swagger hame, the best they dow,
	Some wait the afternoon.
gaps; fellows; bit	At slaps the billies halt a blink,
take off	Till lasses strip their shoon;
	Wi' faith an' hope, an' love an' drink,
	They're a' in famous tune
talk	For crack that day.

As in the past the local country inn is still the venue of the club dinner or smoking concert and is often a stronghold of amateur music-making. Certainly this was the case during the first quarter of the twentieth century, before the more glittering forms of mass entertainment set in. Then the amateur was not afraid to sing or play an instrument in public. His performance may not have been polished, but he gave of his best and gained much good-will by his efforts to make the evening a success. If he lived in a remote country district he was in constant demand and suffered no comparison with the professional entertainer.

In many places there is a happy association between the local brass band and the inn. A room is put aside for the weekly rehearsal and wind playing being thirsty work the choice of quarters could probably not be improved upon.

On holiday some years ago in that lovely Cotswold village, Chipping Campden, I was fortunate enough to meet Bill Nicholls, a great character and veteran folk-singer of those parts. My information was that he could be found in the bar-parlour of the *Red Lion* about 12 o'clock. Local knowledge in such matters is never far wrong and so it proved on this occasion. Despite his seventy-six years, he had only just retired from an active life, with mind and memory unimpaired. In fact his memory might well have been the envy of a much younger man. His replies to my queries were given in a soft voice and that courteous manner so typical of the district.

At the end of the last century he had heard songs sung in the streets at local fairs and had been attracted by them. On many occasions he learned both words and tunes by merely listening to them once or twice, but – and here would come a sly wink – he usually altered a word here and there, "just in case". So presumably some form of copyright was in use in those days and in those circles. Sometimes Mr. Nicholls would buy a broadsheet which normally contained the words of a dozen or more songs. He recalled how, in 1895 at the age of thirteen he heard an old man singing at Stratford Mop Fair. One of the songs attracted him and he bought the sheet for one penny. In this way he obtained a copy of a song, which he renamed "Old Days". His friends in the locals were always delighted to assist with the chorus. As far as he knows no one else ever sang this song, which he made his own.

First Verse
In the days of the past, I was forced to leave home
In the wilds of Australia to toil,
Hard times at home drove me far o'er the sea,
There was no work for the sons of the toil
As I bade my dear father and mother goodbye,
Says I "Dad I'll not be long away"
Now twelve years have passed, fickle fortune has smiled
And I'm leaving Australia today.

Chorus
I,m going back to my dear old home
Far away over the sea,
Back to the scenes of my childhood
Where there's a welcome for me.
Many years have passed away,
Since I left old England's shore
May God speed the vessel that carries me back
To my dear old home once more.

Verse 2
I sailed to the West with a schoolmate of mine
We worked and shared the one claim
We toiled day by day in the heat of the sun
Sharing luck good and bad just the same
Till a cowardly blow struck my dear partner low
Who struck it we never could tell
But here at my heart is the share of the gold
For his mother and dear sister Nell.

106

Chorus (as before)

Verse 3.
Goodbye lads, I'm going, says I to the boys
Let's have one loving drink ere we part,
I'm going to the land that lies over the sea
To my birth place, the home of my heart.
And as rough honest hands held my own in their grip
Somehow the goodbye couldn't come.
They knew there was one who'd gone home long before
T'was my own darling schoolmate and chum.

Chorus (as before)

Broadsheets cost one penny or two pence, never more. As we
have already seen, they could be bought from strolling singers in the
streets, at fairs and in some book shops. If the words of a song
appealed, but no tune could be found, Bill Nicholls would be quite
prepared to make up a melody to suit. He impressed upon me the
fact that he never sang with a piano or other accompanying
instrument. He heard the song "A little bit of string" only twice.
That was in the *Anchor* at Fladbury, "over Pershore way". Here
some of the words may not be the original but the sense of the song
is substantially as he remembered first hearing it in 1900.

A LITTLE BIT OF STRING

Verse 1
Now its nice to see a man's a man
And knock about and shout
But ever since the world began
The girls have knocked us out
They tell you you're the master
But they know you're no such thing
And they wind you round their fingers
Like a little bit of string.

Chorus
A little bit of string, a little bit of string
And then perhaps you'll get a smile
And that's all your reward
For they tell you you're the master

107

But they know you're no such thing
For they wind you round their finger
like a little bit of string.

Verse 2
They let you take them for a walk,
Or to a play at night
And listen to your foolish talk,
And that's all their delight.
They meet a masher in the air
And tell him he's a king
And lead him like a little dog
On a little bit of string.

Chorus

Verse 3
Now you love your Jack, you worship him
And you'll marry him you say
And then you go and meet a Jim
And love him better still
Now Jack 'n says, what shall I do
I've been and bought the ring
She says "You go and hang yourself
With that little bit of string.

An amusing parody on "Cock o' the North" was found in the same broadsheet that contained "Old Days". This was a great favourite in the pubs of the Cotswolds during the early years of this century, and one can well imagine the words of the chorus being roared out with tremendous vigour to this well-known air.

COCK O' THE NORTH

Verse 1
I went into a raffle once
And what do you think I got,
A beautiful bird from off McNabs
Drove the Mrs. right off her dot,
We screwed his neck in the ringing machine
But the Cock o' the North wouldn't die
So we stuffed him into the saucepan then
But every minute he'd cry.

Chorus
Cock-a-doodle, cock-a-doodle
That's what he sang in the broth
We scraped and jacked him
Boiled and baked him
Cooping the "Cock o' the North".

Verse 2
We took him out of the saucepan then
And covered him over with ice
And stuck a pin in his Parson's Nose
And stuffed him with treacle and rice
We put him in the oven and then
We made up the fire so high
That he kicked the door of the oven right off
And then he started to cry.

Chorus

Verse 3
We stuffed 'is poverty corner up
With sage and potato as well
We fired six shots at 'is Marble Arch
And two at 'is Darby Hell,
But all of a sudden he gave a leap
And then flew under the bed
And dipped his head in the washing basin
And wiped his face and said

Chorus

Verse 4
The lodgers came in and the neighbours they
All said its a pity to try
To kill such a bird if he wants to live
So don't let the poor beggar die
So we tied him up to the bedpost then
With a rope and a table cloth
But all he got saying was "let 'em all come
For I'm the Cock o' the North".

What a pleasure it was to meet Bill Nicholls, a fine upstanding old gentleman. He had many an entertaining story to tell of harvest suppers, football socials and tap-room sing-songs in this part of England, which seems less affected by change than many another district.

To the south of the Cotswolds, the landlord of the *Falcon Inn,* Poulton, when asked about music in his house, replied that he did not altogether encourage it. But strangely enough only the previous evening a man from Ampney Crusis had strolled into the bar with his "squeeze-box". Sitting down in the far corner he had quietly played "some of the good old tunes such as *Daisy, Daisy, give me your answer do, Nellie Dean* and others of the same kind, and everybody had joined in". It was obviously a most happy occasion and much to the taste of the customers, who had been very well-behaved. "Not like you get with this rock 'n roll stuff" he concluded.

Today our sense of values has changed; standards of taste and performance are now so often dictated by a screen and loud speaker, and the average amateur no longer feels able to compete.

Occasionally something of interest comes to light, as for example a delightful custom at *The Haunch of Venison* by the Poultry Cross, Salisbury. Here, Mr. Ian Bennet, the licensee, has a most intriguing way of signalling the arrival of closing time. He is an accomplished musician and can make a 7 foot length of ordinary gas pipe sound like a trumpet. When closing time comes round he produces his "instrument" and plays the "Last Post". It never fails.

Another fascinating piece of information of what may be termed present day Tuneful Taverns concerns the *Cross Keys* at Pangbourne. The tenant, Mr. George Raybould has a priceless collection of over fifty musical boxes. It began several years ago when his grandfather left him a musical box. Since then he has made many strange and hurried journeys in search of these treasures.

The museum includes a large cabinet musical box made in 1890 by a Swiss emigrant to America. A magnificent piece, it has an automatic record changer, a speed control and a magazine to hold twenty of the large steel records of the period. The sonorous, bell-like tone comes as a surprise to a generation which thinks of musical boxes as tinkling little novelties. An intricate ormolu cage containing a miniature bird is the showpiece. Made in 1760 for Louis XV of France by a master of his craft, it is probably one of the oldest instruments of its kind in existence. It reproduces the song of the nightingale, while the bird wags its tail, flutters its wings and turns its head from side to side. There is also a splendid Bavarian hand-organ of 1850 which plays paper disc records. In its repertoire are *See Me Dance the Polka, Abide With Me* and *Rescue the Perishing*. The last named is a great favourite and provides a regular and irresistable stimulus to the local amateur tenors.

WORKING MEN'S CLUBS

It will have been noted how, over the centuries changes have taken place in the type of musical entertainment associated with the inn and tavern. These changes in popular music may be compared with somewhat similar trends in the more extreme types of fashion, which wax and wane with such rapidity.

The tavern was responsible for the birth of music-hall and the many musical clubs had their origin in licensed premises. Now, in the second half of the twentieth century interest in the music-hall as such has seriously declined. Only recently it was reported that in Blackpool, a traditional home of this form of entertainment, the number of live theatre shows had dropped from eighteen to fourteen since the end of World War II and that this followed a national pattern. The publicity director stated that there was now a trend towards the more free and easy atmosphere of the cabaret lounge, of which there were fifteen in Blackpool or the resort's twenty-nine clubs, all of which provided live entertainment.

Also, much of the musical life of public-houses, particularly in the great conurbations, would seem to have been transferred to the working men's clubs. Such clubs should in no way be confused with those of earlier centuries, many of which catered for an aristocratic clientele and maintained a strict control over member-ship, which was entirely male. The present-day clubs as a general rule welcome the women-folk of their members and the entertainment provided is geared to the family as a whole.

In the 1960s it might fairly be said that the social club had come into its own and played a most important part in the lives of countless people. An extraordinary feature of the present spread of leisure is to be found in the Working Men's Clubs, situated mostly in the Midlands, the North of England and South Wales. Many of the buildings are tastefully decorated and well-furnished, and some of the lounges might easily pass for those in a first-class hotel. Colour schemes have been carefully considered, with good wood on walls and floors and with attractive lighting. These features all contrive to give an atmosphere of well-being and undoubtedly such premises may claim to be the very antithesis of the old sawdust public bars. The majority of these clubs are affiliated to the Clubs Institute Union and in passing through a working class district one's attention is drawn to the C.I.U. sign prominently displayed outside the buildings concerned. Members of a club attached to this association are automatically granted the same privileges and amenities at any other C.I.U. Club.

The would-be clientele far out-stripped the available accommodation in many districts, hence the feverish amount of new building during that decade. In general the clubs consisted of a large bar for men only, often known as the pint bar for obvious reasons, and a comfortable lounge bar for men and women. A large concert-room, often situated on the first floor and extending over the rest of the premises, would contain a bar and a stage at opposite ends. The latter invariably boasted a piano, in most cases a grand, with a drum set, often quite elaborate, together with microphones and other examples of amplification.

This generalisation may not be accurate for all parts of the country, as my knowledge of these clubs is in no way exhaustive. However, wishing to include some data on this interesting social phenomenon it seemed necessary to gain first-hand information. Through the good offices of a friend I was introduced to Mr. Gavin Read, a director of Scottish and Newcastle Breweries who proved most helpful and suggested my visiting Newcastle, the centre of club-life in North East England. He put me in touch with the department concerned and arranged for Mr. Thomas Hurst, the Area Sales Manager to act as my host and guide. This was in 1965, a fact worth remembering when considering costs and prices. Inflation has no doubt had its effects on the clubs as in every other walk of life. Mr. Hurst went out of his way to show me the various types of club and I feel certain that Chairmen, Secretaries and Stewards would never have answered my queries so willingly had Mr. Hurst not paved the way.

First we visited the Rex Club, Birtley, which started life in a Nissen hut. Now the club boasts palatial premises, with on the ground floor a lounge bar of good design, tastefully decorated and furnished and also a bar for men, comfortable but perhaps a little plainer in decor. Upstairs was the large concert room with stage and bar, and in common with all the clubs visited everything was scrupulously clean.

In an interesting talk with Mr. Scott, the Secretary, I gleaned that this club was completely independent and not affiliated to the C.I.U. The membership, which at that time numbered some four thousand was drawn from the mining community and two large factories in the vicinity. A local vicar, two doctors and several executives of the factories were members and occasionally looked in for a drink and a chat. Although costs must be very different now, at the time of my visit members paid 5/– to join the club with 2/6 as the annual subscription. A regular programme of entertainment was organised by the Concert Secretary who aimed at a different kind of programme each evening of the week. I happened to call on Bingo night and was therefore unable to see or hear a live performance.

As a result we repaired to Mount Pleasant, high above the Tyne at Gateshead. This large and bustling club, a member of the C.I.U. was humming with activity and a sense of expectancy. This was Audition Night. For such an occasion the performers, many of whom making their first appearance, felt very much on trial. Other clubs on the look-out for new talent would be represented in the audience, so it behove the artists to give of their best. Each turn was introduced by the chairman, sitting at a table below and at one side of the stage, the lights were dimmed and after several requests for silence the entertainment began. The items ranged from straight singers, instrumentalists, soubrettes to comedians, in fact the kind of programme presented at the old music-hall of years ago. The performers certainly worked like Trojans until the perspiration ran down their faces. The singers tried hard to set the audience alight and encouraged them to join in the choruses, but with scant success. Most of the songs were well-known and many people mouthed the words but no sound emerged. The applause was generous enough but due either to distortion in the amplification or the fact that the items were unfamiliar, I found some difficulty in following the words.

Another popular series in all the clubs was the "Go-as-you-please" evening in which several performers competed for money prizes. Advertisements appeared in the local press, a typical one being *Go-as-you-please. Every Sunday. Prizes £5, £4, £3, £2, £1. Minimum five. Names to the Chairman by 8 p.m. Copy Pianist.* The artists were judged by a small committee, aided by the applause of the members and the prizes were awarded accordingly. In the club notices of a

Newcastle newspaper (23 July 1965) there were no less than fifty-one clubs announcing "Go-as-you-please" for the current week and this was probably only a proportion of those being held in the district. It was pointed out to me that a really good entertainer could earn a considerable amount of extra money by doing a tour of the clubs.

Rather akin to "Go-as-you-please" but with certain modifications should be mentioned the "Talent Contest". Here the prizes were similar but the chances of recognition brighter as concert agents might be present. Incidentally, many clubs and entertainment secretaries booked their artists through agents. They found this a safer proposition, as performers normally turned up when sent by an agency. It was astonishing where all these entertainers came from – it must have been a question of demand and supply. They were mostly semi-professional, which means that they followed some normal occupation during the day and blossomed out in the world of entertainment during the evening.

I was intrigued by the term "Copy pianist" which appeared in many public announcements. This was something new to me and on inquiry I was told that a copy pianist was one who could read music as distinct from one who played purely by ear. With the increasing number of visiting artists, a resident club pianist who could read at sight competently had become a necessity. The majority of pianists – at least those I saw – were middle-aged men, some of whom showed considerable ability. At one club a young lady suffering from a bout of nerves, found the task of pitching the key rather beyond her. After several attempts she made a final decision which caused the pianist seriously to think. To my delight he juggled about for a space and was able to accompany her in the very low key chosen.

Sunderland was the next port of call where I was taken to the East End Club situated on the riverside in the shadow of the great cranes and derricks. It was therefore no surprise to learn that the vast majority of members were employed in the ship-yards. This club was opened on New Year's Day 1965 and already the accommodation was being extended. Although of considerable size the building was bursting at the seams and enlargement was necessary to cater for the influx of new members. The membership of seven hundred and fifty could be doubled given adequate accommodation I was told. As a matter of interest the builders of this club were given twenty-six weeks to complete the contract.

It was finished in twenty-three weeks. There must be a moral here somewhere. Secretary Victor Brooks was extremely busy with a full house, but in common with all the other club officials whom I met, he took his responsibilities very seriously and put the comfort of his members before all else. One again noticed the spotless cleanliness and the excellent furnishings and I pondered on the effect of this aspect of the clubs on the community as a whole. Although the atmosphere was one of cheerful good-fellowship – it was after all a Saturday night – the standard of behaviour was exceptionally high.

We arrived a little before the entertainment was due to begin. The Secretary called for quiet and introduced the first turn. This consisted of two Scottish performers dressed in traditional style, one being a fiddler and singer, the other an accompanist on the piano-accordian. They worked tremendously hard and in between items exchanged the usual patter. The audience appeared to enjoy the entertainment, but refused all blandishments to join in the well-known choruses. This was followed by a young lady in a tight-fitting frock who proceeded to sing some of the latest pop songs into the microphone. Again, although the words were obviously familiar to most of the audience, there was no attempt to do other than just mouth the words. This was a feature of club life which surprised me and I could not help wondering if this was not just another spectator sport. Maybe in some places the audience would raise its collective voice to good effect.

I was told that very occasionally members would show dis-satisfaction by cat-calling and booing, in which case the artist would receive no payment, but be sent home with out-of-pocket expenses only. This rarely happened however.

Although expecting to find boisterous and somewhat uninhibited enjoyment in the working men's clubs, I was quite unprepared to experience a plush and extremely well-run night club in Sunderland. We arrived at *La Strada* and passed through a distinctly unpromising front door, having first been examined through a spy-hole, in the best traditions of a certain type of film. But once on the other side of the door we found ourselves in a beautifully appointed club with a splendid dance floor, a resident band and a remarkably good restaurant. Mr. Bob Dryden, the Manager, showed us around with a justifiable sense of pride. Youth was more in evidence here and well-dressed youth at that. One portion of the premises was given over to gaming tables where a quiet, sombre atmosphere

115

prevailed. The devotees played and watched with an intensity I have always understood characterised the Casino at Monte Carlo. But perhaps gambling is the same the world over. In addition to the striking decor this club boasted a cabaret inter-linked with *La Strada* at South Shields. As the cabaret was not due to appear for some time I felt the famous and oft quoted statement of Pepys "And so to bed" to be worthy of consideration.

Many of the officials told me that the club movement had rocketted into favour as a reaction to television. Whereas formerly bottles of beer were taken home and consumed whilst watching T.V. now there had been a swing to draft beer in a more social atmosphere, together with friends and acquaintances. This I can understand; I can also understand the warmth of companionship to be found in the clubs. What puzzles me is why so many people should change one form of passive entertainment for another. I did not hear one example of spontaneous singing in the clubs visited, though the performers did their utmost to arouse enthusiasm. This must surely happen sometimes.

In spite of these remarks one must admit that the majority looked to be enjoying themselves and in no case was there anything of a suggestive or unpleasant nature. It was good clean fun, often sentimental but perhaps none the worse for that.

Every day of this somewhat hectic week-end had brought its quota of club visiting and each had proved most interesting. But it was the last that stood out in my memory so forcibly, for reasons not altogether connected with music or entertainment. My host had been firmly resolved that I should see The Jolly Boys, so we crossed the river again, this time for Saltwell Social Club in Gateshead. Here I was fortunate in meeting the Chairman, Mr. D. Mitchell who gave a most interesting account of his club. The various bars were full to overflowing and the steward and his helpers were kept at full stretch attending to the needs of the members. But my object was to meet The Jolly Boys. We therefore made our way upstairs to the Concert Room where a large number of men sat at long tables each with his pint in front of him.

The concert was on the point of starting, but I had an opportunity of a word or two with the Chairman of the Jolly Boys, Mr. T. Lunn. He explained that they were in fact a group of men, and the emphasis here was on men only, who joined this additional organisation and paid extra for the privilege. A Concert was laid on every week with usually paid performers and this cost each member 2/– a time. This enabled an annual outing to some popular venue to be organised, an event that was obviously relished by all. But in a week-end of surprises I discovered here another and more serious side to the Jolly Boys. Many handicapped children were assisted by these men. Toys and articles of clothing were given to local institutions at Christmas time and spastics and the mentally ill received regular visits. Mr. Lunn, who will I hope forgive me if I describe him as a big, burly giant of a man, openly confessed to being reduced to tears when visiting some of these sadly afflicted children.

He then had to dash away to introduce the first item on the programme. Picking up a microphone he asked for, begged for and then demanded quiet for a large, friendly, motherly-looking lady who took the stage. She sang, and her voice was of such quality that she completely ignored the microphone. As a result her words were more distinct and the audience listened more attentively. An obviously popular entertainer she received a great ovation at the conclusion of her act.

Next came a young man – one of the few to be heard during the series attended – who sang and accompanied himself at the piano. A rather serious and patently sincere person, he also received acclamation. We then had to take leave of the Jolly Boys, but the whole scene exuded the sort of bonhomie one might find at a select smoking concert, and I was both amazed and delighted to find it in a quiet corner of Gateshead.

We have seen how in former centuries the social clubs played an important part in the life of the community. Now, in the twentieth century it might be fairly said that there has been a resurgence of this tradition, particularly in the working men's clubs. Although the aims and functions of these organisations have taken a different slant from many of those mentioned earlier, yet there is a sufficient common ground of good companionship to make an investigation one of absorbing interest.

I was much impressed by the club officials. Men obviously with a mission, dedicated to their clubs and all that went on in them. Their wives were chatty, cheerful and friendly and seemed pleased to accompany their menfolk on the nightly ploys. Friendliness was the outstanding feature encountered everywhere and I am most grateful to Scottish and Newcastle Breweries for making such an experience possible and wish to convey special thanks to Mr. Hurst, my congenial and helpful host.

Three part harmony

During the 16th century there was a fashion for works in three part harmony, both vocal and instrumental. The excerpts provided are both attributed to Henry VIII.

Two Psalms

These two psalms by David Peebles are chosen as examples of composition before and after the Scottish Reformation. Psalm III is Pre-Reformation. in Latin with flowing, melodic voice parts. During the Reformation an edict went out that only one word or syllable must be used to one note, thus resulting in block harmony as seen in Psalm I.

Psalm III

Psalm I

David Peebles

The man is blest that hath not bent to wick-ed-ness his

peare Nor lead his life as sin-ners do nor sat in sin-ners

chaire But in the law of God the Lord doth set his whole de-

light And in that law doth ex-er-cise him-selfe both

day and night.

The Cock of the North

The melody of the popular song 'The Cock of the North' was used by Bill Nicholls of Chipping Camden for one of his 'village songs'.

CHAPTER 3

MUSIC in the SCHOOL

Yea though I'm full of music
As choirs of singing birds
I cannot sing the old songs —
I do no know the words.

Robert James Burdette

MONASTIC SONG SCHOOLS

The history of music in the schools of Britain is a fascinating one. Dating back to the early days of Christianity it has known periods of intense activity coupled with those of almost complete neglect.

To understand the position clearly we have to look to the continent of Europe for the first signs of musical education. The responsible body was the church and music was fostered as an essential adjunct of the church service. It was important that the tradition of plainsong should not be broken; consequently the schools paid much attention to its teaching. Those churches which aimed at a high standard of musical performance formed separate song-schools, in which music took pride of place as an educational subject; indeed in some cases it was the only subject.

The earliest song schools were those of Rome, founded in the fourth century, probably during the pontificate of Pope Sylvester I, and which continued for a thousand years. During the early centuries of Christianity these establishments sent out singers as musical missionaries throughout the Roman Catholic church, to ensure proper performance of the chant.

The introduction of plainsong in Britain resulted from the visit of Saint Augustine in AD 597 whose object was to convert King

118

Egbert to Christianity. The court was then situated at Canterbury and Augustine having been successful in his mission, monks from all parts of the country were then drawn there to study the new form of ecclesiastical music. Also, in 680 Benedict Biscop, the founder of Wearmouth Abbey in Northumberland, on his return from Italy, brought John, Archcantor of St. Peter's, to advise the monks in the art of singing as practised in Rome.

This must have been an incredibly difficult task, as no manuscript previous to the eleventh century contained a notation with exact intervals. Instead, singers had to submit to a course of memory training lasting several years. It is little wonder, therefore, that on occasions choristers made mistakes. There was, however, a system of discipline which ensured maximum concentration:

"If the boys commit any fault in the psalmody or other singing either by sleeping or such like transgression, let there be no sort of delay, but let them be stripped of frock or cowl, and beaten in their shirt only . . . with pliant and smooth rods provided for that special purpose."

Each monastery was expected to clothe and feed the children of the song school as a means of payment for their duties in the choir. At Westminster the boys wore russet-coloured fustian, lined in white cotton, bound with black velvet and tied with silken points. The almoners roll for 1319 contained the item:

"thirteen shillings and eightpence to keep little Nigel at school for a whole year for the love of God."

At the Priory of Barnwell, Cambridge:

"the boys who lived on charity in the almonry were to be set to argue against each other and to be kept under the rod, so that they might learn better. On feast days, when not at school, they were to read and sing in church, learn to write on parchment, and repeat by heart their letters and explain the different meanings of words, instead of running about the streets, fighting and disputing. Otherwise the almoner should turn them out and substitute well-conducted scholars in their place."

It will be seen that some of the monasteries provided education apart from music. This was true of Ely and Durham where school masters or monks attended to normal school subjects.

Many of the choir schools attached to British abbeys and cathedrals were founded in very early times; that of York Minster for example dating from the year 627. Hundreds of great religious houses were scattered throughout the land and certainly a goodly proportion of them, those which were well administered, would be found to be havens of artistic endeavour, with music of a high order.

It seems ironic, therefore, that the great majority of these monastic song schools should have perished as a direct result of action by Henry VIII, a genuine lover of music. With the dissolution of the monasteries, over six hundred foundations, all greater or lesser centres of music were extinguished during the years 1523–1539. Thousands of musical volumes, many of exceptional historical interest, went abroad as parchment for book-binding.

THE SANG SCULES

In Scotland many of the song schools fared rather better and some even survived the Reformation. Known variously as Sang Scules, Sang Scuils or Sang Schoolis, these institutions, dating from the twelfth century, were of great importance throughout the country and some were still in existence in the seventeenth century.

One of the most important centres of religious and musical activity was at St. Andrew's. Here the Augustine Priory of Canons was founded in 1144 by Robert, Bishop of St. Andrew's. In the course of time it became extremely prosperous, with a Sang Scule of outstanding merit lasting several centuries. There must have been men of great ability to compose for it, though apart from David Peebles, history affords little information of them. However, Peebles, a canon and described as 'one of the principale musitians in all this land in his tyme', was active during the period of before and after the Reformation. Many of his compositions are of interest, showing as they do the difference between pre and post Reformation music.

Although primarily concerned with music of the church, the Sang Scules would appear generally to be governed by a different type of administration to that in England. In the latter, the school was attached to and was an integral part of the abbey or cathedral concerned, as in fact was the case at St. Andrew's. But normally in Scotland, certainly in the cities and larger towns, the sang scules were under the jurisdiction of the local burghs. Of these, the most famous was Aberdeen, where in 1256 we find reference to boys singing in the choirs of the churches. In that year the master of the scule "was required to see to the due attendance of four singing boys at divine service in St. Nicholas Church". This famous landmark in the centre of Aberdeen has played an important part in the history of the city. Of great dimensions, it is divided into the West and East Churches by the superb and ancient Drum and Collison Aisle which traces its construction back over one thousand years.

In 1437 an organ was installed in this church and as a result a request was made for a greater body of singers in the choir. This was granted but the choir members were all "ruled by and governed and trespasses corrected" by the Council, or else "they will not support them". The council was quite prepared to carry out its threat and in 1453 there was expulsion for those missing from "matins, hiemess and evensong". These were of boys recruited from the sang scule. We are not told if the previous organ was in any way unsatisfactory, but certaily the authorities of St. Nicholas introduced another some years later, and the novel method of paying for it was by a special tax imposed on all sheep and swine brought into the city.

About this time the Sang Scule adopted a progressive educational policy and although its chief aim was to train boy choristers, anyone sufficiently interested could attend classes for what might be termed an extra-mural course in singing. Almost a century later, 18th September 1544 to be exact, the burgh records give details of the appointment of a master at the school:

"The said day, the hale consale being convenit togidder, has feit Sir Jhone Fethy to be one of the prebendaris of their Queir and to haif thair organes and sang scule for the instruction of the men of quid bavins and keeping of thaim in guide ordour . . . farr the quhilk thai haf gifen him XX lib. yeirlie of fee."

Aberdeen's success encouraged others to follow suit and in 1545 a sang scule was founded at Kirkwall in the Orkneys, presumably to assist the music at the magnificent Cathedral of St. Magnus.

In May and June of 1559 the Reformation in Scotland was finally brought about, due in no small measure to the eloquence of John Knox. In a matter of weeks, church services were unrecognisable by previous standards and all music ceased. But we have already noted how some of the sang scules survived. It might be more accurate to state that they ceased functioning, but for a very short period. Within twelve years of the reformed religion being made law in 1560, Aberdeen and Edinburgh had restored their schools with the former masters once more in charge. But with the Reformation came a complete change in the character of the music. Instead of plainsong and polyphony, the choirs led their congregations in the singing of the metrical psalms.

At the end of the sixteenth century, James VI re-established many of the sang scules which had fallen into dis-use, including those of Elgin, Dunfermline and Musselburgh, and in common with other schools of their type, reading, writing and arithmetic were introduced into the curriculum. But in Aberdeen the emphasis was still on music, together with manners and virtue. The other subjects were taught, but in separate schools. One cannot help feeling that the priorities were not entirely wrong and perhaps rather more attention to manners and virtue might not come amiss today. Early in the following century instrumental teaching was added, thus transforming the institution into a music school as distinct from a sang scule. Strangely enough with the introduction of instrumental teaching the words "manners and virtue" were dropped. Was this a portent of things to come?

Success attended this venture for some time, but as experience has shown in more recent times, the increase in numbers brought an increase in trouble. There were regular demands for "rights" and numerous "sit-ins" occurred, then known as "takings of the school". The master, when not under criticism from his pupils, was being censured by the Council for not keeping the students under proper control. The master and the council were engaged in a number of distressing private wrangles and it was obvious that affairs were coming to a head. The last mention of an annual magisterial visitation to the music school was in 1775 when the *Aberdeen Journal* reported that "the visitors were pleased with the performance of Mr. Tait's scholars in music". Soon afterwards the building was sold and the school ceased to exist after a long and honourable history.

During this same year something of a sensation was caused in Aberdeen on the opening of the new West Kirk. Thomas Channon, the precentor of Monymusk Parish Kirk was invited to bring a group of his pupils, mostly country lads and lassies, to lead the music at this special service. The citizens heard such a performance of church music as "nearly drove them out of their wits with surprise to hear". Channon, a former soldier in Monk's Regiment gained an enviable reputation throughout north east Scotland. The

Aberdeen Intelligencer of 26th November 1754 refers to his work –
"We hear that a new method of singing the church tunes has
been lately introduced with success into congregations in this
neighbourhood. The person who teaches it goes from one parish to
another, and carries some of the best singers with him, who join
with and, under his direction, are very helpful to the learners. By
his skill in vocal music, and the use of a small instrument called a
pitch-pipe, he has made a great reform upon this part of the divine
service. We hear that he is to teach the boys in Gordon's Hospital.
It is said that some congregations look upon this as an unwarrantable
innovation and have refused its admittance among them. We are,
however, persuaded that an improvement so highly necessary, and
so much to the honour of religion, will get the better of all prejudices,
and the clergy and everybody of taste must approve of it". Attempts
of a rather similar nature were made to educate English church
congregations about this time.

Also in 1755 Edinburgh Town Council passed a resolution to
the effect, that owing to the "very indecent and offensive way in
which church music was performed, a master skilled in the theory
and practice of church music should be employed to teach in the
city". A scheme was prepared which offered every interested
person an opportunity of learning music. A chorister of Durham
Cathedral named Gilson was appointed as master of music in the
city churches. Schools were opened in various districts and in 1757
eight or nine were in existence, each under the care of a suitable
musician with Gilson in overall control. A fund was raised for those
who could not afford the fees.

THE REFORMATION IN ENGLAND

The Reformation in England had come somewhat earlier, in
1530, and as has been noted, its effect on the song schools attached
to the monasteries was catastrophic. But a number of Oxford and
Cambridge colleges fared better and traditions formed during the
fourteenth and fifteenth centuries have lasted to the present day.
The sixteen boys of Magdelen College were adept at "plainsong and
other song" and good choirs were also maintained at Queens,
Balliol and New Colleges, Oxford, and at King's College, Cambridge.
Two of these colleges, in which music played so important a part,

were closely linked with two schools, both of which were destined for future greatness.

One of these, Winchester, was a monastic school from early times, but was created in its present form as Saint Mary College of Winchester by William of Wykeham in 1382, with its chapel begun five years later. Bishop Wykeham had already established New College, Oxford, originally known as Saint Mary College of Winchester in Oxford and he made precisely the same provision in terms of scholars and staff for both foundations. These were a warden, seventy "poor and indigent" scholars, ten ordained fellows, three ordained chaplains, three clerks (singing men) and sixteen choristers. The scholars were required to be "poor and needy, of good character and well conditioned of gentlemanly habits, able for school, completely learned in reading, plainsong and old Donatus (the standard Latin grammar)". The scholars of Winchester thus became the more mature scholars of Oxford.

The choristers, known as quiristers, had to be under twelve years of age and competent in reading and singing. Their duties included helping the servants in hall and making the beds of the fellows and chaplains. Here we have probably the very first example of a school with its own professional choir. The College Quiristers are still in existence and certainly during the first quarter of this century serving the college boys in the hall was one of their duties. This was probably no bad thing, but as a cathedral chorister at Winchester during that time, I can well remember the revulsion of feeling in our youthful ranks at the quiristers having to perform what seemed to us so demeaning a task. Now, instead of occupying their own school within a school, they share the educational facilities of the Pilgrims School, the home of the Cathedral Choristers.

Imitation being the sincerest form of flattery, Henry VI in the following century used the example of Winchester and New College as a blue-print for his double royal foundation of Eton and King's College, Cambridge. This was known as the "two Colleges Roiall, one called the College Roiall of Our Ladie of Eton beside Windesor and the other called the College Roiall of Our Ladie and St. Nicholas of Cambridge". Dating from 1443 the start was auspicious and by 1447 Eton had reached its full quota of seventy scholars. The staff was much of the pattern of Winchester, but the chapel choir appeared better balanced, as in addition to sixteen choristers there were ten lay clerks instead of three, all of whom had to be knowledgeable in plainsong and polyphony. This was but a temporary advantage however. The Wars of the Roses broke out in 1455 and six years later Henry VI was deposed by Edward IV. Eton entered on a critical period during which all the chapel ornaments and books were confiscated and removed to St. George's Chapel, Windsor. In 1476 Edward IV relented and reversed a previous decision to close the school, but the choir was reduced to seven clerks and ten choristers.

The Choir School at Eton was disbanded in 1968 and the College Chapel now relies on a choir numbering some fifty boys with a larger choir when needed. The members of these choirs are recruited from the normal pupils as in most other schools.

In the period following the introduction of chapel choirs at these two schools, a number of establishments adopted a similar policy, and the influence of William of Wykeham was manifestly obvious. Henry Chichele, Archbishop of Canterbury from 1414 to 1443, a former pupil of Winchester and a student at New College, founded in 1442 a grammar school at his birthplace of Higham Ferrers, Northamptonshire, with a choir of six boys and four men. Later, in 1438 he founded All Souls' College, Oxford, in which the choir numbered three clerks and six choristers. There were eight clerks and thirteen choristers at Fotheringay (1412) and the college in Tattershall in Lincolnshire (1440) maintained a choir of seven clerks and six choristers.

Richard Mulcaster, the distinguished Headmaster of Merchant Taylor's School in the sixteenth century, believed in music as an educational necessity and he included it as one of four subjects to be taught in the elementary school, the others being reading, writing and drawing. He was also of the opinion that it was conducive to both good health and moral sense, and that its practice was essential to maintain belief in the eternal verities. These sentiments will be met with again, and throughout history they appear so often to have been the deciding factor in the acceptance of music as a part of the curriculum.

Several of the ancient song schools were retained, with the proviso that all the words in the musical portion of the church service should be heard distinctly. This was a direct reference to the pre-Reformation polyphonic music, now out of favour. A few schools, such as Christ's Hospital, Dulwich College, Shrewsbury and Westminster all became well-known for their musical education. Christ's Hospital had an especially enviable reputation in the sixteenth and seventeenth centuries and engaged a number of outstanding musicians as teachers, including John Farrant, Thomas Ravenscroft and Thomas Brewer. Not only was singing considered of importance; the boys were encouraged to learn a wind instrument from those available and to play in the school band. This tradition has continued at the school into the twentieth century and the band is used most days to play the school into lunch. The boys assemble outside the dining hall in houses with the band in the centre. In the north of England, Rotherham Grammar School enjoyed more than local fame musically, but these schools were in the minority. Elsewhere the subject was not treated seriously despite the exhortations of many who realised its value.

Roger Ascham, a teacher of Queen Elizabeth when princess, and later secretary to Mary and Elizabeth, had definite views on music as an educational aid. In his book *Toxophilus, The Schole of Shootinge,* dedicated to Henry VIII, one section is entitled "Youth ought to learn to sing". In this he wrote that "All voices may be helped and brought to a good point, by learning to sing. Whether this be true or not, they that stand most in need, can tell best, whereof some I have known, which, because they learned not to sing when they were boys, were fain to take pain in it, when they were men. Of them that come daily to the university, where one hath learned to sing, six hath not".

Twenty years after the first edition, betwen 1563 and 1568, Ascham wrote *The Scholemaster, or plaine and perfite way of teachyng children, to understand, write and speke, in Latin tong, but specially purposed for the private brynging up of youth in jentlemen and noble mens houses.* Again the study of music was urged.

In the following century two other books, popular in their day reflected the same sentiments; Henry Peacham's *Compleat Gentleman,* published in several editions in 1622 and Richard Braithwaite's *English Gentleman* of 1630. Peacham's book discussed courses of study which included history, geometry, poetry, music, dancing, painting, armory and blazonry, exercise and general conduct. He went on to quote a well-known Italian proverb *Whom God loves not, that man loves not music.*

But Peacham was considerate enough to make allowances for some. He pointed out that lack of aptitude excused some gentlemen, who were gentlemen nevertheless. The parents came in for criticism as, not having been markedly successful in music themselves they were hardly in a position to enthuse their children, particularly in the dull routine of practice. Pupils learned other and more academic subjects because of their teachers, who were not prepared to accept low standards. But music was in a different category owing to the pleasure and social benefits to be derived later on. Much depended on the keenness of the child concerned, but even where this was present there was the real difficulty of obtaining suitable teachers.

It is perhaps significant that in almost every age musical historians had cause to lament the standard of the art and in particular its teaching. This was true even during the sixteenth century Elizabethan period, a golden age of English music. Thomas Whythorne's *Autobiography* of 1571 spoke of the low standard of the teachers, whilst in 1597 Thomas Morley, one of the great composers of his day, wrote upon the same subject deploring the state of musical education in the country.

Those living outside the centres of population found it extremely difficult to obtain individual musical tuition. As a result, a number of hand-books were published extolling the advantages of learning at home – a kind of 'do-it-yourself' treatise. In 1596 there appeared *A new booke of tabliture, containing sundrie easie and familiar instructions, shewing how to play on sundry instruments.* We are not told how successful such ventures proved to be. In more recent times one has noticed press advertisements for something rather similar, particularly in regard to tuition for the pianoforte.

The majority of schools at that time were unable to improve the situation in spite of the forward-looking views of a number of eminent men. Apart from the cathedral and collegiate church schools and the Newark Song School, a mere half dozen appear to have taught music. Three have already been mentioned, Merchant Taylor's School, Christ's Hospital and Dulwich College. In addition Rivington Grammar School, the school at Burford, Oxfordshire and possibly Repton School paid some attention to the subject. At Dulwich in 1634 the organist was said "not to be able to instruct the poor scholars in prick song, nor on the viol and other instruments. His incompetency was alleged to be connived at because he was the master's son". Obviously an early example of nepotism.

At the beginning of the seventeenth century Winchester College once more attracted attention, this time in an attempt to improve the organ playing in chapel. To this end, Thomas Weekes, famous as one of the great composers of madrigals, was appointed organist in 1600. There is unfortunately no record of his opinion on the matter, but the remuneration of thirteen shillings and four pence per annum plus board and lodging would appear not unduly generous. Another fine musician who acted in a similar capacity later in the century was Jeremiah Clark, who afterwards became organist of St. Paul's Cathedral. He is perhaps better remembered today over the controversial issue of the Trumpet Voluntary, previously attributed to Purcell, but now generally considered to be the work of Clarke.

THE MUSIC OF FRIENDS

As in the sixteenth century, so the seventeenth was a time for domestic music, but with a noticeable change of emphasis. There was a movement towards instrumental as distinct from vocal music. The recorder had become popular in the homes of educated people and often madrigals were played instead of sung by groups of friends, who formed recorder consorts for the purpose. The viol also proved attractive for ensemble playing and composers were kept busy providing suitable music for their patrons. The composers who specialised in this music were often those who had written for voices, and included Richard Deering, Orlando Gibbons, John Jenkins, William Lawes, Matthew Locke and Thomas Weekes.

Most of the performers were amateurs, with an occasional professional musician to add stability where necessary. They played for sheer enjoyment and their music was made in the home, hence this was genuine chamber music. Although confined to a relatively small section of the community, this period of vigorous musical activity had a considerable effect on the young, who were encouraged to join in the family music-making.

At the present time one is heartened and delighted to see this tradition maintained. In Edinburgh, which city I know best, there are numerous family groups of parents and children playing a variety of instruments and not only aiming at a high standard, but perhaps of more importance, obtaining enormous fun and enjoyment in the doing. This, one feels, is true musical education and in fact reaches beyond. It also makes nonsense of the the so-called generation gap.

THE LOST CENTURY

Despite the interest shown by a small cultured group in the seventeenth century, there followed a marked decline which was to prove of long-standing duration. The eighteenth century was indeed a bleak time for British musicians, both in composition and in performance. Undoubtedly we became a land without music, at least a land without our own music.

The ever-increasing number of visiting musicians perfomred naturally enough the music of their own countries, and perhaps in too many cases their own personal compositions. Music became accepted as a foreign prerogative and Britain listened, but took less and less part in positive music-making. Could it be that an inferiority complex had smitten the land, or were there more pressing matters requiring attention.

Many prominent people spoke against music and considered the effort spent on its practice to be a waste of time, particularly for boys. Another factor which played a part in this general disapproval was that music had increasingly become associated with the stage and the world of entertainment, with the usual implied evils. Fond parents were not prepared to have their sons mixing in such a strata of society. The climate of opinion would seem to have changed somewhat today.

It was suggested that young men should be more interested in preparing themselves for the army and kindred professions and in taking part in more manly pursuits. With this doctrine gaining ground in upper and middle-class circles, it is not surprising that the schools took notice. After all, in the eighteenth century the majority were concerned primarily with the education of the wealthier classes.

In some boys' schools this attitude concerning music lasted well into the twentieth century and has not been entirely eradicated even now. In a few places and by certain people it is still considered a "cissy" subject.

Despite much adverse criticism the church attempted to keep abreast of the times, to introduce new music and methods of popularising it. William Cowper (1731–1800) in his *Essay on Country Congregations* gives a delightful picture of conditions existing at the time. "The good old practice of psalm-singing is, indeed, wonderfully improved in many country churches since the days of Sternhold and Hopkins: and there is scarce a parish clerk who has so little taste as not to pick his staves out of the New Version. This has occasioned great complaints in some places, where the clerk has been forced to bawl by himself, because the rest of the congregation cannot find the psalm at the end of their prayer-books; while others are highly disgusted at the innovation, and stick as obstinately to the Old Version as to the Old Style. The tunes themselves have also been new set to jiggish measures; and the sober drawl, which used to accompany the first two staves of the hundreth psalm, with the *gloria patri*, is now split into as many quavers as an Italian air.

For this purpose there is in every county an itinerant band of vocal musicians, who make it their business to go around to all the churches in their turns, and, after a prelude with the pitch pipe, astonish the audience with hymns set to the new Winchester measure, and anthems of their own composing. As these new-fashioned psalmodists are necessarily made up of young men and maids, we may naturally suppose that there is a perfect concord and symphony between them: and, indeed, I have known it happen that these sweet singers have more than once been brought into disgrace, by too close an union between the thorough-bass and the treble".

In Scotland the year 1854 saw the commencement of the great psalmody reform movement which swept the country and which had its beginnings in Aberdeen. The Psalmody Association was founded in 1855 and immediately set to work on improving church music under the direction of William Carnie. In the short space of two months the Committee was "happy to announce that one hundred and sixty ladies and gentlemen have kindly agreed to form a choir to illustrate the various styles of sacred music".

The movement grew rapidly and involved a great many enthusiasts who attended public meetings, conducted classes and gave lectures in which musical illustrations played an important part. As a result of its two years of intensive effort there were formed one general, three denominational and twenty-six congregational associations with meetings for practice, eight societies for the performance of vocal music, six schools in which music was taught, five schools where singing was practised and five special classes.

Meanwhile, during the eighteenth century a great deal of thought was given to musical education on the continent and the various experiments carried out at that time later affected the pattern of school music in Britain. One man who devoted much time and care to these problems was Jean Jacques Rousseau, the French writer and philosopher. His ideas on music-teaching as with his ideas on many other subjects were far in advance of his time, and he saw his theory for a new notation turned down. His writings on sight-singing and his advocacy of the "movable doh" preceded other educationists by at least a century.

He was followed by two dedicated teachers, the Swiss Johann Pestalozzi and the German Friedrich Froebel. As is normally the case with pioneers, there was a hard fight for recognition, but gradually their methods gained support throughout Europe. They both encouraged children to sing, not with the purpose of them becoming great artists, but in order to appreciate true art. Their work with the youngest children is still much admired and Froebel training forms an important part of kindergarten work today.

SIGNS OF IMPROVEMENT

While these experiments were going ahead abroad, music in Britain at the commencement of the nineteenth century was no more auspicious than during the eighteenth. A fierce broadside from that redoubtable twentieth century authority, Sir Richard Terry stated: "It is now generally conceded that the Victorian era was a great one in Science, Letters and Art, and a deplorable one in Music. In Science and Letters especially there were giants in those days; in Music we had pigmies and the standard of musical taste would seemed to have reached its nadir".

This gloomy pronouncement may well have been true, but there were the first signs of an awakening interest in education and a *Select Committee to Enquire into the Education of the Lower Orders* was formed at the behest of Lord Brougham. Also during the first half of the century several suggestions were put forward that more time and effort should be expended on the teaching of singing in schools. Hitherto there had been a modicum of instruction, too often a case of the blind leading the blind, the musical knowledge of many of the teachers being minimal. It was realised that above all some simple method of reading music was essential, something that would overcome the intricacies of normal notation.

At once there were enthusiasts ready and willing to help and experiment, and of these, John Turner suggested that encouragement of the art would lead to a civilising effect on the youth of the working classes and "contribute largely to the rooting out of dissolute and debasing habits, and establishing the dominion of religion and virtue in their place". In these sentiments we see a reiteration of the policies of Mulcaster, Headmaster of Merchant Taylor's and of the Aberdeen Sang Scule of earlier centuries.

Certainly Turner's argument carried the day and singing was introduced into the time-tables of such elementary schools as existed. This was a great step forward and was destined to have far-reaching effects.

Another pioneer, William Hickson 'father of English school music' appeared on the scene. His approach to the teaching of singing was not altogether in accordance with Turner's. He did not see it entirely as a moral force, but rather as something to be enjoyed as music. But both of these men had high ideals and in their different ways they played a vital part in the early stages of musical education for the many.

Schooling for the poor had always been the responsibility of the church, but the funds available were quite inadequate to do more than scratch the surface. Some help was received by a Government grant of £20,000 in 1833 but this was merely a temporary solution. There was no compulsory scheme of education and therefore the vast majority of children did not go to school. Also of course, there was no defined leaving age and pupils who did attend could be taken away from school at any time convenient to their parents.

Far-sighted people were convinced of the injustice of the situation and efforts were made by Parliament to introduce a scheme of national education. This met with bitter opposition from all quarters. Many members of parliament could see no useful purpose in educating children from the lower classes. Business men feared losing a profitable source of cheap labour and parents were worried at the prospect of diminishing wages coming into the homes. Also the church was concerned that under a state system religious instruction would be more difficult to handle, in which surmise they have been proved correct. In spite of these conflicting interests, a *Committee of Council on Education* was set up in 1839 with Dr. James Kay as its secretary. This was a fortuitous appointment of a man hitherto unconnected with education, but who proved completely dedicated to his task. His first action was to travel through Europe where several countries already had state systems in operation. Finding much of interest in this tour, Kay was greatly

132

impressed with the standard of singing in the schools, which owed much to the methods of two teachers, Wilhelm and Pestalozzi.

On his return to London, Dr. Kay found an enthusiastic collaborator in John Pyke Hullah, whose studies under Wilhelm had made him an ardent disciple of that teacher and his system of sight-singing. As in earlier days, inspiration was once again drawn from the musical reservoir of Europe.

In the meantime a young teacher in Norwich, Sarah Ann Glover had been making a reputation as a trainer of children's choirs. She had experimented with a method of sight-singing which made all keys alike through using a 'movable doh'. Not only was Miss Glover successful in the sphere of sight-singing. Her choirs uniformly sang with beautiful tone and true intonation and Norwich became more than locally famous for its singing. Amateur musicians from other parts of the country made frequent visits to the city to gain help and guidance with their problems in choir training.

Hullah on the other hand favoured the 'fixed doh' used by Wilhelm and the majority of teachers on the continent. This system had enormous success initially, owing to the ease with which pupils could understand its first principles. As a director of music at the Training College of St. John, Battersea and with teaching connections at St. Mark's Chelsea and King's College London, Hullah was in a strong position of influence. And he made certain that his students were fully conversant with every detail before being permitted to teach in the schools.

A glutton for work, he hired the Exeter Hall in 1841 to give a series of demonstration sight-singing lessons to school teachers. These classes were so successful that the general public requested similar facilities, which were granted. Enthusiasm ran high. Hullah now formed a choir consisting of his senior pupils, which in 1847 provided the backbone of four great concerts arranged to raise funds for building a hall for the furtherance of his singing classes. The new hall of St. Martin's, situated in Long Acre was completed in 1850 with a seating capacity of three thousand. Here, Hullah held his classes for only ten years, the building being destroyed by fire in 1860.

Other people were now experimenting in this field, including Joseph Manzer a German, whose ambition was to propagate *Singing for the Million*. His ideas were popular and well received in certain parts of the country, but by now competition was intense. Both his and Hullah's methods gradually declined before the truly amazing success of John Curwen.

A Congregational minister of no outstanding musical ability Curwen's avowed object was to use music as 'the indirect means of aiding worship, temperance and culture, of holding young men and women among good influences, of reforming character, of spreading Christianity'. Curwen had for some time been working hard to improve the musical image of his Sunday school and to this end had been using a 'movable doh' in his experiments. His efforts had not gone unnoticed and when invited to suggest some formula for the teaching of singing, he decided to visit Miss Glover for discussion on the system she had used with such success. As a result, he was able to put forward a clear and concise scheme of sight-singing and to found what is now universally known as Tonic Solfa. Curwen had the gift of expressing himself in simple terms, even to the youngest children and his books on sight-reading remain today models of clarity.

It may be that this very simplicity created difficulties. The method was often taught by teachers of subjects other than music and sometimes by those of little musical taste. In the early days possibly too much stress was placed on sight-singing and it became an end in itself, resulting in less time for song singing. Whatever its drawbacks Tonic Solfa undoubtedly helped countless children to read music quickly and its influence on the adult world was phenomenal. There was obviously a real desire to sing amongst a large section of the community and many people for the first time were able to take part in a wide variety of choral works. This was an important factor in the growth of the British choral society movement of the late nineteenth century.

Music in the elementary schools had been encouraged to such an extent that Matthew Arnold in his capacity as inspector of schools, wrote in 1863 that it was much easier 'to get entrance to the minds of children and to awaken them by music than by literature'. It is not without significance that at this time most of the expensive public schools were left far behind in the study of music.

Then came a sudden change of heart and from a most unexpected quarter. Edward Thring, during his headmastership of Uppingham School (1853–1887) introduced and encouraged music. He was no musician himself, but his German wife was keenly interested and saw its value in education. The whole school was frequently brought together to sing as a community, and well-known professional performers were invited to give recitals at the school. This latter idea was well in advance of the times. Other public schools took note and later followed suit.

The great musical historian Charles Burney, during his foreign travels, spent some time in Italy, where he had ample opportunity of studying the schools of music for poor children at Naples and Venice. This experience filled him with enthusiasm and on his return to London in 1774 he put forward a scheme for a music school to be connected with and administered by the Foundling Hospital. Unfortunately his plan was not well received in official circles and nothing came of his idea. But less than fifty years later the Royal Academy of Music was founded (1822) very much on the Italian pattern, with young pupils, all of whom were boarders at the Academy. There was a headmaster in charge of the children and the first principal was William Crotch, whose work in other spheres has been noted. Since those early days there have been many changes and the Academy now deals with more mature students, most of whom are studying for advanced diplomas to aid them in their professional careers. As one of the great British teaching institutions, it has in its distinguished history, numbered on its staff many fine performers and teachers, who in their turn have produced a long line of equally famous musicians.

Some fifty years later there commenced a veritable rash of music colleges, all of which have played an important part in musical education, and where dedicated men and women have provided training of the highest quality.

The Royal College of Music was founded in 1873 as the National Training School of Music, but changed to its present name ten years later. These two royal foundations combine as the Associated Board for the purpose of the administration of graded examinations in singing and instrumental playing at local centres throughout the country.

Trinity College of Music (1872) also has a wide following in its local examination system and has attracted to its ranks many eminent musicians as teachers and examiners. The Guildhall School of Music (1880) is controlled by the Corporation of the City of London and in particular has gained an enviable reputation for its operatic successes. The Birmingham and Midland Institute School of Music since 1887 catered for the young musicians of its district. Although possibly less well-known nationally than some of the other colleges, I remember being impressed with its extra-mural work in the years following the second world war. The

Glasgow Athenaeum School of Music was founded in 1890 and : now known as the Royal Scottish Academy of Music and Drama. This college has done praiseworthy work for the musical youth of Scotland and plans are afoot for an entirely modern complex of buildings on a new site to replace the present inconvenient and out-of-date premises. The Royal Manchester College of Music founded by Charles Hallé in 1893 has been outstandingly successful in sending forth a regular flow of fine musicians. Now amalgamated with the Northern College of Music, it is housed in an exciting new building, containing everything necessary for the training of music students. Manchester, long famous for its musical associations has spared no effort to produce something exceptional. The building, opened in 1973 is the most modern of its kind in Britain and includes an Opera House, Concert Hall and over ninety individual tutorial rooms. Now known as the Royal Northern College of Music it has the Queen as patron and the Duchess of Kent as President. The Royal College of Organists is in a slightly different category as it caters specifically for organ students. It was founded in 1864 and has filled an important role. From all this activity it will be seen that the nineteenth century was not as musically barren as might have been supposed.

THE TWENTIETH CENTURY

What of the present century? Has the study of music in our schools made progress – is more interest being shown in the subject today? Obviously there are two sides to any question and different replies would be received according to the views of those asked to comment. But truth to tell the impact of really good music has been an exciting feature of modern education. From its traditional place in the embers beside Cinderella, music has leapt ahead to be *almost* a Prince amongst subjects. Its value has now been recognised and in all schools of all types time is given to its study.

Much credit for this state of affairs is due to the great teachers of the early part of the century, as for example Gustav Holst. His twenty-eight years work at St. Paul's Girls' School, London, was characterised by outstanding and selfless devotion to duty. He was of course abundantly gifted as a composer and this gift he used for the delight of his pupils as well as for the wider public.

His daughter Imogen, in her book *The Music of Gustav Holst* wrote, "He was spending more and more of his energy in teaching school children to sing folk-songs and in rehearsing Bach cantatas with his amateur choirs and orchestras. He was also writing easy music for them to sing and play, which meant that he was unconsciously bridging the gap between the contemporary composer and that being known as 'the ordinary listener'. He never realised that he was helping to restore some of the balance of supply and demand between the composer and the public. Teaching had become part of his life and it was inevitable he should compose for his pupils".

Holst set the highest standards in performance and taste and is assuredly one of the immortals every teacher should try to emulate to the best of his ability. Such men set the pattern for others to follow.

But teachers do not always get their own way and much depends on the attitude of the heads of schools. Some are still unconvinced that music is more than a frill, a necessary evil to be taken out of cold storage for the annual concert, with the minimum of dislocation for rehearsal. To the keen and dedicated music teacher this results in serious frustration, a condition quickly transferred to the pupils. This, where it occurs, is a lamentable state of affairs. Every thinking person will agree that the academic subjects are essential for a great number of children and must be given an adequate share of the time-table. Also, the more time devoted to highly technical study – in its broadest sense – the more important becomes an understanding of great literature, great art and great music if our object is to produce well-balanced individuals.

Music has a real part to play in the life of a child. It is a creative activity which helps to develop the imagination and demands a considerable degree of concentration. In addition to its civilising and humanising qualities, music opens the door on a world of unsuspected beauty and undoubtedly leads to a greater enrichment of life.

Given sympathetic backing by education committees or boards of governors and headmasters/headmistresses, given adequate facilities for teaching, given enthusiastic and dedicated staff and not least, pupils who are able and willing to benefit from these advantages, one has an ideal situation in which to nurture the delicate plant. Given only some of these components, the task is obviously more difficult, but as in most other areas of education the vital factors are the teachers and pupils. A common bond of interest and understanding between them will resolve almost any eventuality.

Recently there have been encouraging sounds from head-masters, university principals and others whose utterances receive publicity, several of whom have given music their blessing. Some time ago Mr. D. D. Lindsay, then Headmaster of Malvern College told a rather startled conference of preparatory school headmasters that it was totally unnecessary to start any Latin before the age of eleven. There was nothing to gain from the traditional early start. Use the time, he urged, for foreign languages and English and soak the boys in music.

Reference has been made more than once in this chapter to the supposed value of music on moral and religious grounds; sentiments usually uttered with suitable expressions of piety. Now we have just had the latest version of the same theme, on this occasion from the head of the department of psychology at Manchester University. In addressing the Royal Institute of Public Health and Hygiene conference at Harrogate, he suggested that music could be one of the most effective answers to vandalism. He considered that local authorities could reap enormous dividends by buying instruments enough to give every pupil the chance to play. He was a great believer in the value of music and felt that if a boy played an instrument which gave self-satisfaction, this would probably lead him away from mischief!

At the other end of the scale, at university level, Sir Thomas Taylor, a great principal of Aberdeen University, spoke words of the utmost wisdom in his valedictory address in 1958. He told graduands that the acquisition of factual knowledge was not the only kind of knowledge. The formation of certain standards of judgement, taste and discrimination which were both ethical and aesthetic were of equal importance.

"I am not very easy in my mind about the place that is given to that kind of knowledge throughout our educational system in schools and universities" said Sir Thomas. "It is much too easily assumed in some quarters that if you look after physical health and provide the factual information necessary for life in a technical society, goodness and beauty will somehow look after themselves.

"It does not work out that far, for in a sense every fresh generation is a new invasion of the barbarians which has to be taught what is good and what is beautiful. This is not the kind of knowledge that comes to human beings by instinct. Human beings who were

138

starved of beauty ended, quite often, by hating it and seeking to destroy it". He told the graduands they must beware in their own lives of that kind of malnutrition; it was much worse than night-starvation. The remedies were to be found in the beauty of nature, in great literature, especially in the great poets, in music and all the arts, particularly if you could take a hand in them yourself. He urged graduands not to neglect that side of their lives.

Then there was the purely practical approach. Dr. Greenhouse Allt speaking in his capacity as President of the National Music Council of Great Britain, put forward an eight-point plan "Action This Day" which he sent off to the Chancellor of the Exchequer forthwith. I cannot remember his communication having any marked success with regard to taxation. However, it was a move in the right direction. Of the eight points, the five especially relevant to schools are given.

1. The tax on musical instruments should be ended at once.
2. The tax on gramophone records should at least be halved now and abolished altogether at the earliest possible moment.
3. Greater facilities for the study and performance of music in all schools should be encouraged.
4. No financial barrier to any child or young person in the development of musical talent.
5. Throughout the festival movement, music summer schools, student orchestras and so on, the development of living music among young people should be encouraged.

Certainly points 3, 4 and 5 have been successfully achieved.

THE SCHOOLS TODAY

There can be no doubt that education is passing through a period of great change, much of it due to political strategy and certain aspects have become news. This must be obvious to all who read the daily press, whose coverage is indeed generous to statements by politicians, teachers' unions, the behaviour of pupils and the activities of university students. A visible reminder may be noted on all sides in the recent rash of factory-like buildings, which on closer inspection prove to be yet more over-sized schools. There are probably economic reasons for these mammoth establishments, but one cannot help feeling that the human element has too often been overlooked. As a result, many pupils find it increasingly difficult to pledge their whole-hearted loyalty to what have so rapidly become impersonal institutions.

Morale is of paramount importance to young people, and those in authority, either as administrators or teachers would do well to keep this aspect of school life to the fore. Self-respect and thence morale is achieved by encouraging the pupil to work to his full capacity and not by offering him everything on a plate. This makes demands not only on the young person, but equally on the teacher, who should be ready and willing to guide and counsel at every stage. Ideally the school should be a community in which everyone works and plays, not only to benefit himself, but also to further the good name of the institution concerned. Both in the short and long term this must have a beneficial effect on all connected with education.

At one time, not so long ago, there was a real sense of honour in belonging to a fine school, but one has noticed with sadness the gradual decline of such a spirit. Whereas the games field provided an opportunity for fostering a pride of school and in some instances still does so, in a number of places team games seem to be in partial decline and fewer pupils attend to support and encourage their athletic contemporaries.

Instead, a large number of extra-curricular activities of various kinds have been introduced, some of which appeal to very small numbers. This is commendable, as minority groups should be catered for, but a school needs some unifying force, a sense of community, an activity in which a great section of the school population can partake at one and the same time.

Music may possibly help to fill this gap. Here is a subject ready-made for pupils of a wide age-range and of variable ability. The amount of work involved to attain a standard, the excitement of joining together in a worth-while project bring with it a sense of achievement. Surely here we have a means of uniting large numbers of young people in an enterprise of some importance that will not only give them personal satisfaction, but redound to the credit of their school. It might even nurture a degree of loyalty, which would be no bad thing. I am perfectly aware that many or all of these statements will be laughed out of court by the trendier members of our present society, but all the old-fashioned ideas of corporate action are not necessarily bad because they are old, any more than every new idea is good simply because it is new.

It has been said by certain educationists that training in

musicianship can stimulate general intellectual development, and that academic performance may be improved by thirty per cent if children receive systematic grounding from an early age. Without considering statistics, which so often prove unreliable, those with experience of teaching have long known that a gifted child at music is usually equally successful in other subjects. But perhaps of greater importance is the fact that pupils who find the normal curriculum difficult, are often completely transformed by success in music. It may be that the confidence provided by this newly found ability is transferred to more academic work.

One might make a plea for a little more overlapping in certain subjects. For instance, school history books in the main deal with the lives and action, often in considerable detail, of kings and queens, statesmen, high-ranking members of the armed forces, explorers, inventors, writers and painters, but not so regularly do we find reference to the great musicians. Yet these have done so much to influence the lives of countless people and indeed of whole nations by their creative skill. It is sometimes forgotten that the history of music is an important branch of general history and mirrors the times just as effectively as the work of outstanding architects or master masons. Music, being an international language, need be no barrier to the understanding of the great composers of other countries. Children should receive some information regarding the more significant figures in this art, purely as a part of history.

What is read in the history lesson may be amplified in the music department with heightened effect, and this could be reciprocated equally well. Other subjects which might co-operate with benefit to all are Art and Literature, and Physics could play a part in the explanation of the science of sound. This of course happens in many schools and such integration makes learning more interesting and meaningful.

Considerable progress has been made in school music and this is reflected in the attitude of many of the pupils. Previously, the traditional image of the music master was a figure of fun, whose pathetic attempts at keeping discipline afforded such hilarity. Many are the hair-raising stories told by an older generation of the weekly music period, when almost anything might happen – except music. This is not so obvious today.

But the idea of artistically-gifted people as living in another world dies hard. I remember in my schooldays being in the same form as an outstanding young musician who later bore out his early promise.

On one occasion, sitting quietly at the back of the room as was his wont, he was suddenly galvanised into action by the rasping demand "Repley, what grows in vineyards?" Poor Rapley, not quite sure of his facts, blurted out "Cabbages and things, sir". "Cebbages Repley?" – the master concerned always pronounced his a's as e's. "Cebbages? No doubt I interrupted you in the middle of composing a five pert fugue". Laughter from the class. We always laughed if the master cracked a joke. Things have changed. Such a sally today would bring forth groans or pained expressions all round.

SINGING

Singing has been the basic element of school music as long as music has had a place in education and in the majority of schools today it is still the principal musical activity. The period set aside for its purpose is either a joyous and exhilerating occasion, a time for skiving (doing no work) or a boring exercise, depending to some extent on the methods employed.

As already noted, much time was devoted to sight-singing in the early days. Children were brought up to read music by a variety of methods, some of which have been touched on in this chapter. They may have shown great expertise in this field but they rarely sang any songs. A more enlightened policy is now gradually emerging and although one may sympathise with the aims of teachers and would ideally wish to see generations of good sight-reading pupils going out into the world, the position is not easy. Honesty compels one to state that on occasions too much emphasis has been placed on this subject. The majority of school pupils are not contemplating music as a career and many will never sing seriously after leaving school. It would seem a pity therefore that a distaste for music should develop owing to a lack of gauging intervals correctly. Surely it is far more important that they should gain some pleasure from the vast output of songs composed over the centuries. The keen people will soon learn how to read at sight and this technical knowledge will be further strengthened by singing in one of the choirs.

Certainly suitable songs were in short supply at the beginning of this century and the task of obtaining music must have been formidable. There was however a gradual improvement until eventually a wide literature of singing material was made available for schools. Over the years this has increased enormously and today there is an almost embarrassing quantity from which to choose. The publishers of educational music provide excellent catalogues containing references to part songs, unison songs and folk songs as well as music for Christmas and other special occasions. Also many publishers now have hire departments which prove invaluable when an expensive or extended work is required.

Almost every class of young children contains its percentage of "groaners" who are more often than not blissfully unaware of their musical "colour blindness". Where class singing is concerned it is perhaps as well to turn a deaf ear to many of the peculiar sounds and hope fervently that things will improve. And strangely enough they sometimes do. I have known several cases of "groaners" suddenly finding their singing voices and sense of pitch, so it does not always pay to write off a young voice too soon. Of course one cannot afford to be so easy-going where the choir is concerned and it has to be tactfully suggested to out-of-tune singers that perhaps their turn will come a little later on.

A very small proportion of pupils may always find difficulty in assessing pitch and consequently will never be able to sing in tune. This is not a frequent happening, but it can cause distress or amusement depending on the temperament of the young person concerned. I remember such a case many years ago when teaching in Somerset. The boy involved was a good tempered and delightful character who accepted all my "witty" sallies with a serene good humour. We all laughed with, rather than at him, which perhaps made a difference. In spite of everything, he enjoyed listening to music with a keenness wonderful to behold. During one holiday I met him and asked what his plans were for the vacation. He replied that he had mapped out a cycling tour to take in Bristol, Birmingham, Liverpool, Manchester and Worcester and his stay in each city was timed to correspond with a concert given by a different orchestra. In addition his pocket money was devoted to acquiring a splendid collection of gramophone records. This is the kind of heartening surprise one sometimes experiences.

Another class problem arises with boys at the adolescent stage, which seems to become earlier almost yearly. It is not unusual today to have a group of twelve year olds, the majority of whom can no longer sing treble. This might be compared with the statement regarding the boys' changing voice made in the chapter on Music in the Court. They frequently find difficulty in controlling their voices for a while and as a result become rather sensitive. It is therefore a kindly act for all concerned to give them a rest from singing and to concentrate on listening as a more agreeable method of musical education.

Quite the opposite is suggested for members of the choir. These boys are normally keen enough to wish to continue singing and they should be encouraged to use the register most convenient at the moment. They are able without much difficulty to move from treble to alto and from alto to either tenor or bass as the voices deepen. This transition period they find rather amusing and quite enjoyable, and the majority develop into first rate singers in their new voices and invariably become stalwarts of the choir. Singing during this period does no harm, possibly the reverse, providing the voice is used correctly. Far more damage is caused by shouting over considerable distances as is the practice of many of our young men.

With girls these difficulties do not arise in so acute a form and although some produce a lovely contralto tone as they grow older, most will continue singing the soprano parts. The choice of songs for the class room is most important and warrants much careful thought. Girls perhaps would not derive the same pleasure from a rollicking sea shanty as would a group of boisterous boys. On the other hand boys might find a certain type of song rather "sloppy". In the co-educational school it should not be impossible to find a variety of songs suitable for girls and boys to sing together.

Reverting once more to the choir and to its capabilities, much obviously depends on the type of school. The problems of a boys' school are quite different from those of a girls' or co-educational school, but most choirs are able to give a good account of themselves when put to the test. Some aspire to performing an opera, oratorio or other work of a comparable nature in which the demands on technique are considerable. This is commendable as the music specialists must always aim high and never lose sight of the fact that education in all its branches is for the future.

SCHOOL SONGS

On appropriate occasions such as Speech Days or end-of-term functions many schools join in singing the School Song, often of a traditional nature and well known to all the pupils. Probably the most famous example is that of *Dulce Domun* performed at Winchester. This is a good song set to a fine melody unlike so many others, which tend to suffer from undue sentimentality with quite often dreadful tunes. Perhaps it is time to eliminate such efforts when they become objects of fun or are parodied – although I have heard some parodies which make rather more sense than the originals. However, the idea of the whole school singing together once or twice a year is a good one and providing suitable material can be found one hopes this feature will not completely die.

THE ORCHESTRA

Within a year or two of the end of the second world war, there was an upsurge of musical activity in the schools of Britain. The youngest children were encouraged to learn to play small instruments of percussion, including triangles, drums and castanets. After a period of training they joined together in percussion bands, an excellent and thoroughly enjoyable method of learning to count and to understand simple rhythms. There was also the fun of performing in a team, a new experience for most children of such tender years. One remembers the look of almost seraphic delight on tiny faces as all the castanets entered together on the correct beat. One also remembers the looks of absolute horror as a solitary toy drum made itself heard two bars too soon. Here was a perfect situation for the cartoonist, H. M. Bateman.

After percussion came something more melodious. To this end lengths of bamboo were bought in bulk and the future players helped to make their own pipes, a quite difficult but worthwhile exercise. Later, excellent recorders were available from many sources and recorder groups became popular. These instruments, of differing size and pitch, enabled the young musicians to perform a wide selection of pieces in harmony. Also, the recorder served as an introduction to a normal orchestral instrument as the child grew older. And this in turn led to the school orchestra.

In the first instance very elementary pieces were attempted, often simple arrangements of well-known works, but soon the young enthusiast could graduate to a more advanced orchestra. With the assistance of a helpful staff the pupil would gain in confidence and probably surprise himself by his new-found talent. From such simple beginnings the keen musician would ultimately reach the stage where he might join a senior school orchestra of fine quality, capable of performing much of the standard repertoire, previously undertaken only by professional or first-class amateur musicians.

The value of teamwork in education has long been recognised and here the orchestra plays a most important role. Every teacher who has attempted to form a school orchestra will know the difficulties which present themselves and how gradual is the process of building up. Nevertheless those who have succeeded not only in forming, but in maintaining the musical interest and support of the players, realise what a tremendous asset it can be in musical education and a real power for good in the school.

One of the normal difficulties is the growing-up of the members – if only they could remain static for a litle longer. On leaving school they often leave a serious gap in the ranks. For this reason it is necessary to be continually training young players to assume greater responsibility. One method of obtaining a daily practice is to include the orchestra at morning assembly. Here it can usefully accompany the hymns and the players of transposing instruments receive good training in sight-reading. The advantages of the school orchestra certainly outweigh the difficulties.

Often the timid pupil is brought to the fore and the more aggressive is held back in an attempt to preserve a sense of balance. Personal selfishness has no place in corporate music-making. One usually finds that the older and more experienced players do everything possible to assist the juniors. They set a standard and by their attitude to the orchestra they create an enthusiasm which is handed down year after year. Much is gained from this very real comradeship, each individual working for the common good and striving for excellence in the final result.

One is constantly amazed and humbled by the results achieved and by the obvious delight of pupils taking part in a fine work. Their enthusiasm and sheer hard work are the forces which drive the conscientious music master on to further effort. This infectious spirit makes up for the odd wrong note or occasional bar of harsh tone. Few people have any realisation of what is involved in the preparation of a musical programme in the average school.

Certainly many adults would demand double time if asked to put as much effort into their work as do these youngsters. Often a musical work is quite physically exhausting as well as mentally testing and there is also an emotional strain that saps the strength of many a young person.

But this is character building, and to aim at the highest possible standard of performance brings with it a sense of achievement which lasts long after the applause of the audience has ended. It is something which is remembered and talked about in the years to come.

LISTENING

Although many schools place the emphasis on singing as a classroom pursuit, there are others which make a feature of musical appreciation at certain stages of the pupils' development. One has the impression that a number of teachers do not favour this branch of education. They may feel the time more usefully spent in keeping the children busily employed; yet appreciation classes are important, as they involve those of no great musical prowess, who normally would not partake in musical activities. As mentioned earlier in this chapter, this is particularly true of boys' schools, where the pupils go through the awkward changing voice period.

A theory held by many musicians is that if children are given the opportunity of listening to music, that in itself is sufficient to create interest in the subject. There is unfortunately no guarantee that this invariably happens. Certainly there are compositions which make an immediate appeal to various age groups, but in general it has been found helpful to give a short introductory talk before the listening commences. This is due to the very wide range of musical experience to be met with in an average class. Not everyone is born with a first-class musical ear; certainly not everyone is born with an understanding of great music. Nor has everyone the advantage of a musical home background. In such cases a simple short talk on what to listen for may make the difference between interest and boredom. Such instruction should however be handled with care. A modicum of humour is always an advantage and the light touch with an underlying seriousness of purpose may fit the bill.

There are many methods of obtaining results and perhaps the

first in importance is to know the class with which one is dealing. One group might contain a majority interested in orchestral instruments and their performance. Another might find programme music (that which tells a story) to be their special line, while a third might favour information on the lives of composers, or to know something of the historical nature of the subject.

The teacher should therefore do his utmost to introduce suitable music. There might be some disagreement on what constitutes suitable music and this of course is a matter for individual choice. Certainly every effort should be made to mould taste in the younger generation. If this is not achieved at school, the opportunity may not come so readily later on. Perhaps an emphasis on music of a colourful nature with a well-defined melodic line would make a good beginning.

Young people are much attracted by the rhythmic side of music. They are also interested in anything new and enjoy discovering the latest and discarding that which pleased them only a short while ago. This constant questing is a natural phase in growing-up which, if stimulated by the teacher may lead to an interesting period of musical exploration. It has been found that a number of twentieth century compositions make an appeal and certain works of our present century can be a good introduction to those of the past. The exciting orchestrations and rhythmic complexities of Stravinsky, Ravel, Holst, Bartok and Vaughan Williams are accepted and almost immediately enjoyed. But it must also be admitted that many *avant garde* composers do not appeal. This may in part be due to a lack of sympathy among the older teachers and is understandable. In their young days they wrestled manfully with what must have seemed decidedly unintelligible music and they are now quite prepared to allow the more advanced students to do likewise in their turn.

Much fun, with the motive kept from the class, may be had in taking a piece apart with suggestions as what to listen for; how this follows that, how snatches of tune are repeated at various points etc; and then at a future lesson the whole work can be put together, with the pupils listening carefully for the points previously mentioned. This, it is hoped may lead to an understanding of musical form. It is also possible to compare music with examples of art and architecture. This usually causes considerable discussion, particularly if the visual element be introduced. The imaginative teacher will think up a variety of methods to create interest, but it must be stressed that a light touch helps enormously in dealing with young people. Much of this will be considered obvious and possibly 'old hat', but the class must be encouraged to concentrate and think. Intelligent listening to music is not a passive pastime; it is a pleasure demanding close attention.

In these days, when the youngest of the young have an uncanny knowledge of record-players, amplifiers and speakers, it is imperative that schools should have the finest possible equipment, otherwise the best of intentions will become a mere mockery.

The teacher, in company with the preacher, the barrister and the politician has something of the actor in his make-up. Though not generally as successful in obtaining such rapt attention as those members of the professions mentioned, he is ever hopeful that one day all the conditions will conspire to that end. I well remember taking a singing class of junior-school boys some years ago. It was a good class and we had been enjoying some Schubert songs. The singing had been quite beautiful and in a moment of enthusiasm I stood up and spoke to them about the composer and of his sometimes odd ways. "Do you know" said I, "that Schubert often went to a restaurant in Vienna to meet his friends and while waiting for them he would on occasions write down some of his lovely tunes on the menu". There was complete and absolute silence as every eye met mine. This, I felt, was it. After years of teaching I had at last succeeded. I now knew how an actor felt on having his audience in the palm of his hand. I was savouring the joint success of Schubert and myself when a boy rose very slowly in the front row. "Please sir, my daddy says that in some restaurants they use the same tea twice".

THE BOARDING SCHOOLS

The first half of the twentieth century saw a strengthening of musical traditions in many boarding schools throughout the country. There had been a gradual movement towards the art for some time and the public schools were in a specially favoured position. They had control of their pupils at all times during the term and with a keen music staff and benevolent house masters, it would seem reasonable to suppose that the subject should flourish.

Musically, every public school is more or less a law unto itself and in many ways this is a boon, as interesting experiments may be tried without recourse to any outside body. Consequently, although given a free hand in working out a suitable scheme of work, a considerable burden of responsibility rests on each individual director of music. And this applies equally in the matter of personal enthusiasm.

Over the years, and in some cases over the centuries, a pattern has emerged in which certain priorities have come to be expected. Pride of place has undoubtedly been devoted to music in the chapel. Owing to the religious foundations of many public schools, the chapel has long been the hub of the establishment, where the entire school meets daily during term. Often a building of great beauty, the atmosphere of chapel is unlike that encountered elsewhere in the school, and its effect on past generations of youngsters must be incalculable.

For the music master there has been the constant challenge of providing an accompaniment for the many services, usually aided by a good organ and choir. This traditional focus on school chapel has in the past encouraged singing of much worthwhile church music. Well trained choirs have led their youthful congregations in a most efficient manner and their performances of anthems and settings have reached a high standard. Normally, the choral society is an extension of the chapel choir, the latter body providing the experienced singers and soloists. The music staff spends much of its time in the preparation and rehearsal for various musical events planned for the school year. Some schools are inclined to be rather inward looking and keep their performances to themselves. Others take a wider view and encourage visits to outside bodies, depending on the time available. This would seem a good policy whenever practicable, both for the sake of community relations and as a change of scene for the pupils.

Other features in the school calendar include recitals given by professional artists and music competitions based on the house system. The director of music is also concerned with the development of the musical boy, with the stress on ordinary and advanced level examinations and the prospect of his entering university to read for a degree.

Although individual lessons in a wide range of instruments now play an important role in the life of every school of this type, music as a curricular subject is rare. Little time has in the past been devoted to class music and it has therefore been possible for pupils to pass through a public school without coming into contact with music, except in school chapel. There are now some signs of change in this state of affairs, but at the moment these are tentative.

The second half of the 1960s saw another change which affected many schools. Outside influences, principally those of the entertainment world, had a profound effect on vast numbers of young people, irrespective of background or upbringing. This was the age of the 'protest song', accompanied by amplified guitars and body gyrations, and its aim was the emancipation of the young and the overthrow of authority. The resultant apathy and even open hostility towards anything of an 'establishment' nature was shown also in the attitude towards organised religion. Many headmasters felt it necessary to re-assess the function of the chapel service and alterations were made, often to the detriment of the music and resulting in less participation in singing.

Another, though quite different factor to be taken into account is the much earlier changing of the treble voice. In the not so distant past the public schools could rely on good choral singing in four part harmony, with the top part safely entrusted to boy sopranos. Today the situation is very different. Apart from one or two schools which accept boys at nine and eleven years respectively, the average age of entry is thirteen years. As a result many boys arriving at their public schools will never sing treble again.

Some schools have solved this problem by inviting local girls' schools to collaborate in the performance of suitable works. Despite the obvious difficulties of corporate rehearsal, this would seem the happiest solution. Schools which have already tried this experiment pronounce the result a musical and social success. Also with co-education becoming increasingly popular in certain of our famous boys' schools we shall no doubt witness the full cycle in chapel choirs – the introduction of four part harmony once again, with the top part taken by girls in place of boys.

There is at present great enthusiasm for learning musical instruments, particularly those associated with orchestral playing. The abundance of wind players may have proved something of an embarrassment in certain quarters, but ways and means are being found to cope with the situation. It must be realised that more immediate satisfaction may be gained from playing a wind rather than a stringed instrument and one can appreciate the pupil's point of view. Owing to the much improved repertoire available for wind bands, many school children now have an opportunity of taking part in corporate music-making quite apart from playing in the orchestra. It would however be a pity if our schools followed too closely the pattern of the United States, where most educational establishments have a band, while orchestras are in a minority.

The authorities are however, alive to the problem and increasing encouragement is being given to the learning of strings. Several schools have introduced innovations, as for instance, free tuition for beginners on stringed instruments and in a very few schools every new boy must learn an instrument during his first year. There is also a great incentive to musical boys, in that valuable scholarships are available, many connected with string playing. These scholarships vary considerably in value, some being exceptionally generous, but all are of sufficient importance to encourage prep. schools to develop instrumental work at an early age.

The overall picture of music in the boarding schools is, generally speaking, a bright one. Certainly many of the orchestras are highly proficient and perform works which only a decade or so ago would have been considered the prerogative of professional bodies. It only remains for good singing to re-assert itself in those places which are, we hope, experiencing but a temporary lull in their activities.

It will be obvious that this section on the public schools has been concerned primarily with establishments for boys, but much might apply equally to many of the boarding schools for girls. Some have excellent music departments and they produce young musicians of very high calibre. But their choral work has to some extent suffered from the lack of lower voices. Where the boys' schools have to make do with alto, tenor and bass, the girls are restricted to soprano and contralto. Presumably the co-educational boarding school is the answer. Two such schools would seem to enjoy the best of both worlds in this respect. At Bedales near Petersfield and Dartington Hall in Devon, music has played a vital part as an educational subject and has flourished in the ideal surroundings provided for their pupils.

LOCAL AUTHORITY SCHOOLS

It is good to know that music takes its rightful place in all local authority schools, both junior and senior. In many of the junior schools it is entrusted to the teachers of general subjects, especially those with a love of music. Some of these teachers are quite brilliant natural musicians and produce amazing results. The fact that a number do not play an instrument very well is no deterrent and the musicianly singing from their classes provides evidence of high artistic standards. First of all they are teachers, and as such they are able to apply their professional skills to a branch of education which gives them scope and obvious pleasure. In those schools where the teacher concerned does not profess to being very musical, considerable help is given by a sympathetic adviser, who visits and suggests and generally sees that a satisfactory level of work is maintained.

Throughout Britain most of the go-ahead education authorities, both urban and county, employ musical advisers, who perform a variety of valuable duties. They keep in close touch with all music-making in the area and note promising pupils in the various schools. They usually organise and conduct a central choir and orchestra chosen from talented children and in order to enable young people to continue their musical interests after leaving school, advisers will often make themselves responsible for a youth choir and orchestra. They give lectures, organise courses for teachers, arrange summer schools and order music and instruments for the various groups under their jurisdiction. Large district concerts and the engaging of eminent soloists for educational purposes are also the responsibility of advisers. They also encourage music festivals in the schools, some of which, particularly in junior schools, are of a non-competitive nature. On these occasions the children may listen to one another in an atmosphere without strain. One has heard many fine performances by recorder and percussion bands and also of part-singing by very young children.

Where large authorities are fortunate enough to be within the orbit of a professional orchestra, arrangements are sometimes made for short concerts to be given in their schools. These concerts are usually introduced in a manner suitable for very young people and individual instruments are demonstrated by the players. I well remember, some years ago in Birmingham attending several of these occasions and being much impressed by the behaviour of the children, many of whom sat cross-legged on the floor. It seemed to me that these friendly concerts gained from being held in one school, with pupils being brought in from neighbouring schools. The atmosphere was just right, with the children of the host school helping to make their visitors welcome and at home. Quite apart from the music this was a splendid piece of social education. I have not been as happy where contingents of pupils from a large number of schools are packed together in a vast hall, as sometimes happens.

In the large senior schools there are usually music specialists who do their utmost to continue the good work started in the juniour schools. It cannot always be easy as the growing child is subject to so many influences from the outside world, not all of which are of a cultural character. Musical education has two main aims – to instil an intelligent interest in the subject through participation, and to foster the enjoyment of music by equally intelligent listening. The first of these for the average child means singing, and here there is a wide repertory of songs ranging from regional and national to art songs of fine quality. Also several composers have set amusing words to charming music, which when sandwiched between the more serious fare, cause a laugh and help to relax tension. With regard to listening, most schools have a library of gramophone records which used judiciously in cooperation with a well-prepared lesson of musical appreciation can lead to a most valuable and enjoyable period.

An interesting and thoroughly worthwhile experiment in school music has been carried out in Wales, where a real effort to involve entire classes have proved most successful. The orchestral players naturally perform on their own instruments, a wide range of percussion is used, recorders take a prominent part and other members of the class sing. In this way everybody takes part in a group activity. Much of the work is based on the splendid lead given by Kodaly and Carl Orff in their respective countries. The movement, known as 'Orff-Schulwerk' (Music for Children) has had a profound influence throughout Europe and was first introduced in Wales in 1964. Since then many local authorities have encouraged the system by holding courses for teachers and by providing the necessary percussion instruments so essential to the scheme.

Several Welsh school orchestras have enjoyed considerable prestige for some time and South Wales, with its density of population has generally led the way. The three Grammar Schools of Llanelli, Gowerton and Neath have been outstanding for many years and due to their musical traditions many old boys of these schools occupy positions of influence in the Principality today. Recently these schools have been overtaken by comprehensivisation – dreadful word – and one fervently hopes that the change will not impair the reputations so carefully built up over the years. The success enjoyed by these schools as elsewhere throughout Britain is the result of very hard work by the respective music staffs, backed enthusiastically by enlightened headmasters.

British school choirs and orchestras are increasingly embarking on musical tours abroad and many European countries have been visited in recent years. This is a splendid experience for the youngsters concerned and involves them in a vast amount of serious rehearsal to attain the standard required. It is particulary pleasurable to record the success of the Neath Grammar School Orchestra, which in 1973 under its conductor John Jenkins had the honour of representing the school orchestras of Britain at the Internation Festival of Youth and Music in Vienna.

The interest in orchestral music during the second half of this century has been remarkable. Much of the credit for the success of this work must go to the various education departments. They have been generous in the purchase of instruments and music, and they have provided an ever-increasing pool of excellent instrumental instructors. Children with the desire to learn, now have a splendid opportunity. Although some discontinue their studies at an early age, others become proficient and the results so far established augur well for the future.

As mentioned earlier, a further inducement has come the way of gifted school musicians. First-rate youth orchestras have been established in various parts of the country and these draw their personnel from local schools. Many cities and large towns support such orchestras and in the rural areas there are several thriving county orchestras. The participants meet together for arduous holiday courses under the guidance of specialist teachers and at the conclusion of the period a concert gives evidence of the hard work undertaken by staff and pupils alike.

At an even more advanced level there are the national youth orchestras. In the United Kingdom the National Youth Orchestra of Great Britain, formed soon after the second world war, enjoys a deservedly high reputation. Young would-be members have to be especially gifted and have also to submit to a searching audition before being accepted. The experience of performing in such an orchestra under world-famous conductors and of maintaining the finest standards is a tremendous challenge. Tours abroad and appearances at international festivals have resulted in performances of such maturity unimaginable fifty years ago.

The Welsh National Youth Orchestra is another example of this same striving for excellence by young people. Here the standards have been rising dramatically since its inception in 1945. It is maintained from public funds and is administered by the Welsh Joint Education Committee. Successful tours have been undertaken in Europe and every year the orchestra performs at one of the concerts of the Royal National Eisteddfod of Wales. As might be expected, there is great competition for a place in the orchestra. In these days when we read so much of truancy and hooliganism in schools, it is good to remember the other side of the coin and to realise that many young people are ready and willing to accept discipline of the most exacting nature.

Arising out of this youthful interest in music, which incidentally is world-wide, there has come into operation an International Festival of Youth Orchestras Foundation. This organisation, which arranges an annual festival to include outstanding groups of young musicians, has now decided that it should be held permanently in Britain, the two main centres being Aberdeen and London. Although designated 'Youth Orchestras', the Festival includes singers and dancers as well as instrumentalists, the total number of those participating exceeding one thousand five hundred.

As a point of interest, Aberdeen's unanimous decision to house the first part of the festival was accompanied by a contribution of £90,000 over three years, £20,000 in 1974, £30,000 in 1975 and £40,000 for 1976. This generous and praiseworthy gesture would appear to be patronage at its finest, by bringing together young people of many nationalities in friendship and understanding through the common bond of music.

In 1974 ten orchestras, four choirs, three ballet groups, an opera company and a folk dance troup took part, with contingents from Japan, the United States, Canada, Australia and Fiji. It was an exceptionally busy time for all concerned as in Scotland concerts were given in cities and towns in various parts of the country. All were then moved *en bloc* in two special trains to London for the second part of the festival, and for a great concert in the

Royal Albert Hall. This business of transporting so many people, together with instruments and baggage was in itself a triumph of organisation.

British groups which shared in the music-making included the Gwynedd Youth Choir, Wells Cathedral School Chamber Orchestra, Bedfordshire County Youth Orchestra and the London Opera Centre.

GRANT AIDED AND PRIVATE DAY SCHOOLS

Many of the large independent and grant-aided day schools are of ancient foundation and high academic distinction. They differ from many others schools in that they have their own Preparatory and Junior departments on the premises so to speak, and as a result the integration of music as a subject should prove easier. Members of the music staff normally teach throughout the entire school and are directly responsible for the curriculum. Thus an overall policy is possible, beginning with the youngest children and continuing through to the sixth form. In the early stages, percussion bands, recorder groups and choirs are all encouraged and although some children inevitably fall by the wayside, this work undoubtedly bears fruit. Pupils are given the opportunity of learning orchestral instruments as well as the piano when they are ready and it is remarkable how many become really good musicians when very young.

At Junior School level there is usually a large choir and an orchestra containing many of the instruments found in a full scale orchestra. This appeals greatly to the young idea and at this point there is usually a queue of would-be orchestral players who elect to learn the violin, clarinet or trumpet etc.

Where the school is situated in a large town it is possible to engage a staff of really good teachers, and by their efforts the head of the department is kept in constant touch with the progress of pupils. It is often possible to assess the future outstanding players at this stage and to give that extra modicum of encouragement which means so much.

All classes in the Junior School have at least one music period per week which is normally devoted to singing. This is a crucial stage in the development of the subject as the children are at their most enthusiastic and respond readily to a cheerful but demanding lead. Here are the singers and players of the future. Thus the day school with such a Junior department probably has the edge on the boarding school owing to the degree of continuity mentioned previously.

Another factor which plays a part is the attitude of the parents. Most live within fairly easy reach of the school and have the opportunity of consulting members of staff at frequent intervals. If they are musically interested they will encourage their children in every way, by providing the facilities for practice and by attending the various concerts arranged by the school.

Many establishments build up a pool of instruments by means of gifts and purchases and these are loaned to beginners. Not every child will become a Heifetz or Rostropovitch and some may find instrumental playing not to be their metier at all. Thus parents are saved considerable and unnecessary expense. Where the pupils show keenness and ability they soon become the proud owners of the latest in oboe, 'cello or whatever.

Some schools offer, on a competitive basis, much sought after music scholarships which take effect at the beginning of the senior school. The holders of these scholarships all learn two instruments and the majority continue their studies and include music in their university entrance examinations.

These schools, certainly in Scotland and unlike many of the public schools, continue musical education throughout the senior departments. Every form receives its regular weekly quota, singing for the younger pupils and musical appreciation in the upper classes.

All the effort and hard work of earlier years in the lower school should now come to fruition. A large choir, capable of mastering a series of great works, as well as normal songs, might be confidently expected. Here is a real opportunity to explore music of various periods, both religious and secular and to make every effort to feature works of the twentieth century. The orchestra, now presumably of a high standard, will enjoy coping with the intricacies of a demanding score in company with the choir, as well as providing evidence of its ability in purely orchestral items.

The very finest method of appreciation is to have taken part in the performance of outstanding music, even if one does not aspire to soloist quality. The hours spent in rehearsal are invaluable training in terms of team-work and in attention to detail, and the successful rendering of a fine work brings real satisfaction. But the music must be good – not vulgar or trivial. Experience has shown with almost monotonous regularity, that the first two or three rehearsals are tinged with a certain resentment against the music chosen. But as the new idiom is digested members of choir and orchestra accept the work and end by voting it 'the best ever'.

Several schools and groups of schools have in the past few years commissioned famous composers to write music for special occasions, often to be performmed under the direction of the composer concerned. Such events add to a quickening of interest, and the surmounting of technical difficulties of a contemporary nature extend knowledge and performance ten-fold.

It will have been noted in previous chapters that patrons have played a notable part in the furthering of professional music-making. Perhaps it is not so well known that many schools receive munificent gifts from time to time in order to assist and encourage their pupils. In my own limited experience as a school music master I remember with the utmost gratitude, gifts great and small which so often helped to smooth the way. All were from people with an interest in the school, often as parents or former pupils. These included dozens of instruments of high quality – one being an outstanding Stainer violin of 1699, complete libraries of instrumental music, orchestral scores, books on every conceivable musical subject, articles of furniture and most amazingly of all, a truly magnificent Music School.

The musical activities possible in a lively school are legion. The annual Christmas Carol Service is a great favourite both with parents and pupils. A blend of old and new carols with a judicious choice of well-loved items for the congregation to sing invariably creates the atmosphere of a family service.

School concerts are great occasions, as they normally involve large numbers of pupils, who are very much on parade before parents and friends. The sense of anticipation and excitement behind the scenes prior to the entrance of choir and orchestra, has to be experienced to be believed. If young children are performing, the music master is driven almost to distraction trying to answer all the queries posed by these enthusiastic little people. The fact that all the relevant details have been carefully explained in advance and probably several times, is quite beside the point. The conductor of an adult choir or professional orchestra has usually a little time to collect his thoughts before a performance; not so the music master of a school.

Such concerts also afford a platform for brilliant young soloists, whose example enthuses the next generation, already listening with a critical ear. As distinct from those taking part in the actual performance, many non-musicians are pressed into service and electricians, recording experts, stewards, helpers at the refreshment stalls (an eagerly sought duty), all seem delighted to assist.

Those concerts held outside the school premises are always of special interest. The performing on unfamiliar ground, often to a new audience, tend to create a sense of novelty to the occasion. Also such affairs are often organised in aid of charity, a fact guaranteed to bring out the best in youngsters. For various reasons a smaller, highly trained group of singers and players is desirable for many of the 'outside' performances. It is more mobile and easier to handle where space may be restricted. This also gives an opportunity for selection, with such a group consisting of the best talent available at any one time. Long experience has proved that the extra training and time involved attracts the keenest types and a tremendous spirit of esprit de corps is built up.

This small group can be used for other specialised purposes such as radio and television performances. Although the pupils concerned take these commitments in their stride, they are secretly very proud of having been invited and work extremely hard in advance to ensure the highest possible standard.

Again, where the quality of performance permits, there is always the possibility of going on tour in foreign lands. This is perhaps the ultimate aim and carries with it immense responsibilities for all concerned. The organiser of such tours has to do a vast amount of homework to ensure the smooth running of complicated timetables. This is particularly the case when the music group is constantly on the move, and such details as transport, accommodation and not least, feeding the hungry, have to be carefully planned.

The generosity of local inhabitants is indeed wonderful, notably in the United States and the Scandinavian countries and offers of hospitality are usually in excess of requirements. By staying in private homes the young musicians gain an insight into the customs of a people seldom achieved by normal holiday makers.

But one has to be very certain of the pupils chosen for such an adventure. Their behaviour and manners must be beyond reproach and the V.I.P. treatment they receive must never go to their heads.

They have also to maintain at all times their high musical standards. The many distractions of travelling in a strange land for the first time may have the effect of disturbing concentration, particularly at the outset of a tour. These are extremely important points if the pupils are to give of ther best – after all they are not just tourists.

An experience of this nature has a profound effect on the majority of young people. Many may be away from home and parents for the first time and they return after a few short weeks more self-reliant and assured. They are also happy at having given pleasure to so many foreign audiences and in enhancing the reputation of their school.

The choice of staff is also most important. This is no nine to four assignment and each day brings its minor problems. It is essential to include a doctor in the party to deal with any ailments or accidents which may occur. Changes in climatic conditions and diet can affect children with disastrous results and the doctor, particularly in America, is a necessity. Perhaps the quality most desirable in staff is a sense of humour and an ability to join in the fun and games inescapable from journeying with a school party. One of their most difficult tasks is to ensure that members of the choir refrain from singing when travelling by plane, bus or train. Boundless energy sometimes results in singing of a character not always suitable as preparation for an important concert. Therefore only members of the orchestra are allowed to indulge, often with comic results.

The effects of a tour do not necessarily end with the final concert. Friendships made abroad are frequently of lasting duration and result in exchange visits by the families concerned. Such a foreign tour is of the highest educational value. It is thoroughly constructive, as the participants give of their time and talent and it is of course a source of great enjoyment. And all who engage, however humbly, in a project of this nature lay up a store of never-to-be-forgotten memories.

A PERSONAL NOTE

On looking back over the years, impressions are naturally coloured by one's experiences. My teaching career has been spent in pleasant places and in happy schools; first at Yeovil School, Somerset, then after World War II at Robert Gordon's College, Aberdeen, and finally at George Watson's College, Edinburgh. Undoubtedly I have been fortunate as each school produced an interested group of boys which made teaching a worth-while exercise. At my last school the number of pupils wishing to learn instruments and sing in the various choirs became almost an embarrassment. Of a school population of one thousand five hundred, over six hundred boys were actively engaged in making music out of school hours. As a result one's life was spent entirely in dealing with the musical progress and aspiration of generations of these splendid young people. Due to their dedicated work it was possible to organise several extensive tours which included visits to Denmark, France, Southern England and the United States. A book could be written on these experiences which were heartwarming in the extreme.

One must not forget the many members of staff whose personal kindness and musical ability were of such immense assistance. They were invariably generous in giving of their time and talent and the fact of their presence in choirs and orchestras gave those bodies a greater significance in the eyes of the pupils. The loyalty of former pupils was another outstanding feature. They always seemed delighted to return to their old school and take part in the musical production of the moment. Thus was created a feeling of continuity by people of widely differing age groups, all having roots in the same school.

COMPETITIONS

Where time allows, and in a busy school time seems always to be at a premium, the music competition provides a splendid outlet for pupils of all ages and stages. Although individual prestige is involved, many competitions are organised on a less personal basis, with the gifted pupils earning points for their house possibly in the context of a championship of wider issue.

Such a competition serves as a spur to otherwise 'tired' pupils and if held at fairly regular intervals may act as a method of assessing progress. Talented children are given an opportunity of conducting choirs and orchestras and some even have the thrill of hearing their own compositions performed. In a large school where the number of entrants is considerable, there may be several evenings of preliminary heats followed by a day of finals. Here the atmosphere is inclined to be tense, with perhaps a number of outside adjudicators to give expert and unbiassed opinions. It is quite possible to unearth unexpected talent in this way and usually a healthy and friendly rivalry is established amongst the competitors.

In the great centres of population throughout the land and indeed in many rural areas also, mammoth competitions are frequently organised with a wide coverage of classes for young people. It is possible to hear some splendid performances on these occasions and sometimes to spot a great artist in the making. These potentially excellent musicians are given wise and helpful advice and the really good adjudicator can give enormous encouragement to large numbers of youngsters who may not be in the top flight.

Scotland has its National Mod, a Gaelic speaking competition held annually in a different centre. This in many ways is not unlike the Welsh Eisteddfod and creates much interest and enthusiasm. Children's choirs and young soloists play an important part in the Mod and a high standard of musicianship is regularly attained. The B.B.C. gives wide coverage to this event and undoubtedly stimulates the efforts of competitors, particularly those from the Islands and Highlands.

SPECIALIST SCHOOLS

Although so many schools play close attention to music and encourage talented pupils, few specialist schools as such exist in Britain. The choristers attached to various cathedrals and certain Oxford and Cambridge colleges receive highly professional training, principally from the vocal aspect, but some of these schools go further and encourage their pupils to take instrumental instruction. In this respect mention should be made of Wells Cathedral School in Somerset, which has succeeded in a bold and imaginative experiment. Dating from the thirteenth century, it has throughout its history catered primarily for the boys of the cathedral choir and remained small, after the pattern of other such schools. But since the 1920s there has been a gradual increase in numbers to its present six hundred pupils with co-education well established.

Great store is set on musical education and talented children are drawn to the school by reason of the opportunities offered.

A graded system of entry is in operation, consisting of Specialist Musicians, Serious Musicians and General Musicians. The Specialist Musicians are chosen by an independent board of adjudicators and are required to show outstanding ability and potential in violin playing. At some time in the future it is hoped to widen the scope of this category and to include instruments other than the violin. The children accepted in this grade have to work hard, as in addition to a normal curriculum, they receive two violin lessons per week and tuition in a second instrument. Two to three hours practice a day is deemed essential and for the younger pupils much of this time is supervised. As many of these students will eventually become professional musicians, it is wise to insist on such dedication at an early age. The Guildhall School of Music acts in a consultative role regarding the Specialist Musicians and the Professor of Violin visits Wells at least once every term.

Serious Musicians enter the school as normal members, but are young people who wish to study to an advanced standard. In this grade the pupil has a choice of instrument and is expected to take part in one of the orchestras or chamber groups.

General Musicians are those who are interested in the subject as an additional activity, but for whom the normal timetable is of equal importance. As might be expected with three hundred children learning instruments, the school enjoys a vigorous musical life, with regular concerts given in the glorious Cathedral and chamber concerts held in the Music School. The choir and orchestra have toured in Scandinavia and the chamber orchestra has this year visited Perth, Western Australia on the occasion of the Congress of the XIth International Society for Musical Education.

Another exceptional undertaking is the Yehudi Menuhin School, an excellent training ground for young string players and one which has gained an enviable reputation. The school ensemble has become well-known through its public performances and invariably creates genuine appreciation from discerning audiences. It should be stressed that considerable importance is given to normal educational subjects, as might be expected from its distinguished founder.

In Manchester, Chetham's Hospital School of Music, an independent boarding and day school caters specifically for musical boys and girls. Admission is by audition for children of seven years and above, and in addition to a full musical course, a normal academic training is provided. Pupils are able to study the instruments of their choice and boys with suitable voices are given the opportunity of becoming choristers in Manchester Cathedral.

In an age of specialisation there can be no doubt that institutions such as those mentioned fill a much-needed want, as it is vital that gifted young musicians should be given every encouragement at the earliest possible age.

A SAD NOTE

In spite of all that has been written so far, there is another and less happy side to music in the classroom. It must be admitted that all is not sweetness and light. There is in many a school and perhaps there has always been, an element which seems to reject the accepted axiom of beauty or anything of good repute. It is not surprising that to such a group music is anathema. There may be various reasons for this state of affairs. An unsympathetic home background and in some cases one frankly derisive of such a subject. Associates and friends may play an important part, with the juke box a powerful influence. Also where a certain type of young person is concerned it might well be fashionable to be just anti-establishment. One can expect a degree of apathy from the immature, but it is sad to encounter the reaction of sheer hatred which sometimes exists.

Some years ago there appeared an article in *The Universities and Left Review* entitled *The Anti-Culture Born of Despair*. It described how a class of fourteen year old pupils in a secondary modern school responded when asked to write about the kind of music they disliked. It may not have been very clever to enquire into the musical likes and dislikes of such an age group, but the result was certainly forthright. The children wrote against everything they had been taught by their music master. "Classical music was slow, went on for hours, had no go in it, was full of high notes and had no tune. You could not clap your hands to it, jive to it or even hand jive to it. It had no beat. It did not send you. Bach, Beethoven and their followers are just lucky they are not living today. They would have

165

been chivved up (knifed) by some cool cats".

Classical music was hated because those who liked it were 'old fogies' or 'squares'. Those who went to opera 'talked posh' or were 'queers'. Symphonies gave one headaches, opera singers should be 'done in' and opera banned. Some thought that Covent Garden and Sadler's Wells should be bombed.

We are the 'squares' and we are hated for not 'getting in the groove' with them, for failing 'to get the message'. To these children music is bound up with the 'posh' and is an empty, meaningless attempt at superiority. Unfortunately this is not an isolated case and may indeed be more prevalent in the present age of permissiveness. But one important question requires an answer. Were not these particular children too young to come in contact with Bach and Beethoven. Perhaps they always would be. Maybe a more gradual approach to composers might have gained better results. We shall never know.

SUMMER SCHOOLS

In addition to the splendid work now being achieved in other educational fields, a number of summer schools operate in various parts of the country for the musically interested. Some are specially arranged for young people of school age, while others are intended for a wider range and cater for those of greater experience. Most summer schools include orchestral playing in their schedules and some are organised exclusively towards this end. Many provide a syllabus in which choral singing is studied seriously.

The administrators are invariably friendly and understanding and the courses, which are always held in attractive locations, are organised with the dual purpose of sound musical training, combined with a holiday atmosphere. Professional musicians are engaged to coach the students in every branch of music-making, including assistance with individual instrumental technique. It is often possible to form two orchestras to suit the abilities of the students, and the standard attained at the end of the course is wholly commendable.

The fees are very reasonable and offer wonderful value. Living conditions are good and nothing is spared to give the participants a happy and worthwhile experience. Also local authorities and other bodies are often helpful regarding finance for those who wish to spend part of their holiday in such a pursuit. The venue changes from time to time, but many successful courses have been held at Canford School, Sherborne School for Girls, Roedean, Winchester, Oxford and St. Andrews amongst others.

Owing to its unique tradition of music-making, together with its long and fruitful association with Imogen Holst, Dartington Hall is the ideal setting for a summer school. The buildings, some dating from the fourteenth century and reminiscent of the older Oxford and Cambridge colleges, are surrounded by magnificent woodlands, formal gardens and with wonderful vistas in every direction. These grounds have been described as 'perhaps the most beautiful of English Paradise Gardens'.

Many famous musicians have been attracted to this centre of the arts and in 1947 the Banqueting Hall was the scene of the very first performance given by the Amadeus Quartet. Since then this quartet has achieved world wide acclaim.

THE CHURCH TRIES AGAIN

The modern counterpart of the ancient song schools attached to the monasteries exist in the thirty or so schools whose headmasters are members of the Choir Schools Association. These schools operate primarily to train boys to sing the services in cathedral or college chapel and the standard of work is uniformly high. The majority of these schools are independent and those which cater only for choristers and probationers are very small, having usually less than fifty pupils. These small specialised schools are however becoming increasingly difficult to maintain and several have already closed. Where this has happened provision for the boys' education has been made at larger schools, usually a local grammar school or its equivalent.

The young musicians concerned constitute what may be termed the professional boy singers of the country and they ably maintain a tradition reaching back many centuries. They are in fact justly renowned for their performance of the finest ecclesiastical music. It is sometimes assumed that these boys, robed in gowns and surplices, with angelic faces shining from a recent application of soap and water, are as pure and unsullied as their appearance might suggest. But they are still boys! Certainly they work tremendously hard. From early morning to late evening they know little respite. Services, rehearsals, normal school subjects, instrumental lessons, games and of course meals, have all to be fitted into a complicated timetable. And yet most of them come up smiling, proving that hard work is not a bad thing, provided one is interested in the task in hand.

Apart from the small number of establishments which enjoy the advantage of choir schools, the vast number of church choirs throughout the land have to rely on voluntary help from a variety of sources. Thus it has been difficult to co-ordinate a plan of action and the quality of music, both in performance and taste has varied enormously.

The church, having been responsible for so much musical education in past centuries, has taken a bold step towards improvement in the twentieth. This was largely at the instigation of Sir Sidney Nicholson, one time organist of Westminster Abbey and a man of high ideals and great vision. At the centre of his plan was the formation of a training school for the benefit of all interested in the music of the Anglican Communion.

In 1927 the School of English Church Music, now the Royal School of Church Music was founded and two years later the College of St. Nicholas at Chislehurst was brought into being as its headquarters. In the early days this organisation proved invaluable in its help and advice to church choirs, particularly those of limited musical resources.

But even Nicholson would have been amazed at the success of his brain-child. Owing to the great interest shown by choirs in this scheme, larger premises were acquired at Addington Palace, Croydon, although these are already proving inadequate for their purpose and further building is envisaged. The School offers a wide choice of training courses, covering every aspect of church music and in 1972 it was recognised by the Secretary of State for Education and Science as 'an efficient establishment of further education'. It sends out Commissioners (eminent church musicians) upon request to any of its affiliatd choirs to offer help and advice: it organises festivals of church music and it engages in the publication of music.

Much thought has been given to the encouragement of younger members of choirs, in which grades of proficiency lead to positions of responsibility within their choirs. This is sound sense as many young people give long and devoted service to their church and acknowledgement of this fact is very rewarding.

168

The multifarious activities of this organisation have had a beneficial effect on church music generally, not only within the Church of England. Other denominations, those belonging to the World Council of Churches are free to use the facilities of the R.S.C.M. and many avail themselves of this opportunity. Also a heartening sign is that several of these bodies have formed their own advisory services to deal with their particular problems. The reader cannot have failed to notice in this chapter how important a part the church has played in musical education throughout the centuries. This most recent example by the R.S.C.M is truly a magnificent piece of work.

TEACHER TRAINING COLLEGES

Colleges for the training of teachers may be found in many parts of the country. Students wishing to become specialist teachers of music follow a very full course under highly qualified staffs. Included in this training is sight-reading, class-singing and suggestions regarding the type of song most likely to be successful. Students spend much of their time in the schools observing established teachers at work and are encouraged to do some teaching themselves. The colleges are usually well equipped and many musical activities are available to would-be teachers. One would perhaps wish that more assistance might be given regarding class management. In teaching, discipline is of vital importance. Some young teachers, by sheer personality are able to cope satisfactorily whilst others find some difficulty in the early stages. But the training colleges do good work and take a very personal interest in their students.

UNIVERSITIES

Although not strictly within the limits of this chapter, some reference if only slight, must be made of music in British universities. The concert giving activities at Oxford have been mentioned in a previous section, an example which many of the younger universities have followed with success. It is now quite normal for outstanding performers to visit and give recitals at these establishments when

169

on tour throughout the country.

Most universities now-a-days provide opportunities for participation in music and many have a chair of music occupied by an eminent professor. Where first-class facilities exist and wise leadership prevails, the results can be outstanding. Even in those institutions of higher learning where music is not so professionally organised there will usually be found a group of singers, often very expert, with sufficient instrumental players to ensure the continuity of one or more orchestras.

Some universities tend to stress the study and performance of music of a contemporary nature, as for instance at York. This is a comparatively new approach, but an understandable one. Many of the staff appointments of recent years have been of young men with an interest in composition, and they are of course working closely with a youthful, questing section of the community, which might be expected to comprehend new ideas readily.

One of the most notable musical achievements of this university was some years ago when residential facilities were afforded the Amadeus Quartet, the members of which not only engaged in recital work, but were also available for consultation and teaching. Those students contemplating a musical career had wonderful teaching and advice.

Over a period of some ten years Hull University had a particularly happy arrangement with the Allegri Quartet. At the end of their term of duty, the honorary degree of Master of Music was conferred upon the individual members in recognition of their outstanding contribution to the university.

It is believed that certain other universities are considering similar projects.

As an example of lively endeavour one might quote the example of Edinburgh University, where music has had an enviable reputation over a long period. One suspects this owes something to Sir Donald Tovey, a one-time professor of international standing, whose great learning exercised so profound an influence on his students. In 1915 Tovey brought into existence the Reid Orchestra, named after General John Reid, a keen amateur musician and generous benefactor to the music department. This orchestra still plays a prominent role in university life and consists of many fine players, both professional and amateur in the city. As a result an ambitious concert programme is organised every winter season. Many of the professional players are also engaged in teaching and are able to hand on much of their skill to pupils in local schools, a scheme which usually works well. The university also sponsors the Edinburgh Quartet which takes an active part in local music-making and from time to time departs on British and foreign tours.

But in spite of much fine work around the country, pride of place must still be given to the two oldest universities. Entrance to the music departments of Oxford and Cambridge is very competitive and in order to gain a scholarship a candidate has to be especially gifted. This means that an exceptional standard is maintained year by year, both academically and in music performance.

It might not be without interest to give the briefest sketch of the rather strange method of appointing professors of music at Oxford during the sixteenth and seventeenth centuries. Within the short space of thirty years two chairs of music were established. The first, created in 1596 was named after the beneficiary, Sir Thomas Gresham, a wealthy businessman and founder of the London Royal Exchange. The initial Gresham Professor of Music was the notable Dr. John Bull who was elected on the strong recommendation of Queen Elizabeth. On his resignation in 1607 due to bad administration or worse, a series of appointments was made, none of which went to a musician. Bull was followed by Clayton, a physician, who in turn was succeeded by Taverner, a clergyman, and this extraordinary state of affairs continued for one hundred and fifty years. Eventually commonsense was brought to bear on an intolerable situation and men worthy of the position were appointed. On the other hand, the second chair, founded in 1626 and occupied by the Oxford Professor of Music, has had a distinguished line of musicians since its inception.

Both universities have a bewildering number of musical bodies, offering a wide variety of choice. There are large choirs and orchestras, with smaller specialized groups devoted to a variety of interesting projects. Some of these organisations may be termed official, in that the players and singers are rehearsed by outstanding musicians from within the establishment and on occasions by experts from outside. As a result performances are of an exceptionally high level. A whole range of great music receives attention and the freshness and enthusiasm of the participants always makes for a memorable occasion.

Those whose interests lean towards more esoteric fare may choose between Baroque, Elisabethan, Medieval, Asian,

171

Contemporary or a host of other equally enjoyable pursuits. Societies which exist to further such aims are often the products of undergraduate zeal and they are usually prepared and willing to accept members in return for a modest subscription.

Three colleges in Oxford maintain chapel choirs consisting of men and boys, these being Magdalen, New and Christ Church, the last-named doubling the role of college chapel and cathedral. In every case the standard of music is of the highest quality and a source of justifiable pride to the colleges concerned. The tradition of centuries is being continued and those in search of fine church music well performed would be abundantly repaid by attendance at one or more of the chapel services.

Cambridge is fortunate in possessing King's College Chapel together with a choir worthy of its setting. Broadcasting has brought more than national fame to this magnificent body of singers, which has maintained such excellence over a long period. Its recent director, David Willcocks, one of the great choral trainers of this century, is now Principal of the Royal College of Music. For sixteen years he was in charge of King's College Chapel and achieved amazing results. The annual carol service on Christmas Eve filled the chapel and gave pleasure to a vast listening public.

But King's now has a serious rival – the choir of St. John's College Chapel. This is a splendid group of disciplined singers, with a repertoire probably the equal of any in the country. Although a choir has been in existence here for a very long time, it is perhaps during the past twenty years that the quality has so greatly improved. This is undoubtedly due to the excellent training and enthusiasm of the Director of Music, Dr. George Guest. As is usual in College Chapel Choirs the situation is one of perpetual youth. The boy trebles move on to public schools as their voices change and the tenors and bases are undergraduates holding choral scholarships. This is youth at its most disciplined and brilliant best.

Many discerning musicians are drawn to St. John's College Chapel, but King's College Chapel is a superb building and placed in the centre of Cambridge, it beckons to all.

The Music School at Cambridge has played a distinguished part in the development of the art since the fifteenth century, and the long list of famous composers and other musicians to have passed that way bears testimony to its success. Now, owing to the increased interest in music, it is no longer adequate for its purpose. Consequently it was decided to appeal for funds to build an entirely new school to include a five hundred seat concert hall, library, study and lecture rooms together with ancillary accommodation such as workshops, storage space and offices. Thus while Oxford has the oldest Concert Room, Cambridge has the newest Music School, at least for a while.

Two of the most important aspects of music in a university would appear to be (a) to guide the gifted student through a complex course leading to a degree and a career in music, and (b) to further the appreciation of as many as possible through participation in great music during their university life. In short to expose a large number of young people to the very best that music can offer. This surely is a most laudable object.

CHAPTER 4
MUSIC in the CONCERT HALL

Music, when soft voices die,
Vibrates in the memory.

Shelley

LONDON

To John Banister of London belongs the honour of arranging the first series of concerts for the general public at which payment was accepted. A talented performer and composer of some merit, Banister was for many years a court musician to Charles II. His concerts started in 1672, in which year the *London Gazette* of December 30th carried the following announcement: "These are to give Notice, that at Mr. John Bannister's House, now called the Music School, over against the George Tavern in White Fryers, this present Monday, will be Musick performed by Excellent Masters, beginning precisely at four of the Clock in the afternoon, and every afternoon for the future, precisely at the same hour".

The room used for this purpose had a platform for the musicians and in the prevailing style of the tavern, chairs and small tables for the audience. The price of admission was one shilling "and call for what you pleased". These concerts continued until 1678, though there were several changes of venue during the six years.

Another important series, consisting of a weekly concert, commenced in the year when Banister's ended. This was due entirely to the musical enthusiast Thomas Britton, a coal hawker in private life. A truly remarkable man, he converted the loft over his coal store at Jerusalem Passage, Clerkenwell, into a music-room and there installed a small organ of five stops. Britton, a self-taught musician, attracted a highly intelligent and appreciative audience to his unusual studio and two of the most famous musicians of the century, Handel and Pepusah often performed for him. These concerts had a great vogue and lasted for thirty-six years. The following description of Britton's music-room is taken from 'The London Magazine':

"On the ground floor there was a repository for small-coal; over that was the concert-room which was small and narrow. Notwithstanding all, this mansion, despicable as it may seem, attracted to it as polite an audience as ever the Opera did".

Ned Ward, always ready to comment on anything of an unusual nature, whether seamy or cultural, gave his imagination full rein in the following description of Britton and his enterprise.

Compleat and Humorous Account of all the Remarkable Clubs and Societies in the Cities of London and Westminster (1745)

The SMALL-COAL MAN'S Musick Club

The Musick Club was at first begun, or at least confirmed by Sir Roger-le-Strange, many years before his knighthood, who was a very musical Gentleman, and had a tolerable Perfection on the Base Viol, a very fashionable Instrument in those Days . . . The reasons that induc'd Sir Roger, and other ingenious Gentlemen, who were lovers of the Muses, to honour the little Mansion of the black and blue Philomat with their weekly Company, were chiefly the unexpected Genius to Books and Musick that they happened to find in their Smutty Acquaintance, and the profound Regard that he had in general to all Manner of Literature, beyond whatever had been found before among the narrow Souls of those groveling Mortals, who are content to disguise Nature with such crocky colour'd Robes, and to hazard the Welfare of their Eyes in such a dusty Profession; however, like a prudent Man, though he might justly boast a great many Qualificatios above many of his level, yet he never suffered the Flatteries of his Betters to lift him up above the Care of his Employment; for though he always took delight to spend his leisure Hours in the Studies of a Gentleman, yet he limited his Industry to the Trade he had been bred to; and though he was Master enough of Musick to play his Part tolerably well, upon several Instruments, yet he would not grow too proud, for the profitable Tune of Small-Coal or lay aside his Sack till his Day's Work was over, to dance after a Fiddle . . . Thus the prudence of his Department, among those who were his Betters, procured him great Respect from all that knew him, so that his Musick Meeting improved in a little time to be very considerable, insomuch, that Men of the best Wit, as well as some of the best Quality, very often honoured his Musical Society with their good Company, that in a few years his harmonious Consort became as publickly noted as the Kit-Cat Club . . . Sir Roger continued to be a constant Meeter in the Zenith of his Glory, and many other Gentlemen, who wer fit Companions for so worthy a person of his Wit and learning; so that *Briton*, when equiped in his blue Surplice, his Shoulder laden with his wooden Tinder, and his Measure twisted into the Mouth of his Sack, was as much distinguished as he walked the streets, and respected by the good Hussifs, who were Customers for his Commodity, as if he had been a Noble-Man in disguise . . . everyone that knew him pointing as he passed crying, *There goes the famous Small-Coal Man, who is a Lover of Learning, a Performer in Musick, and a Companion for a Gentleman.*

Britton Street, a turning off the Clerkenwell Road and within a stone's throw of Jerusalem Passage, serves to remind us of this pioneer concert-giver. Such was the success of these early ventures that the first quarter of the eighteenth century produced greatly increased activity in concert-giving. Two of the most popular places for this type of entertainment were the Crown and Anchor Tavern in the Strand and Hickford's Room in James Street. The former was for many years the meeting place of *The Academy of Ancient Music* which met for the encouragement of non-contemporary music. For eighty-two years this society maintained a high standard of selection and performance. The Duke of Abercorn was its first patron, with Dr. Pepusch, who left it the best part of his immense library, its first director.

Hickfords, a dancing school named after its owner, came into use as a concert-room in 1714. Most of the finest musicians of the day frequently made appearances at these rooms. But a study of the programmes shows a sad lack of British music and British performers. With the death of Purcell in 1695 a period of decline set in. This was due in part to the continental style of music introduced by Charles II on his return from exile in France. The taste of those close to the throne gradually changed and now favoured foreign composers. They lavished adulation upon singers and instrumentalists from abroad. Two German musicians already mentioned settled permanently in London, Pepusch in 1700 and Handel in 1712 and they remained there until their deaths in 1752 and 1759 respectively.

The music of Italy (fostered by Handel) and Germany flourished in Britain, with a corresponding lack of opportunity for native talent, especially those who continued to write in the English tradition. It might be interesting to conjecture what would have been the future of British music but for the early death of Purcell.

As a contributory factor in this state of affairs must be mentioned the arrival, in 1714 of the first of the Hanoverians to become a British Sovereign. This had a considerable influence on people of rank and fashion, who naturally took their lead from the newly appointed King. George I was certainly not interested in the music of Britain; he was however very responsive to the compositions of Handel.

In 1932 Dr. Vaughan Williams was invited to the United States to give a series of six lectures at Bryn Mawr College, Pennsylvania. Discussing music of the eighteenth century he delivered, in characteristic fashion, a few trenchant observations which are well worth repeating here: "I am speaking of course of my own country England, but I believe it exists equally virulently in yours: that music is not an industry which flourishes naturally in our climate; that, therefore, those who want it and can afford it must hire it from abroad. This idea has been prevalent among us for generations. It began in England, I think, in the early eighteenth century when the political power got into the hands of the entirely uncultured landed gentry and the practice of the art was considered unworthy of a gentleman, from which it followed that you had to hire a "damned foreigner" to do it for you if you wanted it, from which in its turn followed the corollary that the type of music which the foreigner brought with him was the only type worth having and that the very different type of music which was being made at home must necessarily be wrong. These ideas were fostered by the fact that we had a foreign court at St. Jame's who apparently did not share the English snobbery about home-made art and so brought the music made in their homes to England with them. So, the official music, whether it took the form of Mr. Handel to compose an oratorio, or an oboe player in a regimental band, was imported from Germany".

The aristocracy pandered to and grossly overpaid Italian and German musicians, whose number increased accordingly. The *Daily Courant* was the one eighteenth century periodical devoted to the advertisement of musical events, and a study of its pages will serve to show how foreign musicians held almost complete sway in Britain. On 10 February 1720 a concert was arranged for Signor Castrucci, leading violin of the opera, in which he played several concertos and solos of his own composition. His name is mentioned on many subsequent occasions and he seems to have been a popular performer. On 23 February of the same year we read of Mr. Kytch playing on the German flute and hautbois at Hickford's Rooms. This was followed by a performance on 21 May of trumpet playing by the celebrated Grano. 31 May saw a concert given by Aubert and then came a benefit concert for Francesco Scarlatti.

Also during this year Bonancini arrived in London and soon became a serious rival to Handel. In musical circles there later developed bitter feeling between the admirers of the two men which became further inflamed by the behaviour of the pro-Handel singer Faistina Bordoni and her rival Francesca Cuzzoni, who quarrelled and fought on the stage in full view of the audience. This was in Bonancini's *Astyanax* performed in 1727.

Handel's forty-one operas are now rarely performed, though a few excerpts from them are sometimes heard. Although popular during their day they did not lack detractors. Addison found the foreign singers much to his distaste and several music critics thought the Italian Bonancini the greater composer. Eventually Handel became accepted at the head of British music and Bonancini faded away; the latter was thought to have taken part in a shady piece of work regarding the submission of prize madrigal, the work of someone else.

> Some say, compar'd to Bonancini That Mynheer Handel's but a ninny;
> Other aver that he to Handel Is scarcely fit to hold a candle
> Strange all this difference 'Twixt Tweedledum and Tweedledee
> should be
> On the feuds between Handel and Bonancini.

John Byrom
1692–1763

During 1722 a new type of entertainment, known as Ridotto

was advertised at the Opera House. It commenced with a recital of songs from various operas sung by Senesino, Baldassari and Salrai. This part of the programme lasted for about two hours, after which the audience moved on to the stage and took part in a ball for the remainder of the evening.

Looking through the lists of concerts for February of that year we find a British name, which strikes a note of welcome novelty. A benefit concert was given in honour of Mr. Thomson, the first editor of a collection of Scots tunes to be published in England. A great many people subscribed to make this possible and its publication must be considered largely responsible for the early success of Scottish songs in England.

Another benefit concert announced for 1722 was that for Castrucci's farewell performance, in which he promised a concerto with an echo. Carbonelli, who had been in London but a short while also had a benefit concert during this same year at Drury Lane. The programme was advertised in detail in *The Daily Courant* and is here produced as an example of the musical taste of the concert-going public of the time.

ACT I

A new concerto for two trumpets, composed and performed by Grano and others; a new concerto by Albinoni, just brought over; song by Mrs. Barbier; concerto composed by Signor Carbonelli.

ACT II

Concerto with two hautbois and two flutes, composed by Diepart; Concerto on the Bass violin by Pippo, song by Mrs. Barbier; by desire the eigth concerto of Arcangelo Corelli.

ACT III

Concerto by Carbonelli: solo on the arch-lute by Signor Vebar. Song by Mrs. Barbier; a new concerto on the little flute composed by Woodcock, performed by Baston; solo by Signor Carbonelli; Finale a concerto for two trumpets by Grano.

In 1723 there arrived several more foreign musicians who undoubtedly found an excellent living in Britain. One of these was Guiseppe San Martini, a composer and hautbois player who made his first London appearance at a benefit concert for Piero at the small Haymarket Theatre, where he was advertised as "an Italian master just arrived". One of the musical novelties of the period was that by Joachim Frederic Greta who "blew the first and second treble on two French horns, in the same manner as is usually done by two persons".

The number of programmes given by continental musicians was greatly multiplied during the next few years and resulted in a feverish search for new concert rooms. The Castle Tavern in Paternoster Row proved an ideal setting and the Castle Society was formed there in 1724.

In 1728 there was a halt, though but a temporary one, to the constant performances of Italian music and to music in the Italian style. This was the production of *The Beggar's Opera* by John Gay an Englishman, which took place at the theatre in Lincoln's Inn Fields and proved an immediate success. It was the first of a new type of entertainment, known as ballad opera, in which spoken dialogue was interspersed with songs set to popular tunes of the day. Not a single new melody was written for this piece; instead, well-known operatic and theatre songs, street tunes and the like were collected and arranged by Dr. Pepusch and the complete work was performed in English. Many of the songs were taken from D'Urfey's *Wit and Mirth* and *Pills to Purge Melancholy*. *The Beggar's Opera* was the result of a suggestion by Swift that a Newgate pastoral 'might make an odd pretty sort of thing'.

The story was much to the liking of the public, being simple in form and in words that could be understood. Also it included several references, not always kindly, to important people and affairs of the day, together with a fair quota of dirt and vice. Italian opera was caricatured and fun was made of the government. (Did Gilbert and Sullivan find any inspiration here?). So successful was this ballad opera that others of a similar nature followed very quickly. In 1729 John Gay published *Polly* as a sequel to *the Beggar's Opera* but this was banned by the Lord Chamberlain. It did not in fact receive its first performance until 1777. Other writers were more fortunate however. From 1729 to 1733 no less than seventy-one ballad operas such as *The Village Opera* by Charles Johnson, were performed in London. This particular work was quickly imitated by Bickerstaff in his *Love in a Village*, in which it must be stated, eighteen of the melodies belonged to Arne with additional items from Boyce, Galuppi, Geminiani, Handel, Howard and Weldon.

This form of plagiarism was accepted by all concerned, rather

180

as it is today in the realm of popular music. There followed in the next four years a further twenty-four, after which a decline set in and only single instances occurred until 1753 when a general lack of interest caused the extinction of this form. Thus the popularity of the ballad opera lasted for rather more than twenty years.

Although short-lived, this sudden burst of native musical energy had far-reaching effects. An immediate result was the emergence of two new composers for the theatre, John Frederick Lampe and Thomas Augustine Arne. They took over the positions so securely held previously by Pepusch and Galliard, who until 1732 were the unrivalled composers in this medium. Arne's most notable achievements were his fine settings of the songs in *The Tempest* and *As You Like It,* some of which, particularly 'Where the bee sucks' have rarely been equalled. Outside the theatre the more solid musical fare was undoubtedly that of Handel and Corelli.

The 20th April 1732 was a notable date as being the occasion of the first public performance of Handel's oratorio *Esther.* The *Daily Journal* of the 19th carried the following information:

Never Perform'd in Publick before

At the Great Room in Villiers-street, York-Buildings,

Tomorrow, being Thursday the 20th, of this Instant April,

will be perform'd

ESTHER an ORATORIO

or

SACRED DRAMA

As it was composed originally for the most noble Duke of Chandos, the words by Mr. Pope, and the Musick by

Mr. Handel.

Tickets to be had at the Place of Performance at 5s each.

To begin exactly at 7 o'clock

It was customary during the eighteenth century to employ castrati, male singers who had been operated on in boyhood to prevent their voices changing into a lower register. Many of these artists became very popular and achieved sensational success both in the opera house and concert hall. One of the finest of the Handel era was certainly Senesino, who quickly became an outstanding socialite. His extraordinary vanity was pandered to by the wives of the wealthy, many of whom waited in queues at the end of a performance to kiss his hand. Thus twentieth century teenage behaviour towards its crooner, rock and roll and pop idols is not entirely without precedent. But Senesino was dismissed by Handel in 1733. He, together with Cuzzoni and Montagnana attempted to commence a rival opera, a venture supported wholeheartedly by Frederick, the young Prince of Wales. The latter was prepared to take any action guaranteed to cause embarrassment to the King and by upsetting Handel he effectively hurt his father. This was typical of the scheming and interference which beset the musical world.

Dr. Charles Burney, the musical historian arrived in London in 1744 and frequently played in Handel's orchestra. His comments make interesting reading.

"I performed in his band, sometimes on the violin, and sometimes on the tenor and thereby qualified my eager curiosity in seeing and examining the person and manners of so extraordinary a man, as well as in hearig him perform on the organ. He was a blunt and peremptory disciplinarian on these occasions but had a humour and wit in delivering his instructions, and even in chiding and finding fault, that was peculiar to himself, and extremely diverting to all but those on whom his lash was laid".

Burney further commented on the first performance of the *Messiah* which took place in Dublin. There must have been some doubt at the time whether in fact the oratorio was given in England prior to its Irish premiere.

"In the autumn of this year (1741), Handel went to Ireland. I have taken considerable pains to obtain a minute and accurate account of the musical transaction of the great musician, during his residence in that kingdom; and in a particular manner tried to wipe off the national stain, of the oratorio of the Messiah having met with a cold reception in England, previous to Handel's departure for Ireland; a fact which I am glad to find impossible to ascertain, either by the newspapers of the times, in which all his other public performances sacred and secular are chronologically recorded, or by the testimony of persons still living, who remember the performances of the Messiah in Ireland, and of his oratorios previous to that period in England".

Faulkner's Journals, for 1741/2 have been consulted for the details of Handel's performances in Dublin. The first mention of the composer appeared in the paper dated 19th December 1741. L'Allegro, Il Penseroso and Il Moderato were advertised for the 23rd. On March 27th, 1742 "Mr Handel's new, grand sacred

182

Oratorio called the Messiah" was announced for the following 12th April.

There was probably some justification for Arne's hearty dislike of Handel and all that he represented musically. The English composer looked upon his great rival as a foreign usurper, responsible for introducing competition into the already precarious sphere of music. As already noted Arne refused to copy Handel's style of composition and frequently rebelled against it though with but little effect. Also it must be remembered that Arne suffered a great disadvantage in that his music was rarely so well performed. Handel was always able to provide a better orchestra, a finer organ and more outstanding singers. But in spite of the many difficulties, Arne must be considered the natural successor of Purcell and there are authorities who assert that in the field of secular music he even surpassed that great master in ease, grace and variety. Many of his songs, particularly those written for Shakespeare's plays were very fine. "Blow, blow thou winter wind", "Under the greenwood tree", "When daisies pied" and "Where the bee sucks" are still often sung today and are considered models of eighteenth century writing. And we must never forget Arne as being the composer of the masque *Alfred* from which comes the patriotic *Rule Britannia*. Our nation would be no worse off if a few more heart-warming songs of this nature were written and sung today instead of some of the effete rubbish with which we are so often regaled.

For some time the Gardens entertainments at both Vauxhall and Ranelagh had been proving popular with the citizens of London. Tyers, the proprietor of Vauxhall Gardens provided orchestral performances of a high standard and in 1745 he added vocal items for the first time. On this initial occasion the music consisted largely of the songs of Arne, which were acclaimed with enthusiasm by the audience.

Ranelagh was planned by Lacey, joint patentee with Garrick of Drury Lane Theatre. The great Rotunda was a feature of this place and became a centre of fashion on account of its lavish appointments and the fact that it afforded shelter in inclement weather. At first there were morning performances which consisted mostly of choruses from well-known oratorios. Apparently the younger merchants and apprentices preferred visiting the Rotunda to going to business and as a result of serious complaints all morning amusements were stopped. Nowadays it is the midweek football match which causes dislocation of industry.

William Boyce, the renowned organist was a contemporary of Arne. He wrote music for masques and for the stage, including the incidental music to Shakespeare's *Tempest, Cymbeline, Romeo and Juliet* and *The Winter's Tale*. As a result of his work in this field he and Arne sometimes got in one another's way, particularly at Drury Lane Theatre. Boyce also composed eight symphonies, twelve string sonatas and two odes for St. Cecilia's Day. The strong and stirring *Heart of Oak* was one of his songs. As a result of deafness he retired from active music-making and devoted his great talent and energy to the compilation of *Cathedral Music,* a collection of the finest English church music, covering a period of three hundred years.

During this time there was a school of English composers of string sonatas which, in addition to Arne and Boyce included John Stanley, Babell, Collett, Croft, Eccles, Gibbs, Humphries, Jones, Lates and Vincent. But the majority did not gain much recognition during their lifetime and today their names are mostly forgotten.

The Italian musical invasion of Britain met with some serious opposition about halfway through the century. Not as might have been expected, from the British, but from German performers who were now arriving in ever increasing numbers and whose well-rehearsed operatic productions created a threat to the Italian school. The latter however still had many admirers particularly amongst the influential sections of society.

Michael Festing, the well-known violinist and leader of the opera, died in 1752 and his place was taken by Felice de Giardini. He rapidly became a favourite in aristocratic circles just at the time when members of the nobility were organising private recitals in their homes. As a result, Giardini rarely performed at public concerts, preferring instead to act as soloist at these select functions.

As usual, Dr. Burney writes entertainingly on the situation obtaining, with special reference to Mrs. Fox Lane, afterwards Lady Bingley.

> "The superior talents of that performer (Giardini) were always warmly patronised by this lady to the time of her death; and not content with admiring them herself, she contrived every means that could be devised to make him the admiration of others. As Giardini was seldom to be heard in public after his first arrival, she invited very select

parties of the first people in the kingdom to hear him at her house, for which happiness she did not suffer them to remain ungrateful at his benefit.

"When Mingotti arrived in this kingdom, having united her interests with those of Giardini in the conduct and management of the opera, Mrs. Lane espoused her cause with great zeal; entering into the spirit of all her theatrical quarrels as ardently as if they had been her own. With two such performers, the concerts she gave to her choice friends were subjects of envy and obloquy to all those who were unable to obtain admission. At these concerts Mrs. Lane frequently played the harpsichord herself; as did Lady Edgcumbe and the late Lady Milbanke, both admirable performers on that instrument. Lady Rockingham, the Dowager Lady Carlisle and Miss Pelham, scholars of Giardini and Mingotti, used to sing: and the difficulty, or rather, impossibility of hearing these professors and illustrious dilettanti anywhere else, stimulated curiosity so much, that there was no sacrifice or mortification to which fashionable people would not submit, in order to obtain admission".

Interest in the subscription concerts at Hickford's room declined with the death of Festing and its place as a centre of musical life in London was transferred to Carlisle House in Soho Square. This was in 1760, when the Italian singer Mrs. Theresa Cornelys took over the house and opened it as an Assembly Rooms. This project was an immediate success and in the early days attracted the finest artists and the most discriminating audience. Three years after its opening J. C. Bach (youngest son of J. S. Bach) and Karl Abel, the viola da gamba virtuoso joined forces and promoted a weekly concert at Carlisle House. Although the music performed was almost entirely by Bach and Abel, it was to the taste of musical London and the series prospered. The subscribers, amongst whose names were those of Royal dukes and almost the entire peerage, enjoyed all the amenities of this splendid house. Alas, this happy state of affairs was not maintained. Mrs. Cornelys was alleged to have offered attractions other than music; hooliganism and rowdiness upset the neighbours, who eventually brought a summons charging her with keeping a common disorderly house. An enterprise which started so brilliantly ended tragically sixteen years later. Mrs. Cornelys was made bankrupt and died in a debtor's prison. Some historians are convinced that the charges against this lady were unwarranted and had in fact been laid by unscrupulous rivals.

A small coterie of English composers consisting of Samuel Arnold, Charles Dibdin and William Shield produced a considerable amount of music, but mostly in the fashionable Italian style. On the other hand Thomas Linley and William Jackson of Exeter kept themselves apart from foreign influences and followed in the tradition of the native composers of the past. Though each of these men was successful, they were definitely light-weight and none could be considered comparable with such as Handel.

Needless to say the indefatigable Dr. Arne was still on the war-path and in 1762 his opera *Artaxerxes* was produced as a direct challenge to the music then in vogue. It was an instant success and achieved many performances, not only at the time, but well into the first quarter of the nineteenth century.

On 16th May 1767 there came an announcement from Covent Garden to the effect that Miss Brickley would sing a song from Arne's *Judith* "accompanied by Mr. Dibden on a new instrument called a Piano Forte". In the following year J. C. Bach introduced it to the London public as a solo instrument. It quickly became popular and in 1773 with Clementi as composer and John Broadwood as maker, its superiority over the harpsichord was established. However, no one at that time could possibly have envisaged its immense importance in future years and today, two hundred years later, there is a boom in the making and selling of pianos.

Willis's Rooms in King Street, St. James's were originally known as Almack's Assembly Rooms. When Almack died in 1781 the premises passed to his niece Mrs. Willis who encouraged music-making of a high order. The Bach-Abel concerts were held there from 1768 to 1773 and were followed by other interesting series, particularly of vocal and chamber music. Despite the normal difficulties of concert promotion this hall was closely associated with music until well into the nineteenth century.

The Pantheon in Oxford Street, "the most beautiful edifice in England" according to Horace Walpole, was opened early in 1772 and the magnificence of this hall was a constant source of comment at the time. Obviously no expense had been spared on its design or decoration and it attracted not only the most famous performers of the day, but also the most glittering audiences which often included the king and queen. Unfortunately this delightful building suffered the fate of so many others devoted to music and the theatre.

In 1792 it was destroyed by fire.

In 1776 the Earl of Sandwich was responsible for the instigation of the Concert of Ancient Music, a society somewhat akin to the Academy of Ancient Music in that it specialised in the works of composers since deceased, particularly those of Purcell and Handel. Many noblemen united with the Earl of Sandwich in this venture, until in 1785 George II attended a performance and assured the society of success. The king was a frequent patron from that time and the institution acquired a prestige greater perhaps than any previous establishment.

The Hanover Square Rooms opened in 1775 with a concert by Bach and Abel. This hall became famous for the series of Professional Concerts held from 1783 to 1793 at which many of the works of Haydn and Mozart were first performed in Britain. Also it was associated with the impressario Johann Salomon and the series of concerts which bore his name. Haydn composed his last twelve symphonies for Salomon and personally directed them at the Hanover Square Rooms amid scenes of the utmost enthusiasm.

At the beginning of the nineteenth century, a favourite concert hall was the Argyll Rooms which attracted many famous musicians. It was the home of the Philharmonic Society, which, formed in 1813 used it regularly until its destruction by fire twenty-seven years later. The halls already mentioned became too small for their purpose and were superseded by the Exeter Hall, built in 1831 and associated so closely with the Sacred Harmonic Society, a fine choral society. In 1858 came the St. James's Hall, the outstanding London concert hall for some forty years. This may have been in some degree due to its position, situated where the Piccadilly Hotel now stands. It specialised in concerts known as 'Pops' and held every Monday and Saturday.

Another great centre of music, with the emphasis on *great* owing to the mammoth forces so often brought together, was the Crystal Palace. This amazing building of glass was originally constructed for the Great Exhibition of 1851 held in Hyde Park. Later moved to Sydenham, it drew vast audiences for concerts of widely differing types. Synonymous with the Crystal Palace was the great conductor August Manns who was largely responsible for creating the interest and was reputed to have directed over twenty thousand concerts there.

The following announcement of a ballad concert appeared in

the *Musical Journal* dated 4th May 1867 and probably referred to the programme of one of the first public concerts of its kind to be promoted.

THE CRYSTAL PALACE
Popular Balad Concert
Wednesday next
Miss Louisa Pyne, Miss Edith Wynne, Miss Julia Elton
Mr. Sims Reeves, Mr. Lewis Thomas
Solo Flute, Mr. Lewis Thomas
Conductor, Mr. Manns
Admission, One Shilling; Children, Sixpence or by season
tickets.
Reserved Seats, Half-a-crown extra, now ready.

It must have been a rather special occasion, as no mention was made in the advertisement of the other delights to be enjoyed at this popular venue. Normally there would appear such titillating extras as 'Fine Art Courts, Salmon Hatching, Monkeys and Parrots, Display of Spring Flowers, and the thousand and one attractions of the Crystal Palace'. The disastrous fire of 1936 was far more spectacular than any of the massive extravaganzas organised by the authorities and the 'Palace' was reduced to a heap of twisted metal, a sad and bizarre sight.

The Queen's Hall, built in 1893 was held in special regard by generations of music lovers and there must be many today who look back with a feeling of nostalgia to summer evenings spent at the Proms. The young people of between the Wars who stood shoulder to shoulder around the gold-fish pond, seemed somewhat quieter than their successors of the present era, but they were a knowledgeable and friendly crowd, deeply appreciative of the programmes provided. Destroyed by enemy action during the second world war, the loss of the Queen's Hall left thousands with a sense of almost personal bereavement.

EDINBURGH

As the great social centre of Scotland in the eighteenth century, Edinburgh boasted musical fare of a high order. Its first concert was given as early as 1695 in honour of St. Cecilia, the patron saint of music. It is recorded that an orchestra of thirty performed on that occasion, consisting of nineteen gentlemen of the 'first rank and fashion' while the eleven professionals were termed 'masters of music'. The orchestra was composed of seven first violins, five second violins, six flutes, two hautbois, five 'cellos and five viols-da-gamba together with a harpsichord. The music was mainly of motetti by Bassani and the sonatas of Corelli.

It was, then, members of the aristocracy in Scotland who first established concert-giving in Edinburgh. They were genuinely concerned with music of quality and they fostered and maintained interest throughout a complete century. These concerts could not be considered public by present-day standards, but they established a pattern and tradition which proved invaluable for the future. In any case it is highly unlikely if the ordinary man-in-the-street would at that time have relished such concerts.

On 29th March 1728 the Edinburgh Musical Society was founded and according to some authorities this was the oldest of its kind in the world. The first place of meeting was Steil's Tavern, Old Assembly Close and as with the London Catch Club of some years later, Lord Eglinton was a founder member. This club numbered amongst its members the Dukes of Argyll, Buccleugh and Hamilton, the Earls of Aberdeen, Breadalbane, Cassilis, Dumfries, Haddington, Kelly, Roseberry and Selkirk. The meetings were later transferred to St. Mary's Chapel, Niddry Wynd, a part of the city steeped in history. In order to ensure that these Gentlemen's Concerts were kept select, soldiers were posted at the doors as 'Centrys' to bar entry to 'low mean folk', a duty which earned them one shilling per night.

The feast of good things provided at the weekly concerts was such that the Society was inundated with requests for membership. At first the subscription was fixed at a guinea. It was subsequently increased to a guinea and a half and finally to two guineas. Every Friday 'during the time of Session a Consort of Musick was performed at 6 o'c in the afternoon in summer and at half an hour after 5 in the winter.

As might be expected, many foreign musicians settled in the city, as they still do, and orchestral and choral activity was considerable. Two of these musicians with London reputations were John Lampe, the composer and Pasquali, the eminent violinist. It was here that Pasquali wrote his celebrated treatise on figured bass which became the standard work for musicians during the remainder of the eighteenth century.

In 1729 the *Gentle Shepherd* was first performed. This was a ballad opera in the Scots dialect written by Allan Ramsay, the poet and wig-maker. Published in 1725 at Ramsay's shop 'at the sign of the Mercury opposite the head of the Niddry Wynd' it is thought to have influenced John Gay in writing the *Beggar's Opera*. Swift probably had it in mind when making the remark regarding a Newgate pastoral quoted earlier in this chapter.

Handel's music was as popular in Edinburgh as elsewhere according to a contemporary article by George Thomson. "Every year, generally, we had an oratorio of Handel performed, with the assistance of a principal bass and tenor singer, and a few chorus singers from the English Cathedrals, together with some Edinburgh amateurs who cultivated that sacred and sublime music. On such occasions the hall was always crowded to excess by a splendid assemblage, including all the beauty and fashion of our city. A supper to the directors and their friends at Fortune's Tavern generally followed the oratorio".

In June 1738 the Directors were wrestling with the problem of admitting 'too great a number of strangers'. It was decided that the Governor was 'to give tickets to and admit no more than ten strangers' to certain concerts arranged for the ladies, while each Director was 'to admit no more than three strangers to every private Concert'. Then, 'to prevent the Crowding of the Room or the admission of Low Mean folks at private Concerts', the Clerk was instructed 'to lett no person pass' without a ticket regularly signed. Was this desire to keep out mean persons accountable, one wonders, for this item in the Accounts for 1751: "By 2 Centrys attending at the Concert 25 nights at 1/– each night". Again, on 9th November 1748 Andrew Blair was bluntly told that if he admitted any person who was not a member without a ticket, he would forfeit 'such a proportion of his salary as the Directors shall think fitt'. Occasionally trickery was involved, as for example, in the case of the Master of Napier and Captain Halden, who gained entrance on 26th January 1750 by tickets which 'had been erased and alter'd in the Date', an offence which resulted in no tickets being available to either of them for the following year.

The Society was much honoured by the interest shown in its work by Handel. In December 1753 the directors wrote a letter of considerable length couched in the flowery style of the period requesting 'a copy of the Recitatives and Choruses to some of your oratorios'. This met with approval and a short reply: 'Mr. Christopher Smith at the Blue Periwig in Dean Street, Soho, has

190

Mr. Handel's orders to let the Gentlemen of the Musical Society at Edinburgh have any of his Compositions that they want, if they write to Mr. Smith he will obey their Commands'.

In 1772 we read that *Acis and Galatea* was given on 24th July, *Messiah* on 4th December and on 22nd December, 'the celebrated and truly sublime musical performance, the Oratorio of the *Messiah* was repeated. This was the music of fashionable taste and also it accorded with the wishes of the professional players and singers. But many of these musicians, although first-class artists, were extremely difficult to manage. Money troubles and unbusiness-like behaviour on their part caused the Society constant worry and frustration.

The Ladies' concerts, started as an experiment, were successful from the outset and an announcement in the *Edinburgh Evening Courant* of 16th January 1755 shows how the ladies gave their whole-hearted and practical co-operation. "We hear that on Tuesday last Signor Pasquali had a general rehearsal of the music that is to be performed at the Assembly Hall for his benefit, and as it is expected that the company will be numerous, many ladies have resolved to go without hoops as they did at the last St. Cecilia's Concert".

This mention of a benefit is deserving of a short explanation. Many of the professional players were drawn from Italy and were induced to settle in Edinburgh for varying periods. In most cases their salaries were very small, but on their engagement they were informed that their income from the Society could be greatly augmented by private teaching and possibly by a benefit concert. Pasquali seems to have been rather more successful financially than some of his contemporaries. Engaged in 1753 as 'First Fiddle' at a salary of £55 a year, he increased his income with a benefit concert, "which by his obliging behaviour turn'd out generally from Twenty to Thirty pounds and upwards. With this and what he had by Teaching he made a very handsome living, for he had as many Schoalers at a guinea and a half a month as he could attend, and a guinea of Entry".

On Pasquali's death in 1757 Martini Olivieri became his successor, on the recommendation of Lady Torphichen. In this same year the Society engaged Peralto Mazzanti, another Italian who had 'sung a whole season at the Opera and at Mr. Handel's oratorios as likewise at Ranelagh'. She was 'young, of very genteel appearance', and of 'a very Decent Life and Behaviour'. Mazzanti's contract was to sing four songs, and to attend the rehearsals of, and perform in the oratorios. 'Her concert (benefit) the Treasurer wrote to an interested party, 'depends intirely on herself in being Discreet and Obliging'.

In March 1760 Mazzanti demanded a higher salary and ten weeks leave of absence. This was refused and the Directors, in their reply were quite brutally frank. "When you was told that by teaching and a Benefit you might make a hundred a year it was likeways told you that both of these would depend upon yourself and the favour of the Publick . . . You must be sensible that you never was heartily Inclined to teaching or to gain scholars . . . You may remember your first Benefit, which was a very good one, how much the Publick was disposed to favour you, how much respect, and how many Civilitys were shown to you by everybody. Had you cultivated this Disposition on your part we are confident you might have made more than the above sume, and been in high favour with all the People of fashion in the place who alone can make a good Benefit.

"In Place of improving your voice at home and learning new songs you gave the Concert every night a repetition of the same. You brought to this place about a Doz^n songs, and since that you have acquired about half a Doz^n more, and these we got from you over and over, so that everybody knows what they are to expect, and even these are sung by you often with an unconcerned air and without any previous study by yourself . . . All this the Publick is very sensible of and must be disgusted with."

Mazzanti was dismissed in November 1761 and was replaced by a Signora Barbarini, a Venetian. It will thus be seen that the aforementioned invasion by foreign 'masters' was not confined to London. However the Society prospered to such effect that St. Mary's Chapel soon proved too small for its purpose. As a result, in 1762 the new St. Cecilia's Hall was built at the lower end of Niddry Wynd. This was a great undertaking and the committee wisely commissioned as architect the famous Sir Robert Mylne. His design was based on the Teatro Farnese, Parma and consisted of a first-floor concert room, oval in shape and roofed in glass. The seating was arranged around the hall, five rows in all, each row five inches higher than the one in front. There was a space in the centre where the members would stroll during the intervals and converse with their friends. This attractive room was gained by a handsome staircase leading from the entrance hall, into which the sedan chairs were carried, enabling the occupants to alight without having to face the elements.

The architect's fee was £10–10–0 (ten guineas) and the cost of the building was defrayed by generous subscriptions from the members. This splendid new hall meant vastly improved conditions both for the audience and performers and owing to its greater seating capacity the membership was increased by twenty to a total of one hundred and seventy. At this stage, had the committee wished, the number could have been greatly enlarged, such was the public interest.

Italian singers and instrumentalists were still in favour though in view of their behaviour one might question why. They came and went with monotonous regularity, many not fulfilling their contracts, others obtaining advances of salary and promptly drifting away. Signora Cremonini was a case in point. She was brought from Rome at considerable expense and proved a heavy drain on funds, as the following items from the Accounts for 1761 testify.

By Signor Cremonini, one year's Salary			£112-0-0
By	„	„ Travelling expenses	100-0-0
By	„	„ Her Journey Stop't by	
Sickness on the way			56-6-0
By Signora Cremonini Her allowance to buy			
clothes at Rome			25-0-0
			£293-6-0

The following year she left for London without excuse, never to return in spite of every inducement from the Directors. This lady was however prosecuted for failing to honour her contract.

Giusto Ferdinando Tenducci was perhaps the greatest and certainly the most popular singer engaged by the Society. He sang many of the lovely Scots songs with great feeling and his interpretations undoubtedly inspired the compilation of the *Melodies of Scotland*. This collection, edited by George Thomson in collaboration with Burns, had a great success in Scotland and in England and to this day has remained an outstanding anthology. In his youth Tenducci was an acquaintance of Mozart, he had sung at the Handel Festival and had toured with Dr. Arne. But extravagance was his downfall and after receiving several payments in advance, Tenducci followed the others on the path to London.

How the members of the committee must have suffered. In

spite of their help and thoughtfulness in dealing with the musicians, the majority of the latter seemed unable to reciprocate in like manner. However, Domenico Corri, appointed to succeed Tenducci, remained in Edinburgh some eighteen years, far above the average in those days and he undoubtedly influenced the musical life of the city. There followed in quick succession Thomal Pinto, Johann Christoff Schetky, Pietro Urbani, Guiseppe Puppo, ad Signora Sultani. Hieronymo Stabilini who was engaged during the Spring of 1784 was probably the last notable artist employed by the Society.

Throughout the first half of the eighteenth century the distinguished patrons of the concerts lived in the vicinity of St. Cecilia's Hall, in the tall buildings of the Canongate and the nearby closes. But by the end of the century the splendid houses of the New Town, now the area of Princes Street, George Street and the adjacent Squares and Crescents, proved an ever-increasing attraction to the aristocracy and the wealthy. Also, the Assembly Rooms in George Street had been completed and concerts – now public instead of subscription – were held there. This was the final blow for St. Cecilia's Hall, which being in a back-water, gradually declined in popularity. The last concert at this musical venue, which had drawn such names as Arne, Boswell, Burns, Hume, Johnson, Scott and Smollett during its great eighteenth century period, was given in 1798.

George Scott-Moncrieff in his interesting book *Edinburgh* published in 1947, wrote of St. Cecilia's Hall, "It remains one of the most deserving of the City's misused structures. It would take very little to convert it again into a concert hall, or even a small theatre, and it remains conveniently central". We shall see later in the chapter how this historic building was brought back to life and made, in a glorious setting, to serve music once again.

ABERDEEN

The musical life of eighteenth century Edinburgh has been fully described in many excellent publications, but it is doubtful whether quite as much is known of a similar activity in Aberdeen. This northern city has a long and honoured history reaching back to the time of the Sang Scules and its concert-giving activity closely followed on that of the Capital. Music clubs normally began in a small way and the Aberdeen Society was no exception. A group of seven keen musicians had met in one of the local taverns for some years and such was the pleasure derived from these meetings that it was decided to form a society, the number not to exceed thirty members. To this end they drew up a set of regulations for the future. It is interesting to note that whereas the Musical Society in Edinburgh was organised largely by the aristocracy, that of Aberdeen consisted, at least in its early days, of townspeople and senior members of the university. The rules for this Musical Society are so eminently sensible that I have considered it worthwhile to record them in full.

At Aberdeen, 29 Janry 1748.

The following persons, vizt. The Revd. Professor Pollock and Mr. Peter Black, Dr. John Gregory and Messrs. James Black, Andrew Tait, Francis Peacock and David Young, having agreed to erect themselves into a Musical Society to meet for their mutual Entertainment in Musick once a Week, for the better Management thereof they have come to the following resolutions.

I

That every Member shall contribute a Crown pr Annum for defraying the Expenses of Coal, Candle & other Necessities; the Overplus to be laid out on proper Musick for the Use of the Soc.

II

That liberty be given to such Gentlemen of the Town as incline it, to enter [as] Members of this Society on paying each a Crown pr. Ann[um]. Only the whole Number of these additional Members not to exceed Twentyfour.

III

That the present Members, on whom the burden of keeping up this Concert lies, shall be the sole Directors or Managers in all matters relating to the Society. That they shall choose all Members afterwards to be admitted: In which they must be unanimous, and none to be chosen against whom any of the Original Members shall object. The Person to be chosen shall first be regularly proposed by Letter or Petition, and ly on the Table Eight Days before he be admitted. That They shall annually choose their own Preses for calling them together; and shall appoint a Clerk, and Cashier to be accountable to them for Money Received and disbursed, and

195

shall give him Directions for what Musick is proper to be purchased.

IV

That, as this is still designed as a private meeting only, no Member shall have Liberty to bring in any other person, not a Member, along with him to the Concert, except the Preses only, who shall have the Privelege of bringing in two or more each Night, or of granting two tickets for Men only, and the Privelege to be used by him chiefly towards Country Gentlemen, or other strangers that happen to be in the town, or, when the Number of the Members is completed, to any of the Towns Gentlemen also.

V

That if a sufficient Number of Hands can be got to perform without such Gentlemen as don't incline to do it in any more publick way than the present, a particular Night, now and then as the Directors find convenient, shall be appointed, in which the Ladies may be present. In which case every Member is to have the Privelege of Supernumerary Tickets to be disposed of by the Consent and Advice of the Preses and Directors: but no Person that is not a Member is to have the Liberty of purchasing a Ticket upon any pretence whatsoever. The Tickets to be sealed with the Preses's Seal, and such subscribed by him or the Clerk; and the Lady's Name to be put on the Ticket, to serve only for her, & not for any other in her place. That the Ladies are only with the Concert Musick to be entertain'd and not with Dancing; which is expressly prohibited in this as in all other Musical Societies of this kind.

VI

That a plan be laid down every Night of the Musick to be perform'd at next Meeting, which is to be kept to, and no Member to propose any other Musick till at least that is finished. That the Plan be so contrived as to be divided into three Acts, in each of which some of Corelli's Musick shall be performed; each Act also, if a Voice can be had to end with a Song: and the whole so contrived as to end at Eight O'Clock at Night, and not to exceed two Hours in Continuance. That such Members or others as are Hearers only, shall take their Seats, and not mix with the Performers, in time of Musick, and strict Silence to be kept, except in the Intervals between the Acts.

That Martinmass Day be appointed for holding the Annual
Meeting for chusing Members, Preses, Clerk and Cashier,
for examining and Clearing Accots, with the former Cashier
and looking into the other affairs of the Society: betwixt wch.
time and St. Cecilia's Day all Members are to pay their
Quotas for the following year and such as neglect to pay it
within that time to forfeit their Membership for that Year,
and others to be elected in their Place.

It is assumed that during the first session in 1749 private meetings
of the Society were still held in one of the taverns which boasted
a room large enough, but the earliest public concert was given in
the Trades Hall on St. Cecilia's Day. Word went around very
quickly regarding the success of this occasion and the public
appetite was thoroughly whetted, in part possibly due to the difficulty
of obtaining tickets. Popular demand was such that eventually
the committee gave way and increased the Society's membership.
This had certain immediate effects, one being a move to larger
premises and the other a change of musical programme to suit the
taste of an entirely different clientele.

A new Concert Hall was built in Broad Street, but this soon
became too small to accommodate the ever-increasing numbers
and there were complaints of lack of comfort at the concerts. Even
more worrying were the accusations regarding the undemocratic
running of the Society, particularly the choosing of committee
members. Another source of annoyance amongst a certain section
was the lack of Scottish music in the programmes. This has ever
been a bone of contention and periodically flares up even in the
present-day Edinburgh Festival. One cannot help feeling a genuine
sympathy with this point of view, as much of the native music has
a simplicity and a haunting beauty that is most moving.

By the year 1754 we note a subtle change in the membership.
with the inclusion of such famous names as the Earl of Kintore,
the Earl of Aboyne, Lord Adam Gordon, the Right Honourable
the Lord Boyd and the Honourable the Master of Braco. Five years
later the Earl of Aberdeen, the Earl of Errol, the Earl of Buchan,
Lord Macduff, Sir Alexander Gordon of Lismore, Sir Thomas
Burnett of Leys and Lord Strichen of Strichen joined the ranks,
thus bringing the Society more in line, aristocratically speaking,
with that of Edinburgh. However, King's and Marischal Colleges

still provided a great many interested and valued members.

Two features of special interest were the concerts given in aid of charity, in which the Infirmary was a particular beneficiary and the Mourning Concerts in memory of outstanding stalwarts of the Society, when music of a suitable nature was performed. In 1772 further alterations and improvements were made to the Concert Hall. The Society was now at the height of its popularity, not only musically but socially, and all the quality of Aberdeen and district wished to see and be seen at the concerts.

Various professional musicians were engaged from time to time, usually for short periods and one's mind boggles at the salaries offered and accepted during the eighteenth century. Mr. Roche of London became Leader of the Concerts in 1758. He would appear to have been unusually talented as he was prepared to teach 'the Fiddle, the German Flute, Hautboy, Bassoon, Violoncello, French Horn etc'. He also taught singing and the Guitar. But like so many of his foreign contemporaries he did not last long. Temperament may have been responsible; certainly he was at variance with the other musicians and he was not re-engaged in 1759. There followed as Leader Thomas Pinto previously noted as one of the Edinburgh performers. During this period there was considerable movement of players between the two cities. In 1761 a Mr. Putti was appointed at a salary of £15 for the season, with the addition of a Benefit. He remained for just one year but in 1771 he made his bow in Edinburgh as Leader of the orchestra. Next we read of Martini Olivieri, nominated Leader in 1765. He had held a similar position in Edinburgh since 1757 and his Aberdeen contract was worth £50 for the year, much more than usual. In contrast Andrew Lunan received a mere £5 per annum and remained on that scale for many years.

The programmes consisted mostly of music by eighteenth century composers, many of whom are almost unknown today. Usually one only hears their music now in specialized recitals devoted to the period. However, a few names are familiar to twentieth century listeners, as for example Arne, Corelli, Gluck, Handel, Rameau and Scarlatti. Others whose music appeared regularly were Arison, the Newcastle composer, famous during his day as a leader of the anti-Handel movement, Barsanti, Gemimiani, Masse, Stanley, the blind organist, Lampe, San Martini, Brebner, the composer of Scottish music, Festing, Marcello and Pasquali. Of the remainder, a name or two may mean something to the connoisseur, but certainly not to the average music-lover. It might perhaps seem strange that Purcell and Bach appear so infrequently in the lists of Aberdeen Concerts.

During April 1785 the old established title of Preses lapsed in favour of Governor and the Clerk and Cashier was now known as Treasurer. The subscription was raised in an effort to cope with rising costs, but it was becoming increasingly clear that the great days of the Society were on the wane. What had in its palmy days been such a brilliant social success now began to lack support. Perhaps other attractions had appeared or maybe it was just another example of a fickle public. In spite of herculean efforts on the part of the committee the writing was quite obviously on the wall and the concert budget could no longer be balanced. The last concert was given on 23 December although attempts were made to continue into the following year. But at a meeting of Directors called for 20 May 1801 to decide on future policy, only two put in an appearance.

The world of music has ever been one of fluctuation. One organisation having enjoyed fame for a while, suddenly finds its popularity in decline and its place in public esteem taken by another. This is fairly common experience and the example of Aberdeen must mirror the situation elsewhere.

In 1847 an instrumental group, the Euterpean Society was formed, only to close down after a year of so, when the majority of its members merged with the newly-founded Haydn Society. This latter gave much pleasure and drew large audiences by reason of its excellent concerts. The formation of the Harmonic Choir took place in 1849 with William Carnie as its conductor, to be followed three years later by the Aberdeen Musical Association. This Association lasted some thirty-three years and was responsible for bringing into being an orchestral group known as the Philharmonic Society. In the meantime the Choral Society, a choir of working men had began operations. The type of music performed was in no sense competitive with the Musical Association, consisting rather of a heartier type with glees and part-songs forming much of its fare.

Yet another choral group, one destined for a great future was commenced in 1858. This was the Choral Union, whose strict rules regarding attendance at rehearsal paid handsome dividends and its two hundred and thirty eight members set a high standard of performance. An orchestra was formed to accompany this choir and the initial concert was given in the presence of the Prince Consort at the formal opening of the Music Hall on 14 September 1859.

Music in the city has continued to flourish up to the present time with a Choral Society and an admirable Chamber Music Club for which there is inevitably a waiting list. Much else is deserving of congratulation, including an Organists' Association of one hundred and ten members and a particularly lively university department supporting a full symphony orchestra. This northern city has a long and glorious tradition in music, a fact sometimes lost sight of in more southerly areas.

OXFORD

Probably the oldest building of its kind in Europe, designed exclusively for the performance and study of music apart from opera, was the Music Room, Oxford, opened in 1748. I have taken certain excerpts from Anthony Wood's *Antient and Present State of the City of Oxford* published in 1773 to show something of the various aspects of this historic undertaking, though unfortunately some of the earliest details concerning concert programmes are not available.

"In this Street (Holiwell) stands an elegant Stone Edifice, appropriated to Music, and therefore called the Music Room. Its Dimensions are 65 by 32 and 30 feet high. The North End, being a Segment of a Circle, is occupied by the Performers. The Orchestra rises gradually from the Front, where the Singers stand, partly screened by a Balustrade. On the uppermost Stage, in the Center, stands an excellent Organ built by the late Mr. John Byfield.

"Here are weekly Performances of Vocal and Instrumental Music, every Monday evening, except in Passion-Week, all the Month of September, and the Quarterly Choral Performances; which are usually Oratorios; and these with very little foreign Assistance. Benefit Concerts are also here for such Performers to whom they were allowed.

"The Building was begun upon the Strength of a Subscription, set on Foot about the Beginning of 1742, which soon accumulated to the amount of 490L. 4s. 6d of which 100L was laid out in the Purchase of the Ground whereupon it stands. Afterwards 120L were raised by two Oratorios

performed in Christ-Church Hall; this served only to pay off
some of the Arrears due, and not sufficient to encourage a
Prosecution of this Undertaking; so that for some Years
the Building stood a mere useless Shell. But the instituting
of a separate Society, for a monthly Performance of Choral
Music at the *King's Head* gained new Credit, and induced both
the Workmen and the Managers to proceed with Cheerfulness;
for such was the Success of this Scheme that by the Opening
of the Room in July 1748 the Fund was increased to 176L 13s. 3d
to which the Profits of the Oratorios performed at that time
added 106L 1s.5d".

It would seem almost certain that Handel's *Esther* was the first
work to be performed in the Music Room. There is in existence
a book of words, entitled 'Esther, an Oratorio Set to Music by Mr.
Handel. As performed at the Opening of the New Music Room in
Holywell, Oxford".

An order dated 16 June 1757 repealed all former rules and orders,
but there being no fewer than forty-one clauses, it is here considered more practical to give a precis of the constitution with
an occasional paragraph of special interest.

It was unanimously agreed that there should be twenty members
on the committee, one to be chosen from each college. The member
was required to be a Fellow, Scholar, Exhibitioner, or Chaplain,
a Vice-Principal or one in some public office in the University.

There was to be a concert, either choral or instrumental every
Monday during the year, the only exception being the Monday in
Passion Week. The music for the instrumental concert was the
responsibility of the steward, but the full committee had to agree
on the programme for the choral concert. Clause XVI read: "It
/the concert/ shall begin precisely at Seven o'Clock by which time
all Gentlemen Performers are desired to attend, but if any of those
Performers who receive Pay, shall be negligent in observing that
Time, they shall be punished at the Discretion of the Steward, by
a Mulet not exceeding ONE SHILLING for each offence".

This is interesting as lady performers were frequently engaged.
Were they more conscientious in arriving on time and if not, were
they punished? A nice point. Perhaps the gentlemen of the committee could not bring themselves to lay down hard and fast
rules for the fair sex.

Every member of the elected body was required to do duty as
Steward, the period being not longer than one month, unless for

201

some exceptional reason. There were strict and businesslike rules for the change-over of stewards each month:

> "he shall deliver up all his Books, Accounts, Bills, Receipts, Money, Keys and etc. to his Successor, who shall give a Receipt for the same in the Stewards Book, to be witnessed by all the members present".

The stewards were wise in human behaviour; no doubt from time to time they had experienced a certain artistic temperament amongst some of their musicians:

> "All performers who receive pay from the society, shall attend at all concerts in their own Persons, and when absent, shall forfeit their pay for that evening. And if they are negligent in their attendance, or continue absent for two evenings successively, without giving notice to the Steward, they shall, upon Complaint against them at an ordinary meeting, be discharged from all future service of the Society."

Then, just to make certain there could be no misunderstanding the last clause, No. XLI read, "An Extract of these of those Orders that relate to the Performers who receive Pay, and to the Servants of the Society, shall be fairly transcribed, and hung up in the Steward's Room, that none may plead Ignorance thereof".

The earliest information regarding a complete series of concerts is for the year 1763 when the subscription was one guinea. There was a weekly concert every Monday at 6.30 p.m. with the exception of August and September, consisting of vocal and instrumental music. In addition an oratorio was given every term. Those advertised for the session were *Judas Maccabaeus* on 9th May 1763, *Hymn of Adam and Eve, Daphne and Amaryllis* and 'music by Pergolesi, Jomelli, Galuppi, Handel and other celebrated Masters' on 13th June 1763, *Belshazzar*, 7th November 1763 and *Messiah* on 19th March 1764.

However, in the fifteen years prior to this date there had been a veritable glut of oratorio, some fifty-eight performances in all, but it must be stated that this number consisted largely of repeats. For instance *Acis and Galatea* was given fifteen times, *L'Allegro* thirteen, *Alexander's Feast* thirteen, with fifteen performances of *Messiah*. It will surprise no one with a knowledge of music in eighteenth century Britain that all these works were by Handel.

The choir would be considered less than adequate by today's standards. In many of the oratorios during the early 1770s the amateur members sang the choruses in unison, while the professional soloists sang the same choruses in harmony. By 1777 this was not deemed good enough and an advertisement of a performance of *Messiah* on 15th March of that year stated, "the Choruses are intended to be particularly full".

Returning to 1772 this was a year notable for the first appearance of the clarinet in collaboration with the orchestra. The instrument had recently been introduced into the orchestras of Europe and then only sparingly. This is an example of the forward-looking policy adopted by the society. Then again, in 1774 in the programme for 21st February we read of a 'Symphony with Clarionets' by Gossec. The symphony as a classical work in four movements was a very modern composition at that time. Perhaps the best method of ascertaining the achievements of the Music Room stewards, who in England produced results akin to the princely courts on the continent, is to glance at one or two of the old programmes.

A benefit concert for Mr. Mahon (Clarionet) 11 November 1773:

Act I

Overture	– Occasional	– Handel
Song	Mr. Norris 'Padre Sposa	– Piccini
Quartetto	6th Op. 7	– Haydn
Song	Miss Reynolds	– Sacchini
Organ Concerto		– Dr. Hayes

Act II

Song	– Miss Reynolds. Accompanied by Clarionets 'Not unto us'	– Arne
Sonata	– Harpsichord, by a young lady, who never appeared in public	
Trio	– Voices 'The Flocks shall leave the Mountains'	– Handel
Concerto	– Clarionet Mr. Mahon	

Another programme, this time of an ordinary concert as distinct from a benefit.

MUSICK ROOM   6 December 1773
Act I

Overture		
Song	– Mr Matthews 'Soon shall that state'	– Piccini
Trio		– Scwindl

203

| Song | Mr. Norris | 'Loverin her Eyes sits playing' | – Handel |
| Symphony, 6th | | | – Ricciotti |

Act II

Overture	–	'Saul' with the Dead March	– Handel
Song	–	Mr. Norris 'Pallido il Sole'	– Hasse
Concert, 12th			
Duet	–	Messrs Norris and Matthews 'When Myra Sings'	– Purcell
Symphony			– Richter

This programme contained an item by Purcell, whose music later became so popular with the society.

In 1776 there appears to have been an important change in programme planning. It was proposed that in future *Messiah* should be performed as usual in the Lent Term, with another oratorio in Act Term. But in Easter and Michaelmass Terms a 'Grand Miscellaneous Concert' should take the place of the traditional oratorio. This was a major policy upheaval. Furthermore it was agreed that 'one capital Vocal Performer and one capital Instrumental Performer' should be engaged.

Owing to the comparative nearness of London it was possible to obtain the finest artists. Amongst the singers who graced the Music Room were Miss Barsanti, Miss Linley (who married Sheridan), Mrs. Barthelemon and Signora Davies. The instrumental soloists included Pinto, Hellendaal, Cramer and Salomon, all famous violinists; Crosdill, the outstanding 'cellist of his day and teacher of George IV; Fischer, the world famous oboe virtuoso, Florio, the flautist, Miller, the bassoonist and Edward Jones, the harpist. Tenducci, the outstanding male soprano mentioned earlier, was also engaged on several occasions. But perhaps where the committee excelled was in discovering new young musicians of great promise who had not yet attained international fame. In this way they were enabled to present fine artists crying out for recognition and at a fee within the budget of the society. Signora Pozzi was given her first engagement at the age of nineteen, Crosdill at eighteen and Miss Linley was only sixteen on her first performance. Signora Sestini's gifts were recognised in Oxford before she became famous in London and it is possible that her appearance in the university city helped her future considerably. Salomon and

Cramer had been in England a very short time when invited to perform at the Music Room. All this shows a keen devotion to duty and business on the part of the stewards.

In addition to the special concerts under review there were the ordinary bread and butter Monday concerts to be maintained and these probably proved more difficult in many respects. A small but admirable resident orchestra played for all the musical occasioons, but as with other societies, members of the orchestra had to depend on teaching to augment their income. The following advertisement in the *Oxford Journal* of 24 February 1781 was typical of the period. 'Hardy, a Pupil of Mr. Pinto and other Masters, having been engaged by the Gentlemen of the Musical Society as a Resident Violin Player in their Band, humbly acquaints the Gentlemen of the University that he teaches on that instrument'.

Strangely enough, the earliest details regarding the composition of the band was furnished by Philippe Jung in his French *Guide d'Oxford* published in 1789. Jung, himself a member of the band, stated that the instrumentation consisted of six violins, two violas, one 'cello, one double bass, two oboes, two bassoons, two horns (one of whom doubled on the flute) and two singers. Norris, 'the finest tenor-singer in the kingdom' was one and the other was Matthews. They must have been excellent artists as both sang as soloists at the Handel Festival in Westminster Abbey in 1784.

The orchestra, though small compared with those of today, was probably very similar to most of those in existence during the eighteenth century. It was directed by the Professor of Music in office at the time.

Over the years the Society built up a splendid library of music, both instrumental and vocal. In its innocence, it generously loaned copies to performers and others interested and unfortunately paid the penalty – music unreturned. This led to much inconvenience and constant appeals to borrowers, even through the local press.

The first signs of serious trouble occurred in 1789 when the weekly concerts were discontinued, after a period of almost forty-one years. As in other societies under review in this chapter, finance was once again a determining factor. But there would appear to have been other causes. A section of the audience, known in modern parlance as 'a minority' had behaved badly and disorderly conduct had been in evidece at the concerts. As a result many people stayed away and subscriptions no longer kept pace with expenses. But the stewards were courageous men and in 1792 a private concert was organised for 26 January. A report on this undertaking contained the following statement: "Last Thursday Evening the Music Room here was opened under the new Subscription, when the Company was select and highly respectable".

The following year subscriptions slumped again and the concerts had once more to be abandoned. Various experiments were tried with varying degrees of success but suffice to say that at the beginning of the nineteenth century the Music Society was still in operation.

As might be expected there were changes in taste at the turn of the century and these were mirrored in the programmes. Although *Messiah* and *Acis and Galatea* received fairly regular performances, the symphonies of Haydn had become firm favourites. Mozart's music was slower in gaining recognition and of Bach there is still no mention. Also Beethoven received scant attention. Some authorities have suggested that the Napoleonic war was responsible for this lack of familiarity with the great European composers mentioned. This may well be true, but also the music of Beethoven would probably have required larger instrumental forces than were available at the Music Room at the time. In any case, when peace came it was Cherubini's Overture to *Anacreon* and the Rossini Overture to the *Barber of Seville* which became firm favourites.

But there was no lack of performance of the music of earlier and established composers. Purcell featured frequently in the programmes with works such as *Macbeth* and *The Tempest* and his many individual songs. Arne also retained his popularity, as did many of the best composers of glees. And at last, in February 1815 there appeared a 'Symphony' by Sebastian Bach.

Of local composers the music of Dr. William Crotch was most often performed. His was an amazing career. A child prodigy, he was giving organ recitals in London at the age of four and frequently appeared at the Music Room as a very young soloist. When only fifteen he was appointed organist at Christ Church, Oxford and seven years later he became Professor of Music.

Regular concerts in the Music Room were discontinued during the greater part of 1820 due to the Society being in debt. Great efforts were made and as a result the amount was paid off and concerts were restarted in the following year. During the suspension of concerts, the stewards did their utmost to keep the orchestra together by arranging benefits for the members, but this was only a temporary measure. From 1821 onwards there was a constant fight to maintain interest and solvency.

The pattern of concert-giving changed. There was now a demand for larger forces, both orchestral and choral and the Music Room was no longer in a position to cope. As a result, the much larger Town Hall and the Sheldonian Theatre were increasingly brought into use. The tendency was for famous instrumentalists as well as singers to be brought from London and gradually the resident orchestra drifted apart. The programmes were liberally bespattered with big names, one being the famous singer Madame Cataloni, who gave her final performance in Oxford in 1824.

Clara Novello sang during 1833, and this and the following year were notable for the music of Rossini, Weber and Auber when the overtures to *La Gazza Ladra, Tancredi, Wilhelm Tell, Freischulz, Oberon* and *Masaniello* were all performed. In addition, Mozart's *Jupiter Symphony*, Gluck's Overture to *Iphigenia* and Beethoven's *Egmont* all received an airing in the subsequent year or two.

There was no concert in 1838 and the last despairing attempt at the Music Room took place in 1839, after which the building passed into other hands. First it became an auction room and was let to various organisations for exhibitions, some far removed from its former purpose and eventually it was made into a museum. There is, however, a happy ending to this account of a unique piece of Oxford history.

In 1901 the University Musical Union took over the building and transformed it into the handsome room of today, where music is in a flourishing state. Its size precludes concerts employing large forces, but it is ideal as a venue for chamber music. The festival of 1951 included a course of lectures on the Arts of seventeenth century England illustrated by a series of chamber concerts. Acoustically perfect for this type of music, the Music Room attracts the best of professional chamber music ensembles, as well as affording good facilities for the various undergraduate organisations. These latter contrive to produce music of many periods, Twentieth Century, Baroque, Elizabethan and even earlier.

The Music Room contains a number of small rooms each with a piano which may be used for practising and in fact the main hall is much in demand as a rehearsal centre. Even the large University Symphony Orchestra and the various choirs use it for this purpose, but their concerts are given in more spacious premises such as the Town Hall and the Sheldonian Theatre.

As an indication of the interesting musical fare to be heard in Oxford, it was recently announced that the University Opera Club had received a grant form the Prime Minister's charity trust to produce an authentic seventeenth century opera. This work, Cavalli's *Rosindo* was heard again after three hundred and twenty years of neglect. The strings of the orchestra were required to play with baroque bows and the continuo section included harpsichords, an organ, several lutes and a chitarone (large lute). The singers were trained in the art of baroque ornamentation in order to improvise in performance as did their seventeenth century predecessors.

FESTIVALS

In the meantime the performance of oratorio had swept Britain. There was enormous enthusiasm for this form of music by a people essentially God fearing and devoted to choral singing. The oratorio as now understood consists of a work based on a religious text and performed by a choir, orchestra and soloists without the use of scenery or acting. Where an orchestra could not be engaged, either for reasons of finance or accommodation the organ proved an excellent substitute.

This intense interest in oratorio was reflected throughout the land in cities and towns, large and small. Committees were set up, choirs organised and conductors enlisted. Often more than one work was prepared and two or three days earmarked for the performances. Thus the great era of choral festivals was ushered in, sometimes in the most unlikely places. Usually given in a church or concert hall, the oratorio owed its initial success to Handel, whose many great works in this idiom caught the imagination of the British public. Other composers, some of native stock were inspired, or at least encouraged to write in somewhat similar vein, though truth to tell many did not make the grade.

Some sixty-four miles north-west of Oxford, in the then slightly less rarified atmosphere of Birmingham, was created in 1768 a very significant music festival destined to become the centre of oratorio. In the early years the chorus numbered forty, with an orchestra of twenty five members, and this body of musicians under the guidance of Capel Bond devoted itself entirely to the works of Handel. Many of the performances were given in the present cathedral, then known as St. Philip's Church; but with the completion of the Town Hall in 1834, a new era was entered upon.

In that year the Birmingham Festival gave the first performance of *David*, a work by the currently popular Austrian composer Sigsmund von Neukomm.

In 1837 Mendelssohn accepted an invitation to conduct his *St. Paul* and three years later he returned to direct the *Hymn of Praise*. The 1846 Festival was marked by the same composer conducting the first performance of his *Elijah*. This was followed by a long list of first performances by composers well-known at the time such as Costa, Sterndale Bennett, Benedict, Sullivan, Gounod, Parry, Stanford and Elgar. Few of the works written for those occasions are heard today and indeed some of the composers are almost forgotten. But Elgar is certainly not forgotten. One of his out-standing works *The Dream of Gerontius* received its initial performance at Birmingham in 1900, though according to reports a very poor one. It is still, however, a great favourite with choral societies and the public. His two succeeding oratorios which constituted the trilogy, *The Apostles* and *The Kingdom*, first heard in 1903 and 1906 respectively, are now less often produced.

The famous Hans Richter was appointed conductor in 1885 and the choral body was quickly put on its mettle, as during that year the programme included Gounod's *Mors et Vita,* Stanford's *Three Holy Children,* Dvorak's *Spectre's Bride* and Cowen's *Sleeping Beauty.*

The great industrial centres of the north had no intention of being left behind and the year following the commencement of the Birmingham Festival saw the emergence of the Sheffield Festival, produced at irregular intervals until 1896. In that year it was decided to hold the festival on a triennial basis with the Sheffield Festival Chorus entrusted with the choral parts. This choir and indeed the festival as a whole was bound up inextricably with Henry Coward, a very remarkable man. Born at Liverpool in 1849 the young Coward moved to Sheffield where he trained to become a cutler. His thirst for education impelled him to pick up knowledge wherever possible and at the age of twenty-two he became a school teacher. His interest in music led to his founding the Tonic Sol Fa Association in Sheffield. There can be no doubt that this comparatively painless method of sight-singing assisted immeasurably those blessed with fine natural voices and brought to many the very real thrill of singing together in a large choir.

He much enjoyed working with childrens' choirs and on the occasion of Queen Victoria's visit to the city in 1897, we are told that he conducted a choir of fifty thousand children and two thousand teachers in her honour. Coward's success as a choral trainer led to his acting in that capacity with the Sheffield Choir until 1908. His great work in the city was recognised with a knight-hood in 1926.

As with other British festivals of the late nineteenth century, Sheffield produced a mixture of outstanding and mediocre music. At the inaugural triennial event no fewer than four large scale works were performed, Mendelssohn's *Elijah*, the *Golden Legend* by Sullivan, *Job* by Parry and Berlioz's *Damnation of Faust*. Dvorak promised a choral composition for 1899, but it was not finished in time. However, the society was able to put on new works in 1905, *Two Choruses* by Weingartner and in 1908 Coleridge-Taylor's *Meg Blake*. This 1908 festival must have been a memorable one as it also included the first British performance of *Sea Drift* by Delius and Debussy's *L'Enfant Prodigue*. From 1903 to 1913 Sir Henry Wood was the regular conductor, but the festival lapsed from 1914 until 1933. It was revived in 1936 with the London Philharmonic Orchestra (founded by Beecham) in attendance and Wood as conductor. Owing to changes in the personnel of the orchestra, including the departure of the leader Paul Beard to the BBC Symphony Orchestra, a bitter controversy broke out between the two conductors mentioned. This was most unfortunate and for a time the festival was placed in jeopardy. Whether this unhappy episode had any bearing or not, the Sheffield Festival ceased as from that year.

The year 1858 saw the beginning of the Leeds Festival which from 1874 onwards was held triennially as other cities were now doing. There was probably sound sense in this move – a festival of oratorio every year tended to lose its impact, whereas one every three years had a revitalising effect on the local community. The Leeds committee commissioned new works and although most of these have rare outings today, the 1931 festival produced something very special. This was Walton's *Belshazzar's Feast*, an exciting work of great power, which rightly receives frequent attention from large choral bodies throughout the country at the present time.

THE THREE CHOIRS FESTIVAL

One of the earliest of British festivals was that centred on the three cathedral cities of Gloucester, Hereford and Worcester.

Beginning in its original form in 1715, it was based on the even earlier festival devoted to the Sons of the Clergy, held in St. Paul's Cathedral.

The Three Choirs Festival was an annual event, each city taking its turn as host, a tradition which has remained until today. This festival has thus continued for a longer period than any other in Britain. The choral resources of the three cities, with the cathedral choirs taking an important part, are brought together every year for a feast of music lasting several days.

There has evolved a tradition that the cathedral organist of the host city should act as conductor and this custom has worked well. The respective choirs could be depended upon to produce good results, but on occasions the amateur orchestral playing was less successful. This led, some years ago to a change of policy and to the engaging of one of the great professional orchestras for the duration of the festival. As a result audiences were able to hear the greatest orchestral works superbly played.

Musical programmes are not confined entirely to church music although the natural tendency is to encourage music of a type suitable for performance in a cathedral. Over the years the organisers have been forward-looking and the list of works specially commissioned is considerable. But despite these good intentions the majority of pieces heard in the past are rarely performed today. This is particularly the case with nineteenth century compositions and is in keeping with the experience of other festivals during that same period. Glancing at some of the programmes one notices works by Sullivan, Stainer, Lee Williams, Bridges, Parker, Cowen and others, few of which have maintained any interest for present-day musicians.

But the festival does not depend on the compositions of contemporaries of any specific period. A programme of music is provided each year in which the finest choral and instrumental classics are performed. Elgar was very interested in the 'Three Choirs' and frequently conducted his own compositions, one of the most popular being *The Dream of Gerontius*. Vaughan Williams also added his particular genius to this festival. Both men were born in the west country and they undoubtedly enjoyed composing for and taking part in this unique gathering.

An unusual feature was introduced at Worcester in 1938. Every morning, before the daily programme began, the trumpet and trombone players of the London Symphony Orchestra mounted the many steps to the top of the Cathedral tower and from there performed Bach chorales. These impromptu recitals caused much interest down below and people on their way to work gathered in the streets to listen. Sir Ivor Atkins, then organist of the cathedral was responsible for the idea of this 'Tower Music'.

POST WAR FESTIVALS

Following the drab years of World War II there was an understandable desire to bring music and art back into circulation once again. One manifestation of this movement has been the proliferation of festivals throughout the land during the past thirty years. Many cater for a wide range of interests and normally include music, drama, ballet, together with a goodly sprinkling of exhibitions. Those festivals that have become established, particularly the larger ones, are administered by professional directors aided by first-class staffs at all levels and are invariably well-organised.

THE EDINBURGH INTERNATIONAL FESTIVAL

Commenced in 1947 under the expert guidance of Rudolph Bing, this festival has become an annual event of the utmost importance in music, art and drama and has developed into one of the greatest in the world. Naturally with such a huge undertaking controversy has raged from time to time, usually on the grounds of finance, although other less business-like features have caused the raising of eyebrows on occasions. It has variously been suggested that the majority of Edinburgh residents left the city for the duration of the festival, or conversely, that the people of Edinburgh became so satiated with culture for three weeks of the year that they could not stay the course for the other forty-nine. Neither criticism appears valid today.

The Festival has always followed the maxim that only the best is good enough and only rarely has it failed to live up to this ideal. The finest orchestras, opera companies and soloists are engaged and it is a fascinating experience to hear artists from many different countries in the space of a few days. Nor has the Festival

Committee neglected local talent as the excellent choirs which perform regularly with famous orchestras and conductors amply testify.

Anyone fortunate enough to have attended concerts annually at this festival will have cause to remember especially great moments which will never be erased from the memory. Different people will have their various highlights but a personal never-to-be-forgotten experience was the singing of Kathleen Ferrier in Mahler's *Das Lied von der Erde*. It was a truly wonderful performance and the entire audience on that occasion was moved to a standing ovation, with scenes of enthusiasm rarely witnessed in the concert hall.

There is also a strong tradition of drama and some memorable acting has been seen at the Assembly Hall, where the play-goers sit on three sides of an open stage. Some years ago the performance of ballet was successful, but more recently this branch of art has fared less well, probably due to the only theatre with a suitable stage being given over to Bingo. Exhibitions of paintings and other works of art are arranged, some on a spectacular scale. One remembers with considerable awe the magnificent collection of the works of Epstein some years ago.

An interesting feature of this festival is known as The Fringe. From the early days numerous amateur dramatic societies, many from universities, have descended on the city and taken over every possible hall. At first this was a rather happy-go-lucky adventure on the part of the organisers and a certain coolness developed between Fringe and the Festival proper. Things are now better organised and a Fringe office is in being to advise the various groups and to act as a centre for their activities. The Fringe has gained in respectability and the official Festival brochure mentions its existence. Things have come a long way since the early festivals. In addition the Edinburgh Film Festival is held simultaneously, so the visitor in search of entertainment can be fully occupied every day.

With all these multifarious activities taking place at one time, it is not surprising that vast numbers of people from all over the world congregate in the city during the three weeks of late August and early September. But Edinburgh is able to cope. It is indeed a favoured city in many respects. Its history, its architecture, its gardens and its shops appeal to those of widely varying tastes. Its communications system is good, whether by air, rail or road. It boasts excellent hotels, several of recent date and can offer a range of accommodation to suit most pockets. Its concert halls are splendid, but its theatres sometimes provoke discussion, largely on the grounds of inadequacy. A very large hole dug some years ago in Castle Terrace still remains a very large hole. It is the site for a new multi-purpose theatre/opera house and one occasionally wonders if and when the proposed new building will materialise.

The historic Assembly Rooms and Music Hall in George Street fills a very special need as a Festival Club and caters for thousands of visitors. This busy centre deserves special mention for its magnificent display of flowers. All in all, this great Festival upholds the finest traditions of music and all the kindred arts and is a pattern for others to follow.

ALDEBURGH

A festival of quite a different nature was brought into being in 1948. This was the Aldeburgh Festival of Music and the Arts, the brain-child of Benjamin Britten, who had close associations with this attractive coastal town for many years. The atmosphere here is more personal, as one might expect in a smaller community. But over the years the Festival has spread across the neighbouring countryside and several fine East Anglian churches have been brought into use for concerts and recitals.

The Maltings at Snape, now an integral part of the festival, were first introduced in 1967 when the Malt House was converted into a first-class concert hall/opera house. This was an important step forward, as hitherto no hall of sufficient size had been available. The conversion was made possible by the generosity of many musical people and the opening ceremony was carried out by the Queen. As often happens, a building erected for some totally different purpose produces excellent acoustics. Whereas despite the marvels of science a modern hall requiring clarity of sound has difficulty in providing it; acoustically the Malt House was so perfect that recordings became a regular feature.

But as experienced so often in the public halls of previous centuries, fire destroyed the Malt House on the opening night of the 1969 season. Thanks to the determined spirit of all concerned the hall was rebuilt and ready for use in the following year. It was re-opened on 5th June 1970 with the Queen again present for a programme of Music for a Royal Occasion. Aldeburgh has gained a special place in the hearts of music-lovers, largely on account of the superb quality of the artists engaged, the care taken in programme building and the presence of its founder.

Some festivals have a distinctive character, as for instance, Haslemere, which celebrated its fiftieth anniversary in 1974. This is very much a family affair, owing its inception to Arnold Dolmetsch and now continued by his son Carl. The festival is devoted in the main to music of a bygone age faithfully reproduced by instruments associated with the period. There is a considerable interest in this type of chamber music and many of those who attend are themselves keen amateur players of no mean talent.

Canterbury has its festival week of Cathedral music and with its unique history stretching back into the mists of time, no finer setting could be imagined for its purpose.

The Cheltenham Festival originated as a centre for the performance of contemporary music and as such gained an enviable reputation. The committee commissioned works from a variety of composers, some of whom are well-known, with others on the threshold of future greatness. But recently there has been a change of direction towards more traditional fare, owing to the number of new works commissioned by other organisations, and also due to the old enemy 'finance', that bugbear of festival organisers, which has necessitated some pruning of the programme.

The city of Bath with its magnificent Roman remains, its famed Georgian architecture and its setting amongst the North Somerset hills, is another home of festival. As a place of fashion during the eighteenth century era of the dictatorial Beau Nash, it would seem an ideal choice for a cultural revival. Despite the many fine things produced during recent years and the number of eminent men associated with it, one sometimes wonders if the festival has fulfilled its potential. However, with its Theatre Royal now completely refurbished, a future of considerable interest may be expected.

York, with its age-old history of medieval guilds and their associated mystery plays is a city where the festival spirit might well flourish. It has everything to delight the discerning visitor in search of musical and artistic pursuits. The incomparable Minster, now being restored to health, ancient and modern halls suitable for concerts of great music, fine museums and galleries in addition to venerable narrow streets of enchanting shops, all add up to a city ready-made for a festival, and one hopes the far-seeing efforts of its promotors may be crowned with success.

It would be a monumental task to even mention all the festivals being held in Britain during the year and in a book of this nature there must unfortunately be many ommisions. But reference to two events of a more intimate nature might not be out of place. The lovely Cotswold village of Guiting Power has proved an attractive venue, which though necessarily smaller in scope is no less ambitious in the quality of its offerings.

Another small festival was that planned by Julian Bream, the famous guitarist, at Semley on the border of Dorset and Wiltshire. Mr. Bream invited a few of his musical friends to take part and they as well as the audience thoroughly enjoyed the experience. There are also many villages which in a modest way advertise festivals of music and flowers. Usually held in the local church with an enthusiastic organist and a keen group of villagers these are delightful occasions bringing pleasure to thousands living in rural communities.

MUSIC IN WALES

Wales has always been known as the Land of Song. Many people outside as well as those in the Principality believe this to be true. Certainly wherever Welsh people foregather there will be singing, with voices of an unmistakably rich quality. Even on the most informal occasions, groups of people will break quite naturally into four-part harmony, characterised by an intensity which bears some resemblance to Russian singing. To hear a vast crowd of Welshmen really letting themselves go – as at an International rugby match, may be uplifting or frightening, depending on one's nationality. There are those, who while granting the natural ability mentioned are less certain of the standard of musical taste. I remember talking with an eminent musician some years ago who scornfully remarked that he had yet to meet a musical Welshman, a remark I considered far too sweeping and patently absurd. But there have been, from time to time murmurs from within Wales itself doubting if all was well.

A passage from Dr. J. Sutcliffe Smith's excellent book *Impressions of Music in Wales* paints a vivid picture of a personal experience, while at the same time wondering if there was room for improvement.

"Arrived at Llanrwst I found the streets crowded with people who were to be seen wending their way in one direction namely towards the Zion Calvinistic Chapel. This set me wondering and asking myself as to whether anything like a gathering of this kind could be found in England – or in Europe for that matter – on a Saturday afternoon.

"And how these people sang! The bright tone of the women and children – most of whom occupied the body of the chapel. As to the men, ranged in force along the galleries, they gave out such a power of tone which I think never to have heard equalled in any place of worship.

"And what of music itself – the hymns, chants and anthems – which held principal place in the book of selections? Well, here I must confess myself to have been disappointed. These singers with their fine voices appeared capable of interpreting compositions of larger calibre. Their hymns, good in their way, and often effective, seemed hardly sufficient for these voices and so much native talent. I can imagine with what effect the anthems of Gibbons, Attwood and Wesley could have been voiced by these Welsh singers".

THE NATIONAL EISTEDDFOD

The earliest British festival is certainly that associated with Wales. The National Eisteddfod, a meeting of the bards, dates back to ancient times. It is a little difficult to establish an actual date, but its history extends to one thousand years. Some authorities aver that Eisteddfodau existed as early as the seventh century, but others mention the year 1100 when such a festival was held at Caerwys under Gruffydd ap Cynan. Traditionally, the Eisteddfod has been linked with the performance of harp music and with Welsh poetry in addition to singing, and this has continued through the centuries.

Formerly, North and South Wales each had its separate Eisteddfod but in 1862 at Caernarvon they joined for what proved a memorable occasion. This has remained the situation until today, there being one event but held in alternate years in the south and north of the country. It is run on a competitive basis and the rivalry between contestants adds an element of drama to the proceedings. Many are the great and exciting choral performances, particularly those of the male voice choirs for which Wales has always been distinguished. These famous choirs draw enormous audiences, enthusiastic and knowledgeable, with sometimes perhaps just a hint of partisanship. It is no mean feat to become premier choir in one's class and every well trained team of singers strives manfully to gain this honour.

In addition to the National, local Eisteddfodau are held throughout Wales and on occasions in other parts of Britain where a sufficient number of Welsh people are gathered together. These smaller festivals are important, acting as they do as forcing grounds for the less experienced competitors.

LLANGOLLEN

The International Music Eisteddfod at Llangollen came into being as a direct result of World War II. During and after the hostilities Britain was host to a large European population, whose musical element was attracted unerringly towards the National Eisteddfod of Wales. The standard of singing and genuine enthusiasm engendered by this ancient but ever new feast of music impressed the visitors to such an extent that a request was put forward for a special class to embrace foreign choirs. This the National Eisteddfod was unable to grant owing to the already overcrowded timetable. But a seed had been sown and a group of enthusiasts headed by the truly remarkable W. S. Gwynn Williams, set to work to organise an Eisteddfod on international lines. The difficulties of such an undertaking were immense, but a spell of incredibly hard work resulted in the triumphant opening in 1947 of a quite unique project.

The little town of Llangollen, with a population of only three thousand was chosen as the venue, and was destined to become world famous as an annual centre of music and dance. Set amongst glorious scenery in North Wales, it became the magnet for choirs, instrumentalists and groups of dancers from Britain, Europe, America, Canada and many other areas.

Although much of this festival is of a competitive and educational nature with its various classes for adult, youth and child performers, many of the evening concerts qualify for inclusion in this chapter. Perhaps Music in the Tent would be a more apt description, as a vast marquee holding some twelve thousand people is annually erected for the week of music making. In addition to the colourfully dressed competitors in their native costumes, great orchestras under famous conductors, ballet companies and even professional opera companies take the stage. This feature has had a tremendous impact and is undoubtedly one of the factors responsible for the interest in the wider sphere of music now found throughout Wales. It has, in its way, continued the great pioneering work of Sir Walford Davies, who worked so enthusiastically, during the first quarter of the century, to introduce much new instrumental music to Wales. The Llangollen International Eisteddfod has succeeded in fostering friendship and a better understanding amongst people of many nationalities. And this at a time of noticeably cool political relationships in certain quarters; achieved quietly, without fuss or undue publicity.

In addition to the exciting events held every July at Llangollen, much musical activity is to be found in the more populous south of the country. Cardiff houses the greatly improved BBC Welsh Orchestra, which provides a regular service of high class programmes. The Swansea Music Festival flourishes and gains in importance year by year. Given in the splendid Brangwyn Hall the emphasis is on orchestral music and many of the great British orchestras take part in a festival which is increasingly pointing the way ahead. Although at first the programmes consisted of well-known works, gradually a more adventurous spirit has crept into the planning and music by native-born composers has rightly been included. Welsh composers are now producing instrumental music of high merit, and the names of Alun Hoddinott, Daniel Jones, William Mathias and Grace Williams are known to a wide public far beyond the boundaries of Wales.

Some years ago a young man, John Metcalf conceived a delightfully original idea, viz. a Vale of Glamorgan Festival. This venture came to life in 1970 with a series of recitals in various churches and historic houses in the district between Cardiff and Swansea. Small groups of singers, instrumentalists and dancers as well as soloists performed in the attractive surroundings of Penllyn Castle, St. Donat's Castle, Merthyr Mawr House, Cowbridge Church and Ewenny Priory.

A praiseworthy attempt to foster the appreciation of music was initiated in 1919 with the formation of the National Council of Wales. The Director was Sir Walford Davies, then Professor of Music at the University College of Aberyswyth who will be

219

remembered by an older generation for a series of broadcasts on the art of music. These talks, illustrated at the piano, were simple and friendly and conveyed much of the true educationist's enthusiasm. Certainly they appealed to a vast public which previously had shown no interest in the subject.

The National Council went out of its way to raise standards wherever possible and organised concerts by small groups of musicians in village halls, schools, chapels and churches. This far-seeing project bore fruit and led to a greater participation in instrumental work, so long considered a weakness in Welsh music.

Certainly all the signs point to a flourishing musical life with chamber concerts and music clubs enjoying excellent support. Also there is an awareness of native composers with the Guild for the Promotion of Welsh Music assisting in a very practical manner. No one body has catered more successfully for this new found enthusiasm in instrumental music than the Welsh Arts Council. It has been busy throughout the country in promoting concerts, not only in the large centres of population, but also in areas where orchestral music by first-class artists might not be normally expected. As an example, during the 1970/71 season the following tours were arranged.

Leipzig Gewandhaus Symphony Orchestra
　Haverfordwest, Barry, Aberystwyth, Wrexham, Llangefni and Rhyl.
Munich Philharmonic Orchestra
　Swansea and Barry.
Berlin Radio Symphony Orchestra
　Aberystwyth and Cardiff.
Royal Philharmonic Orchestra
　Swansea, Aberystwyth, Fishguard and Barry.
Hallé Orchestra
　Wrexham, Llangefni and Rhyl.
London Chamber Orchestra
　Monmouth, Harlech and St. Asaph.

Although the National Orchestra of Wales failed in the 1930s, it may have been brought into being too soon. Perhaps the time is now opportune for another effort to be made. There are many local instrumental players of high calibre and the obvious interest and good-will of the public might be harnessed towards this end. The Welsh National Opera has been in operation for thirty years with marked success and the suggestion has been made that a full-scale permanent orchestra could double the role of accompanying the opera and perform as a National Orchestra. There is a precedent in Scotland where the Scottish National has been very successfully engaged in a similar project. The answer, as always, is finance.

Naturally, the changing times bring with them the inevitable casualties. Those to suffer most would appear to be the very large choirs with their long tradition of oratorio singing. These seem to become less each year and in their place has arisen a number of smaller, highly trained chamber choirs, able to perform a wide variety or works including the intricate scores of contemporary composers.

Probably the inadequacy of halls suitable for concert-giving is the most depressing aspect of music in Wales at the moment. This is bound to have a frustrating effect on those living some distance from the towns, and some of the towns are not well catered for. If this difficulty could be overcome, the musical situation would indeed be healthy.

THE ORCHESTRAL SCENE: THE PROMS

The Promenade Concerts, which have become such a feature of British musical life, owe their origin to a series given at the Colosseum in Regent's Park in 1838. They in turn were based on concerts held in Paris, in which the audience was permitted to stroll about and talk during the performances. The London proms began on 12 January with an orchestra of sixty conducted by Pilati. *The Musical World* commented in slightly aggrieved terms on this innovation remarking "that to a promenade audience the music was really of secondary concern. The chief interest lies in the elegant perambulators themselves, who wander in pairs, finished by Stultz and the St. James's Street milliners and arranged to orchestrations accompanied by Strauss and Musard".

This criticism could hardly be levelled against our present-day promenaders, whose dress generally speaking is not particularly elegant. Also the average prom. is so well attended that there is barely space enough to take a deep breath, let alone promenade. But much more important, the young people who often queue for hours and then stand in a solid phalanx throughout the concert, come for the music which they understand and so obviously enjoy.

During the winter of 1840–1 there were no fewer than three series of promenade concerts running in London, all in competition with one another. Eventually the majority of people attracted to this form of concert-going patronised those organised by Louis Jullien, a conductor of somewhat eccentric behaviour, whose extrovert antics drew large audiences whether his performances took place at *Covent Garden, The Lyceum, Her Majesty's* or *Drury Lane* theatres. On his death in 1860 the concerts continued under the direction of Sullivan and Cowen. But in 1895 the most amazing series of promenade concerts began at the newly built Queen's Hall of blessed memory. The name which springs immediately to mind in association with this annual phenomenon is that of Sir Henry J. Wood. He was engaged by Robert Newman, the hall's exceptional manager, to conduct his first concert at the age of twenty-five. Fifty years later he was still in command. The British public owes him a tremendous debt of gratitude for one of the greatest pieces of musical education ever established. In the early days the programmes reflected public taste, but Wood kept just ahead of his audiences until he was able with confidence to present the type of music now accepted at the normal symphony concert. Although Sir Henry and the Queen's Hall have both passed away, the spirit remains and enthusiasm increases year by year in the vastness of the Royal Albert Hall.

Whereas previously one group of players, the Queen's Hall Orchestra under its indefatigable conductor provided the musical fare for the entire promenade season, now several orchestras with many differnt conductors are engaged. The BBC, responsible for the administration of the proms since 1927, has increasingly encouraged this policy, particularly since the death of Sir Henry. As a result the quality of performance has undoubtedly improved. Orchestral players like everyone else, become tired and stale without a break in their labours.

It might possibly be of interest to those who enjoy the present-day proms to consider part of the very first programme given on 10 August 1895, and to ponder on the musical changes which have occurred in roughly three quarters of a century. Here is the second half of the programme.

Grand Selection   Carmen   Bizet
                      (arranged by Cellier)

Song	Largo al Factotum Mr. Ffrangçon-Davies	Rossini
Overture	Mignon	Ambroise Thomas
Solo Cornet	Serenade Mr. Howard Reynolds	Schubert
Song	My Mother bids me bind my hair Madame Marie Duma	Haydn
Solo Bassoon	Lucy Long Mr. E. F. James	
Song	Dear Heart Mr. Ivor McKay	Tito Mattei
The Uhlan's Call		Eilenberg
Song	Loch Lomond Mrs. Van der Vere Green	Old Scottish
Song	The Soldier's Song Mr. W. A. Peterkin	Mascheroni
Valse	Amoretten Tanze	Gungl
Grand March	Les Enfants de la Garde (orchestrated by Harold Vicars) First performance	Schloesser

The front page of the programme bore an advertisement by a tailoring establishment of particular interest to the aforementioned 'elegant perambulators'. It signified their willingness to make an evening dress lined throughout with silk for five guineas.

As a tribute to Sir Henry Wood on achieving his golden jubilee as a conductor in 1938, Vaughan Williams wrote his incomparable *Serenade to Music*. Composed for orchestra and sixteen solo singers, all of whom had performed on numerous occasions with the conductor, this work created a great impression on its first performance, given at the Royal Albert Hall on 5 October. Based on words taken from Act V, Scene i of *The Merchant of Venice* 'How sweet the moonlight sleeps upon this bank', this is memorable music and its magic is undimmed to this day.

The proms continued up to and during a large part of World War II and the musical public was eagerly anticipating another great occasion. This was due in 1944 when Sir Henry was to celebrate his seventy-fifth birthday and fifty years of conducting at the promenade concerts. Coincident with the planning for this jubilee was the suggestion that a sum of money should be raised to commemorate this astonishing feat, to be distributed at the behest of the recipient.

In his long life devoted to music Henry Wood had much enjoyed his work with young people and in particular rehearsing and conducting the student's orchestra at the Royal Academy of Music. It was not therefore surprising that he advocated a rehearsal centre for students, in which they could practise without interruption, with possibly a hostel to house those whose homes were not in London.

This scheme had to be turned down on various counts and Sir Henry then put forward an alternative; the building of a concert hall to replace the bomb-destroyed Queen's Hall. *The Daily Telegraph* most generously helped towards this end by promoting a concert at the Royal Albert Hall in March 1944 at which the London Symphony, the BBC Symphony and the London Philharmonic Orchestras combined before a vast audience. The programme, which contained music by Elgar and his beloved Bach resulted in several thousand pounds being handed over to the fund.

On 10 June of the same year the Royal Albert Hall was again packed to suffocation for the first concert of the new promenade season. Before the end of the month the authorities decided reluctantly to close the hall owing to the new menace from the air-flying bombs. Sir Henry died shortly afterwards on 18 August, but *The Daily Telegraph* sponsored two further concerts in 1945 and 1946. From all sources including gifts from various bodies and individuals, the total reached £70,000. This was a magnificent tribute, but unfortunately the money could not be used due to the obvious difficulties of building restrictions. Today, with the accrued interest swelling the amount considerably, the sum is still not enough for its original purpose. Also, in the meantime the superb complex of buildings on the South Bank of the Thames, comprising the Royal Festival Hall, the Queen Elizabeth Hall and the Purcell Room have done much to nullify the need for another such centre.

Many changes have taken place at the proms since the war years. The debonair Sir Malcolm Sargent, much beloved of the promenaders, became the chief conductor until his death and introduced a number of exciting young soloists to the public during his term of office. The season has been extended to eight weeks and many of the nightly offerings bear a distinctly new look. A recent innovation provides for some concerts to be held in buildings other than the Royal Albert Hall.

It might not be inappropriate at this juncture to pass a comment on audience behaviour at the Promenade Concerts, not necessarily in criticism but as a matter of interest. It has seemed to one listening regularly to the radio performances that the noise, consisting largely of whistling and shouting, has increased greatly over the years. This impression was quite dramatically exemplified on Sunday 15th September 1974, the day following the prom season. A programme taken from the BBC Sound Archives of a 1936 concert conducted by Sir Henry Wood was broadcast. The applause for the various items and artists was warm but decorous, without a hint of hysteria. Has youth become less inhibited, or has television played its part in pandering to a certain form of self-advertisement, or is it just noise for noise sake? Some more able authority might care to provide an answer. However, with those few remarks out of the way, there can be no doubt that the annual Promenade season is a phenomenon well worthy of the title *The Greatest Music Festival in the World*.

ORCHESTRAS TODAY – LONDON

To see and hear a great orchestra in full cry is a thrilling experience and quite apart from appreciating beauty of tone or intensity of attack, the superb discipline shown by all departments is an object lesson in concentration. But until comparatively recent times the lot of orchestral players was hard and precarious. Even today the life is a strenuous one. The performers have not only to be artists of the highest class, but must have tough constitutions to cope with their multifarious activities. The work is demanding, both mentally and physically and no player can afford to fall below a very high standard.

Much depends on the conductor, regarding his ability and equally his method of dealing with a group of highly proficient and distinctive personalities. For instance, nothing is guaranteed to bore the normal orchestral member more than a rehearsal liberally besprinkled with the conductor's reminiscences or a series of lectures on some obscure feature of the music. They much prefer to get on with the job. The average player can sum up a conductor quickly and decide instinctively if he be a genuine master of his art or not.

There is however a glamour attached to a fine orchestra not exceeded by a famous cricket or football team. In all these cases there is a real concern with team-work of a high order and all have their soloists, usually known as stars in the realms of sport. Concerts, television appearances, recording sessions and foreign tours all make for an exciting life and one that is entirely at variance with the average person's experience. From time to time orchestras are featured in books, illustrated magazines and films which pinpoint their history and achievements. They in fact live in the glare of a constant publicity and however satisfying to the corporate ego, the ultimate effect can be one of strain.

London is the acknowledged centre of world music and is the only city which supports five full symphony orchestras as well as a number of chamber groups of the highest calibre. The recording studios are kept busy coping with the ever-increasing demand for records and the orchestras concerned earn international prestige as a result. And the previously mentioned buildings on the South Bank and the Barbican seem always to be in use and to act as a magnet for large nightly audiences.

Four orchestras, the London Symphony, London Philharmonic, Royal Philharmonic and the Philharmonia are all independently run and being exceptionally expensive undertakings, substantial subsidies are a necessity. Many orchestras on the continent are maintained at the expense of the State, but in Britain the approach is rather different. The Arts Council, financed by the Government, has to assist a large number of enterprises throughout the country, including orchestras, opera, ballet, art and drama. This unenviable task must be a constant headache to the administrators of the available funds, which by no means meet requirements. Large orchestras are finding it increasingly difficult to balance their budgets and players are constantly being asked to increase productivity. The situation is rapidly approaching the point where 'all play and too much work' will have an unfortunate effect on standards.

Throughout the ages there have been generous patrons of music and it is good to know that such people and organisations still exist. Where formerly kings, courts and the church carried the burden, now industry, the board room annd the occasional wealthy music-lover have taken over some of the responsibility. It cannot have escaped notice that many sporting events, such as those associated with golf, tennis, horse-racing and cricket have been sponsored by large firms as a means of advertisement. One is therefore happy to record that music is not excluded from this form of patronage in which tobacco companies, insurance offices, banks, breweries and building societies are amongst the commercial enterprises interested in the future of great orchestras.

If the future appears brighter and a sense of confidence pervades the orchestral scene, it was not always thus. The past history of many British orchestras is a troublous one. Conditions of employment were often unsatisfactory, as many orchestras operated for only six months in the year, with no provision for the players in case of illness, accident or retirement. Also arrangements for rehearsals were invariably poor, taking place in cold, draughty halls with few civilised amenities. Unfortunately this last mentioned situation has not been greatly improved today. Under such circumstances one may regard with sympathy the lot of the players and understand the need to squeeze every penny from their profession. It was due to insecurity that the deputy system evolved. An established orchestral musician, on being offered a more lucrative engagement elsewhere, would arrange for a substitute to take his place, either at rehearsal or performance. One can also understand the position from the conductor's point of view.

THE LONDON SYMPHONY ORCHESTRA

The London Symphony Orchestra was formed as a direct result of Sir Henry Wood's policy of no deputies. Because of this decision forty or so members of the Queen's Hall Orchestra left *en bloc* and took the unusual step of founding an orchestra in which all financial and artistic matters were in the hands of the players. This was in 1904 and at the time constituted a revolutionary move in orchestral circles. The members worked quickly. Additional players were engaged and the finest conductors invited to direct in order to raise and maintain the standard of performance. The orchestra prospered and its reputation soared. Like everything else in this mortal world, orchestras have their ups and downs, but the London Symphony is one of the great orchestras of today. During recent decades several successful foreign tours have been organised and in the August of 1973 it had the honour of being the first British orchestra to perform at the Salzburg Festival.

THE BBC SYMPHONY ORCHESTRA

In 1930 the BBC put into effect its decision to form a full-scale symphony orchestra as a permanent feature of the growing radio medium. Although intended for studio performance it was planned on very substantial lines and hopes were entertained for something special in orchestral music. By offering generous financial terms and good conditions of employment, the BBC brought together a splendid body of players. Dr. Adrian Boult, until then conductor of the City of Birmingham Orchestra was entrusted with the important task of welding one hundred and nineteen performers into a great orchestra. A musician of immense integrity, his quiet and gentlemanly manner earned the respect of his players and together they achieved magnificent results. The orchestra came more and more 'out of purdah' and played to delighted audiences in Britain and overseas, a policy which has been continued to the present time. This is the only one of the five leading London orchestras which does not manage its own affairs, being wholly maintained by the BBC.

Since the late Sir Adrian's resignation several conductors have occupied this key position. In addition, there is a policy of engaging guest conductors, which is sound planning on many counts.

THE LONDON PHILHARMONIC ORCHESTRA

This famous orchestra was established in 1932 by Sir Thomas Beecham. A period of intense rehearsal preceded its first concert, which was given on 7th October of that year in the Queen's Hall. The programme consisted of music so often associated with the conductor, including works by Mozart and Delius, and according to reports the performance was magnificent. But in spite of its brilliant start the orchestra suffered a series of nasty shocks in the early years. It lost several key players due in part to the incredibly long hours spent in rehearsal at Covent Garden and also because of better conditions obtainable with the BBC Symphony Orchestra. Then, in common with other orchestras it had to contend with even greater difficulties on the outbreak of World War II in 1939. This posed serious problems for those engaged in concert pro-motion and there was for a time utter confusion regarding its future. Also many of the players were mobilised into the services and famous regimental bands suddenly found themselves with an almost embarrassing richness of wood-wind and brass performers.

In the spring of 1940 Beecham left for the United States, where apart from a short tour in Australia he remained until 1944. On his return from America he was anxious to renew links with the London Philharmonic once again. Previously, Sir Thomas had been responsible for everything connected with the orchestra, the choice of music and soloists, the engagement of players and their payment; the last mentioned incidentally not always honoured. But during his absence there had been administrative changes within the orchestra. It became self-governing, on rather similar lines to the London Symphony and the members were not prepared to be employed by Beecham as hitherto. Instead he was offered the post of salaried director of music with a contract which denied him the advantages he had always considered his by right. Sir Thomas refused.

The orchestra continued to function by engaging a series of guest conductors, a policy which has since been changed. As already mentioned the orchestra is run by a board of directors, all except one being playing members elected from the orchestra as a whole. They in turn employ an office staff headed by the managing director who is the only non-playing director, and whose function is that of administration. There is also an advisory council to assist on artistic matters and to raise funds for certain activities such as foreign tours.

Some years ago the orchestra visited China, the very first British organisation of this nature to tour in that land. Such a venture called for detailed co-ordination from various sources and the British Council, the LPO Council and the Foreign Office all played their part, but the actual tour was proposed and organised by the Chinese Government, which contributed a large share of the cost. The result was an overwhelming success and the concerts, given in Peking, Shanghai and Canton, were greeted with boundless enthusiasm. The players were deeply moved by their reception and this aspect of the tour was plainly evident in an excellent television documentary, *The Red Carpet*.

As with the other metropolitan orchestras, the London Philharmonic is to be seen and heard frequently at the Royal Festival Hall and the other centres, but one unusual aspect of its activities is the three month Glyndebourne Opera season each year. This affords a break in the normal round of concert work and its entirely different role is performed in a glorious Sussex sylvan setting.

Another thing to be seen in connection with this orchestra is its magnificent new instruments van – if van be not too commonplace for so superb a vehicle. Its black exterior bearing the orchestra's name is most dignified and the interior contains a bed, a boon to the driver on long journeys.

THE ROYAL PHILHARMONIC ORCHESTRA

After his salutary experience with the London Philharmonic, Sir Thomas Beecham decided to form yet another orchestra. He enlisted a number of players at a somewhat difficult time when men were being demobilised from the forces. However, his new organisation, named the Royal Philharmonic made its first appearance before the public at the Davis Theatre, Croydon on 15 September 1946. As with the initial programme given by his previous orchestra, this one also included works by Mozart and Delius. The performance did not receive the 'rave' notices to which Beecham's orchestras had become accustomed. There were in fact some weak links here and there to which the conductor gave his immediate attention. In a matter of months everything was progressing smoothly. The orchestra, with Beecham in command, visited the United States in 1950 and a whirlwind tour consisting of some fifty-two concerts brought notices of the highest praise. The old magic had been rekindled once again.

Sir Thomas was a brilliant conductor much revered by his players, in spite of, or perhaps because of his eccentric behaviour. Which brings to mind a story that has been told on numerous occasions concerning the attitude of orchestral players towards him. It referred to a statement that the orchestra – in this instance the London Philharmonic – played especially well for Beecham. Sir Henry Wood in his fascinating book *My Life of Music* recounts how he asked the members of that orchestra if this remark could be taken seriously. One famous player replied at once to the effect that such a statement was unjust to any orchestra. He added that when he was in good form he played well. If he was not, no conductor could make him play any better. He always gave of his best; they all did. This is probably very true, but I well remember talking with some of the rank and file members of the Royal Philharmonic at an early Edinburgh Festival and being interested in their statement that no other conductor could obtain from them the really stylish performance as could 'Tommy'.

Beecham was an extraordinary person by any standard and the stories told of him are legion and legendary. Some at least must be true, but there has grown up what may only be described as Beecham-lore. He was a somewhat wayward character whose public utterances often caused controversy. He gloried in a rapier-like wit, amusing to all except the subject of his remarks. But Sir Thomas will always be remembered for his untiring efforts on behalf of opera in Britain and for his staunch support of the music of Delius, whilst his superb readings of Mozart have rarely been surpassed.

231

THE PHILHARMONIA
ORCHESTRA

The youngest of the London Orchestras is the Philharmonia. It was founded in 1945 by Walter Legge essentially as a recording orchestra and consisted of a group of specially chosen instrumentalists of virtuoso quality. It made a tremendous impact throughout the world due to its outstanding series of gramophone recordings. Some years later the orchestra was officially disbanded, but the players refused to be split up and in 1964 they formed themselves into a limited company. The aims and principles were similar to the other orchestras already mentioned. The Philharmonia has a council of democratically elected members which meets at regular intervals to discuss all matters affecting the orchestra. Although now one of the great public concert-giving bodies, the orchestra is still famed for its recordings and may be heard in many excellent operatic performances, now produced by a number of different companies, instead of one as formerly.

The deputy system is allowed but strictly controlled. Special permission for absence has to be obtained and the engaging of substitutes is in the hands of the personnel manager, in order that the standard of playing may be maintained.

Several foreign tours have been arranged for the orchestra over the years ahead, always subject to world conditions and other equally delicate circumstances. The Philharmonia has travelled vast distances and concerts in Europe, the USA and the Far East are almost as normal as in London. Of one thing we may be sure; this orchestra will maintain the prestige of British music wherever it goes.

Earlier in this section reference was made to the wretched conditions often suffered by orchestral musicians during the necessary and indeed vital periods of rehearsal. Happier prospects are now emerging. The London Symphony and London Philharmonic orchestras jointly took steps to rectify the situation by obtaining the lease of Holy Trinity Church, Southwark, empty since 1959. This building, with its excellent acoustical qualities, was an ideal choice, having every modern facility, including the latest equipment for recording purposes. Two delightful touches in connection with this project were that the Southwark Diocesan Board offered to lease the building to the orchestras at a nominal rent of £5 per annum and that it was to be named the Henry Wood Hall. It may be remembered that Sir Henry's original desire to provide a rehearsal centre in London was turned down. The trustees of the fund allocated money to this cause, which one feels would have gladdened the heart of that outstanding musician. We must now hope that the other two orchestras may find a suitable permanent base from which to work.

CHAMBER MUSIC ENSEMBLES

In addition to these great symphony orchestras a number of excellent smaller groups is based on the capital. Ranging from some fifteen players upwards, they specialise in true chamber music. The standard of performance is incredibly high, as may be judged from the many recordings now on the market.

Particular mention should be made of the English Chamber Orchestra, the Melos Ensemble, the London Sinfonietta, the London Mozart Players and the Academy of St. Martin in the Fields. The last two are normally conducted by their directors. The other three orchestras engage guest conductors, often young men with a special flair for the type of music to be performed. The London Sinfonietta has gained an enviable reputation for its masterly playing of contemporary music and has given many first performances and has commissioned several British compositions.

Quite apart from the vast quantity of music available for such ensembles there are other advantages. The orchestras are extremely mobile, they do not require large concert halls for performances and with smaller numbers, their expenses are obviously less than for a full symphony orchestra. All of these groups undertake a great deal of travelling including frequent visits abroad.

THE ORCHESTRAL SCENE —
OUTSIDE LONDON

Outside London the large symphony orchestras may be a little thin on the ground compared with some countries, but this in no way implies any lack of professional skill in provincial orchestras. In fact the quality of performance is extremely high and there are certain advantages in belonging to a more locally orientated body. Many players are justly proud to be associated with a certain city or district and they become well-known personalities to their audiences. Owing to their integration in the community one hears genuine expressions of sorrow at the loss or illness of a particular instrumentalist. The great industrial cities of Birmingham, Glasgow, Liverpool, Manchester and Newcastle are well catered for and the surrounding districts derive benefit from these strategically based orchestras. In each case the population is such as to ensure the large audiences necessary to achieve continuity. And a special word of congratulation to Bournemouth, that charming resort which maintains a fine orchestra to the delight of residents and visitors alike.

THE HALLÉ ORCHESTRA

Of all the present day British orchestras the oldest is the Hallé of of Manchester, whose history is certainly not without interest. Few famous orchestras can trace their origins back to eighteenth century music-making, but the Hallé has a definite link with the Gentlemen's Concerts which began in 1774. These concerts catered for an upper-class clientele in which there would appear to be something of a parallel with the venture in Edinburgh, discussed earlier in this chapter.

The Concerts committee raised an orchestra of some twenty-six local players, though truth to tell of rather variable quality. At this time the side-blown flute, recently imported from Germany, was enjoying enormous popularity in England and performers on the instrument were assured a wide measure of social prestige. Inevitably there were too many flautists in circulation and it is recorded that all twenty-six members of the first Gentlemen's orchestra played the flute, which must have resulted in a certain similarity of tone colour. But the great days were not far off and we shall see how in the following century sound plans were laid and a great orchestra born.

In 1848 the eminent musician Charles Hallé visited Manchester, where he had several friends, members of the Gentlemen's Concerts. He was invited to one of their 'evenings' and furthermore urged to take over the organisation and throw in his lot with Manchester's musical life. Hallé was by no means impressed by what he had heard, but having regard to the pressure put upon him, he accepted the offer on one condition – that he should be given a free hand in the choice of players. This having been agreed, Hallé engaged a number of very good professional instrumentalists from various sources and very soon the improvement in standard was obvious to all.

An important Art Treasure Exhibition was held in Manchester during 1857 for which Hallé and his orchestra were engaged to provide programmes of first-class music. Large numbers attended the Exhibition, many of whom previously had had little opportunity of hearing music of this nature so well performed. They were captivated by the orchestra, further strengthened for the occasion and so success-ful was the venture that Hallé was loath to part with any of his players. He therefore went ahead with a series of concerts in and around Manchester, which initially suffered a financial loss. But with the ever-increasing interest and support of people in every walk of life, apparent failure developed into a success story such as few could have imagined. This was genuine pioneering and thus was the Hallé Orchestra launched upon its memorable career. In the following years an enviable reputation was built up; international artists were invited to perform with the orchestra and Manchester became one of the great centres of music. Since that time Man-chester folk have taken an almost partisan interest in the Hallé – it is a part and very important part of the city's life and the citizens are proud of their orchestra.

Sir Charles Hallé died in 1895 and understandably a vacuum occurred for a year or so. But a number of well-to-do music-lovers came to the rescue and formed the Hallé Concerts Society in

1898, a splendid piece of patronage. The members worked quickly and were able to persuade Hans Richter to become permanent conductor. Richter, considered one of the finest conductors of his day, remained with the orchestra for twelve years and brought it to a pitch of perfection envied by the musical world of the early twentieth century. In addition to being the greatest interpreter of Wagner, he was a genuine admirer of Elgar and did much to make that composer's works known in Britain.

Richter was followed by Michael Ballin, who continued as director of music until 1914 when, being a German citizen he had to resign on the outbreak of World War I. Sir Thomas Beecham took over the reins until 1920 when he was succeeded by Hamilton Harty. Harty's work with the Hallé was noteworthy, so much so that his eventual resignation was a sad blow to all concerned. When the BBC Symphony Orchestra was formed, players were recruited from many other orchestras including the Hallé. Several of the most prominent section leaders left for London, thus denuding Manchester of some of its finest players. Sir Hamilton Harty, depressed at this turn of events, felt unable to continue his work with the orchestra and left in 1933. There was, virtually for the first time, a long break without a regular conductor and this was reflected in performance. The BBC in an effort at restitution allowed members of their Northern Orchestra to play for the Hallé, a helpful gesture if somewhat impermanent.

Sir Malcolm Sargent stepped into the breach during the early years of the second World War, but the orchestra, due to the familiar difficulties of the times was but a pale shadow of its former self.

The Hallé had always favoured the policy of engaging a permanent musical director of outstanding quality and now in this crisis the need was greater than ever. But as so often happens, the hour produces the man, and the man in this case was none other than John Barbirolli. This exceptional musician, fresh from his success with the New York Philharmonic was offered the challenge of reviving the fortunes of the Hallé. The task was enormous as the orchestra, consisting of players from the Hallé and from the BBC Northern had no true identity. Barbirolli's first concern was to place the organisation on a sound basis and to this end the players were offered the alternative of remaining with the Hallé full time or joining the BBC. Only twelve stalwarts decided to join Barbirolli, but fortunately these were outstanding musicians. The new conductor had now to assemble and train an almost new body of players, many of whom had little or no experience of orchestral work.

That the project was brought to a successful conclusion speaks volumes for the dedicated work of Sir John Barbirolli, who brought the orchestra once again to that standard of excellence long associated with the Hallé. As in the case of certain of his predecessors Barbirolli *was* the Hallé, and his reputation and that of his orchestra reached new heights.

To choose a successor to an old and trusted friend is a sad task and one often fraught with misgivings, especially when looking for someone to follow a man of Barbirolli's uniqueness. On Sir John's death the Hallé committee had to face up to this problem. They chose well. James Loughran, director of the BBC Scottish was appointed and soon established a rapport with the players and audiences. A fine conductor with a cheery personality and a gift for getting the best out of people, he continued in the tradition of the famous Hallé conductors of the past. Loughran recently retired to engage in free-lance conducting.

BOURNEMOUTH SYMPHONY ORCHESTRA

For a town of such comparatively recent growth, Bournemouth would appear to have had music as an attraction for a considerable part of its history. 1976 saw the centenary of their first band. This was not an orchestra of its present dimensions or capabilities, but a small military band of sixteen players. As will have been noted in previous instances, such a seed can grow into a wonderful blossom if tended and nurtured aright. This small group of players became, in 1892, the first Corporation Band, judiciously augmented with a few additional instrumentalists.

The following year saw another change, one which was destined to have a far-reaching effect on music in Bournemouth. This was the appointment of Dan Godfrey as bandmaster. He commenced what was to become a highly successful career, with a band of thirty wind players whose duties consisted of a series of regular popular concerts on the pier. His band had been well chosen and several members were able to play more than one instrument. As a result of this advantageous state of affairs a small orchestra was formed to perform in the old Winter Garden Pavilion.

Bournemouth, in addition to having claims as a holiday resort was also becoming a favoured residential area with an all-the-year round population which might be expected to support an imaginative musical undertaking. The Town Council wisely sensing the situation made Godfrey musical director of the first permanent Municipal Orchestra in the country. This was in 1894 and gave the conductor his great opportunity. The small orchestra was increased in size and a series of concerts planned. In the early days the programmes were not unlike those of Sir Henry Wood's proms, in that they were popular in content. But very gradually changes took place; the orchestra was built up to one of symphonic proportions and programmes of the highest merit were performed for a discriminating public.

One sometimes wonders why other south coast towns with large residential populations have not been successful in like manner. Certainly Hastings supported a good orchestra years ago under the direction of Julius Harrison and Torquay attempted something similar. But Bournemouth alone appears to have weathered the many difficulties which have perhaps affected other rather similar towns. This may in part have been due to the personality and drive of Godfrey, whose work was rightly recognised by a knighthood in 1922. When Sir Dan retired in 1935, after forty-one years devoted service, the Bournemouh Symphony Orchestra of some seventy players had achieved lasting fame.

It was also adequately housed in the modern Winter Garden Pavilion and this permanent centre added much to the well-being of the instrumentalists and to the comfort of their audiences. Excellent musical directors have been attracted to Bournemouth and in recent years both Sir Charles Groves and Constantin Silvestri have acted in this capacity. The orchestra has now considerably widened its sphere of influence and travels throughout the west country catering for the needs of music-lovers. This short account has an unhappy ending. According to normally reliable sources, there would seem to be trouble at Bournemouth between the local council and the orchestra. As a result, it is possible that both the Symphony Orchestra and Sinfonietta may cease to function in Bournemouth and be offered a home elsewhere.

THE SCOTTISH
NATIONAL ORCHESTRA

The most northerly of our great British orchestras is the Scottish National based in Glasgow, but seen and heard in all the principal cities of Scotland. It has a long history, having originated as an accompanying body for the Glasgow Choral Union. This was during the nineteenth century era of choral singing which swept Britain. Hans von Bulow, who conducted this orchestra for the 1877-8 season was but one brilliant exponent in a succession of distinguished directors. He was followed by August Manns who stayed with the Choral Union Orchestra for several years before moving to London to direct the Crystal Palace concerts. Then in 1891 the Scottish Orchestra was founded and superseded the previously named body. Its first conductor was Sir George Henschel who came to Glasgow direct from the Boston Symphony Orchestra. This fine pianist and singer directed affairs from 1893-5 and was followed for a spell by Sir Frederick Cowen.

The first world war caused the cessation of concert-giving by the Scottish and for some years afterwards no regular conductor was appointed. Instead, the administration relied on a number of guest conductors. Among these were many outstanding musicians, including Koussevitsky, Weingartner, Albert Coates, Landon Ronald and Malko. But they were not in control for any length of time and the orchestra suffered. There was, however, a dramatic improvement with the appointment of John Barbirolli as musical director in 1933. Unfortunately for the orchestra and for music in Scotland this greatly endowed conductor only remained for three years before being lured away to direct the New York Philharmonic.

After World War II the orchestra, in common with many others, had something of an uphill task to find its best form. The difficulties of those times have been touched on before and every allowance should be made in view of the exceptional conditions. Undoubtedly the great modern revival came with the appointment of Alexander Gibson as musical director. All the troubles were not of course resolved immediately, but the orchestra soon gave the impression of being well rehearsed and a complete unity. The young Scottish conductor knew what he wanted and made certain that his plans were carried out. The general improvement was further confirmed with the arrival of Sam Bor as leader. The orchestra has had its ups and downs, but at the moment of writing the graph stands very high.

Now known as the Scottish National Orchestra, it is patently national in more than name. Its reputation throughout the country may be gauged from the financial assistance received from local authorities, industrial concerns, banks and private individuals. The corporations of Glasgow, Edinburgh, Aberdeen and Dundee with Lanark County Council provide large public funds, but no fewer than one hundred and fifty-five smaller authorities make annual contributions.

The musical programmes are well chosen, being a blend of the known and lesser known, and encouragement is given to local composers by the inclusion of their works on occasions. Normally the orchestra is responsible for twenty-two weekly concerts in both Edinburgh and Glasgow, with a further eight in Aberdeen and four at Ayr. The orchestra also sponsors a six day public forum in collaboration with the University of Glasgow dealing with contemporary music. There are public rehearsals, lectures and composers' seminars, all culminating in a final concert.

Every now and then it descends on the Royal Festival Hall in London just to show that music north of the border is in good heart.

During the summer months the orchestra accompanies Scottish Opera, which has had so phenomenal a success in the past few years and not merely in Scotland. Gibson has been the unifying force in all these activities and has proved that to earn a great musical reputation it is not necessary to look constantly to the south. In addition to the many activities here enumerated, the orchestra manages to fit in a delightfully informal series of promenade concerts in Glasgow's Kelvin Hall.

Several factors have contributed to the success of the SNO. The admirable policy of attracting youth by its formation of an orchestral club and the interest fostered in many schools and universities accounts to some extent for enthusiastic and appreciative audiences in which young people are increasingly noticeable. Also many of the more experienced players remain with the orchestra for considerable periods, probably finding living conditions less harassing than in London. This leads to a sense of continuity which is reflected in the standard of performance. Excellent guest conductors and soloists of high repute add to the general interest.

A choral body, the SNO Chorus has added an exhilerating quality to the musical scene. Trained by John Currie, this choir of predominantly young voices is highly disciplined and strong in every department. After hearing the choir on several occasions, I have no hesitation in naming it as one of the finest of my experience. Such is the enthusiasm that vacancies seldom exist and a waiting list of would-be members ensures a high standard for the future, thus proving the old adage 'nothing succeeds like success' to be very true.

Several years ago the splendid St. Andrews Hall in Glasgow was destroyed by fire and this was a grievous loss to the orchestra and to music-lovers alike. Now plans are in being for a new and magnificent complex of buildings in the centre of the city, to include a concert hall, a theatre and accommodation for the Royal Scottish Academy of Music and Drama.

THE ROYAL LIVERPOOL PHILHARMONIC ORCHESTRA

Liverpool is fortunate in its music-making and is justly proud of its great orchestra. This body was brought into being as a direct result of the Liverpool Philharmonic Society which commenced its illustrious concert-giving activities in 1840. The enthusiasm engendered by the society made possible the building of the magnificent Philharmonic Hall in 1849, said by many to be the finest in Europe. It was completely destroyed by fire in 1933, but the society with great courage, at once went ahead with plans for a new hall. Their courage might have failed had they known that the opening, in 1939, would more or less coincide with the outbreak of war.

Although the future was uncertain the society was able for some time to continue organising concerts. It had access to a pool of orchestral players, many of whom were employed by the BBC, but eventually this source of supply dried up. Meanwhile there was in existence an orchestra known as the Merseyside Orchestra, formed by Louis Cohen in 1923 as the Merseyside Chamber Music Players. This group had from time to time added to its playing strength and had given a successful series of concerts at Wallasey over the years. Also the Corporation of Liverpool allowed the orchestra to use St. George's Hall in the city centre for Sunday concerts. But with the outbreak of hostilities the hall was required for other purposes.

This was to prove something of a cross-roads in the musical life of Liverpool. The Philharmonic Society had its fine hall but hardly any orchestra and was seriously in debt. The City Authorities had an orchestra and no hall but ample funds. In 1942 the parties struck a deal of immense importance to the future. The corporation took over the hall and paid the debts; the society was able to continue its concerts, with the Merseyside Orchestra, now augmented to sixty players providing the nucleus of the war-time orchestra. Thus was orchestral music kept alive in North West England. At this juncture Malcolm Sargent was appointed principal conductor with Louis Cohen acting as assistant.

Since that time the orchestra has gone from strength to strength. Its schedule is a particularly busy one, almost two hundred performances being given annually. It is in a happy position in dealing with an enlightened authority, which each year makes itself responsible for any loss, thus leaving the orchestra free from financial worry.

In 1958 the prefix 'Royal' was added to the name of both society and orchestra by command of the Queen.

The Royal Liverpool Philharmonic Orchestra has had a number of eminent Directors of Music, none more popular or hard working than Sir Charles Groves. He did much to broaden the musical scope of his audiences by the inclusion of many large-scale first performances. As with other British orchestras, overseas tours have been a regular feature during the past years, including visits to Germany, Switzerland, Holland, Poland, France and Luxembourg. In Britain it performs not only in Liverpool, but may be heard in other parts of the country including the Royal Festival Hall and at the Promenade Concerts.

An innovation of vital importance to British musical life has been the series of seminars for young conductors. This has enabled a number of brilliant musicians to undergo an intensive training with a great symphony orchestra and to learn by experience something of that most demanding of professions.

THE CITY OF BIRMINGHAM ORCHESTRA

Although Birmingham could lay claim to great musical achievement from the eighteenth century onward, particularly for its choral excellence, it was not until 1920 that its own City of Birmingham Orchestra was finally brought into being. The Festival Choral Society was a splendid body of singers, keen and able to tackle any work however difficult. But orchestrally the situation was less satisfactory. It was therefore not surprising that a number of interested citizens, including Mr. Neville Chamberlain at that time Lord Mayor of Birmingham, suggested the formation of a professional orchestra. As usual on these occasions, opposition was very real, particularly when it was realised that payment for this 'frill' was to be met from the rates. Nevertheless the project was successfully carried through and the orchestra was launched under the conductorship of Appleby Matthews, a well-known local musician who remained in charge for four years.

The financial situation during this period was far from reassuring, but it was then that the committee made a wise move. Dr. Adrian Boult was invited to become Director of Music in 1924 and thus began the great days of orchestral playing in the Midland city. As was the custom at that time, the players were engaged on a six-monthly contract and had perforce to find other employment during the rest of the year. This usually meant joining a light orchestra at a seaside resort for the summer season. Boult pressed for better terms for his players to enable them to remain together for a longer time, but to no avail. Despite this disappointment orchestral music improved until in 1930, when the conductor left for London and the BBC, Birmingham had a highly efficient body of instrumentalists. Deserving of special mention in the fortunes of the orchestra was the young Paul Beard, who was destined to make his reputation as one of the outstanding orchestral leaders.

Once again the committee was fortunate in finding a replacement for their very gifted director. This was Leslie Heward, a brilliant young musician who created a tremendous impression

243

on performers and audiences alike. He brought the orchestra to a high pitch of excellence and to the notice of an ever-increasing public. His untimely death in 1943 was a sad blow to all concerned and his place proved difficult to fill. So difficult in fact that the committee decided on the somewhat unusual course of appointing a successor by open competition. The choice fell upon George Weldon, who had the invidious task of following the distinguished and much beloved Heward. To his credit Weldon overcame any oppostion that may have been present and built up a reputation particularly as a champion of British music. Also young and at the height of his popularity, he died. Since then there have been various conductors and Meredith Davies is one who has rendered invaluable service to the orchestra and city.

THE NORTHERN SINFONIA ORCHESTRA

Based at Newcastle upon Tyne, the Northern Sinfonia Orchestra is the youngest and smallest of the British regional orchestras. It is a chamber orchestra of twenty-seven performers and is, to the best of my knowledge the only permanent professional ensemble of its kind in Britain. The instrumentation consists of six first violins, five second violins, three violas, three cellos, one double bass, one flute, two oboes, two clarinets, two bassoons and two horns.

The schedule is an exceptionally demanding one, regular visits being made to Carlisle, Middlesbrough, Darlington, Leeds and London as well as a host of other towns in the neighbouring regions. The orchestra undertakes unusual and thoroughly worthwhile projects. As an example, some time ago three days were spent at York University. During this visit two concerts were given and those students studying music had the opportunity of attending rehearsals and meeting members of the orchestra.

Programmes are chosen with care and although, as might be expected, eighteenth century music plays an important part, the orchestra does not neglect the nineteenth and twentieth centuries. One notices works by Janacek, Martinu, Nielsen, Goehr,

Schoenburg and Bartok and new works are commissioned from time to time.

The Concert Society engages artists of international status to appear with the orchestra and such names as Pierre Fournier, Radu Lupu, Stephen Bishop, John Lill, Geza Anda, Henryk Szeryng and Joan Dickson goes to prove that the musical life of Newcastle and district is well catered for.

Foreign tours have included France, Canada and the United States, Belgium, Germany, Poland, Hungary, Yugoslavia, Italy, Holland and Latin America, and in every case audiences have responded more than favourably to the high standard of performance.

It would be a fascinating experience to be allowed a peep into the future. Will this orchestra remain as a small group of highly efficient and dedicated musicians or will it emerge eventually as a great symphony orchestra comparable to Manchester's Hallé? Time alone will tell.

The situation in Yorkshire has always seemed rather strange. In a county famed for its great choirs as well as magnificent brass bands, it yet falls short in the matter of a first-class professional orchestra. Efforts have been made from time to time to improve the situation, but no body of players such as may be found in Lancashire has taken permanent root. With cities the size of Sheffield, Leeds and Bradford one might have expected ample and indeed enthusiastic support for a Yorkshire symphony orchestra.

The BBC maintains three regional orchestras, known respectively as the BBC Philharmonic Orchestra, with its base in Manchester, the BBC Scottish Symphony Orchestra at Glasgow and the BBC Welsh Symphony Orchestra housed in splendid quarters near Cardiff. Although originally planned as studio orchestras they have increasingly come before the public in recent years through frequent concert performances. These orchestras are hard working and produce an amazing variety of programmes throughout the year. They have also proved to be the forcing ground for many excellent conductors.

The BBC Philharmonic is perhaps fortunate in being stationed at Manchester, a tradiitional centre of music, with a knowledgeable public and the famous Hallé just round the corner. Although possibly rarely mentioned in musical circles, the fact of having two orchestral bodies in close proximity must lead to a certain feeling of competition, a not entirely unhealthy situation.

245

Also the fine College of Music in the city brings certain advantages, not least as a source from which to draw young players into the orchestra.

Glasgow is in a rather similar position to Manchester in having two orchestras, nor does the similarity end there. It also has two famous football clubs, which over their long histories have been locked in fierce rivalry. With the Scottish National Orchestra and the BBC Scottish Symphony Orchestra there is a friendly reciprocity regarding players. In the case of illness, and with engagements permitting, one organisation will gladly help the other. I may not be certain of my facts, but I have rarely heard of such an event happening with Celtic and Rangers. The BBC Scottish now quite often appears in public and takes an important part in the various music festivals held in Scottish cities. It is rightly held in high esteem and one hopes sincerely that financial stringency will never cause this fine orchestra to be wound up or reduced in size.

The BBC Welsh has no opposition in Cardiff or indeed anywhere in Wales. It is a thoroughly competent body and one which has made great strides in recent years. As noted elsewhere, Wales has become very orchestral minded and with the number of fine young players graduating from the schools into the music colleges and universities, there should be no dearth of suitable material for this orchestra for a long time to come. Its services are sought throughout the Principality for the important festivals and it has gained a reputation for dealing with new music, in which the works of Welsh composers play an increasing part. Its broadcasts give genuine pleasure over a wide area, far beyond the confines of Wales.

Another successful musical venture by the BBC worthy of comment was the formation, some years ago of a Training Orchestra, situated at Bristol. This was designed especially for young professional players to gain experience and to learn the standard repertoire before passing on to the wider sphere of orchestral work. The Training Orchestra, known as The Academy of the BBC, achieved a high standard of expertise and toured extensively in the West Country. Less satisfactory perhaps has been music on television. In orchestral concerts the cameras have little scope apart from dwelling on the conductor and moving to various instruments or sections and back to the conductor. After a time this can become tiresome and many people would rather listen to music without such interruptions.

But one programme has caught and held the interest over a long period and has gained exceptional popularity. If future historians are puzzled over a title *Face the Music*, they might care to delve into the cause of its hold over a large section of the viewing public.

It is a brilliantly contrived programme in which a panel, usually of three, is asked to answer a series of musical questions. These questions are normally in the form of excerpts, played on the piano or on records. All manner of ingenious twists are introduced and the viewer at home has the fun of trying to beat the panel. There is, however, far more to the programme than just another quiz. At a time when we are subjected to so much that is crude and unpalatable and when many figures who appear on the screen are argumentative and aggressive, this programme is intellignet, civilised and happy. This is due in no small measure to Joseph Cooper, a magnificent pianist and a friendly personality whose buoyancy of spirit and complete naturalness carries each episode through to a triumphant conclusion.

All in all, the BBC Music Department has made a remarkable contribution to the cause of music throughout the nation and deserves congratulation for the standard of service regularly maintained. In addition to orchestral performances, it broadcasts frequent recitals by the finest talent in the land and from abroad. The music ranges through the centuries and the Corporation acts as a patron by commissioning works for special occasions.

Music, as a living art must move forward and seek new methods of expression, although some might feel that the pace is a shade too rapid. We are living in an age of constant change and it is becoming something of an effort to keep abreast of contemporary thought – not only in music. The following statement by a composer of today is not without interest. "As we no longer consider tonality to be the overriding power, it is no longer logical to employ these forms, sonata, rondo and fugue, which rely for their true meaning on it. As we no longer, therefore, have these forms it is equally invalid to think in terms of the symmetries which they condition". It might have been added that melody, such as we understand the term, is no longer an important ingredient either.

These new ideas tend to constitute a formidable obstacle for many listeners and help to explain half-empty halls and a lack of enthusiasm when such music is performed. In fairness it should be added that predominantly youthful audiences appear to enjoy this new music. It is the older generation that finds difficulty in appreciating the idiom. But this is not intended to be a condemnation of modern music, as history has provided many examples of composers writing before their time and indeed such innovators lead the way, often to be revered by later generations. Some present-day composers will undoubtedly achieve posterity, although it is possible that this aspect does not worry them unduly. They write for the present and if they are not understood it is just too bad.

Much has been written here about the professional aspect of music, but this would not exist without a vast and enthusiastic musical public. In addition to attending concerts, thousands of people throughout the country belong to amateur choral societies, orchestral bodies, brass bands and church choirs, whilst in private homes small groups of friends and neighbours join together to make music. These are the true amateurs of music who not only set for themselves high ideals, but expect a superlative quality from their professional brethren. In this they are rarely disappointed.

It would be stupid and unchivalrous to deny the tremendous impact of foreign music, past and present on the culture of Britain. An inspection of programmes from the earliest concerts to the present day shows the predominance of works by the great composers of other countries and this is understandable. Quite apart from the obvious numerical position, their music has given genuine pleasure to large and enthusiastic audiences over the years. These same audiences are no less appreciative of the many fine foreign artists who visit or live permanently in our country. The British are sometimes considered parochial in their tastes, but this accusation could not apply to music.

The purveyors of gloom, of which there are many, appear to delight in informing us of falling standards in almost every walk of life. But perhaps enough has been written here to show that we are not entirely without native talent and that in the realms of music the old country can still hold its head high.